Total Telemarketing

Robert J. McHatton

JOHN WILEY & SONS, INC.

New York • Chichester • Brisbare • Toronto • Singapore

Publisher: Stephen Kippur
Editor: David Sobel
Managing Editor: Ruth Greif
Editing, Design & Production: G&H SOHO, Ltd.

DIAL-IT®, Megacom®, PRO®, and Reach Out® are all registered service marks of AT&T.
Readyline^{SM} is a service mark of AT&T.

This publication is designed to provide accurate and authoritative information in regard to the subject matter covered. It is sold with the understanding that the publisher is not engaged in rendering legal, accounting, or other professional service. If legal advice or other expert assistance is required, the services of a competent professional person should be sought. FROM A DECLARATION OF PRINCIPLES JOINTLY ADOPTED BY A COMMITTEE OF THE AMERICAN BAR ASSOCIATION AND A COMMITTEE OF PUBLISHERS.

Library of Congress Cataloging-in-Publication Data

McHatton, Robert J.
    Total Telemarketing.

    Includes index.
    1. Telemarketing. 2. Telephone selling. I. Title.
HF5415.1265.M38   1988   658.8′5   87-21547
ISBN 0-471-62754-2
ISBN 0-471-62755-0 (pbk.)

Printed in the United States of America

88 89 10 9 8 7 6 5 4 3 2 1

*This book is dedicated to the many salesmen and women
who throughout the years have formed my telemarketing crews.
Their successes, trials, and errors have made this book possible.*

Acknowledgments

Not many people are fortunate enough to be given the opportunity to sit down and look over a lifetime and attempt to acknowledge and thank the friends, family, and colleagues who have helped mold their lives. I count myself lucky and grateful for this opportunity.

My heartfelt thanks to:

Bob and Julia McHatton, my parents, whose love and affection gave me the fortitude to succeed.

Wanda, my partner in life, my beloved wife, the mother of my children, for her courage and devotion.

My children, Bob, Audrey, Doug, Julie, Mike, Patty, and Charlie, for their patience.

Joe Donovan, my friend; he was there when I needed him.

Murray Feinberg, friend, partner, and co-author of my first book.

Don and Vivien Romine, friends, supporters.

George "Duddy" Feinberg, former employer, teacher, idea man.

Fred Campbell, who helped me reach for the stars.

Allen Beugen, friend and former partner.

Sumner Brown, my first telemarketing teacher.

Syd Brown, friend and supporter.

Jimmy Cannon, who helped me get started on my own.

Mary (Mumm) Barfoot, secretary, accountant, supporter, friend, untiring worker.

Don Tomsche, who introduced me to correctional industries.

The following associates whose efforts provided the million-dollar months:

Jimmy Carter	Fred Coward	Darryl Richardson
Bob Simpson	Bert Sherman	Bob Fleming
David Reed	Dorothy Peelman	Eddie Garcia
Al Ciancetti	John Noble	Chuck Tucker
Dennis Simonton	Al "Rex" Nersesian	Sharon Vick
Gary McKinney	John Aguirre	Dan Webster
Jerry Pino	Jim Terry	Mary Costa
Tom Thompson	Dave "Mad Dog" Maddox	Rita Dunlop
Mike Welch	Gene Morales	Ted Pickard
Hugh Hagen		

Special thanks to my son, Robert J. McHatton, Jr., for the many hours of labor and assistance provided me in the development and writing of this book.

Contents

1. **Dialing for Success**
   An Introduction to Telemarketing   *1*

   Getting Preferential Acceptance ▪ *Coordinating Uses Pays
   Off* ▪ *"Canned" or Taped Calls* ▪ *Common Marketing
   Mistakes* ▪ *No Quickie Experts* ▪ *Dollars and Sense of
   Telemarketing* ▪ *Time, Contacts, and Sales*

2. **Managing the Phone Operation**   *16*

   Setting Your Goals ▪ *Factors for Success* ▪ *A
   Checklist* ▪ *Facility Requirements* ▪ *Some Questions* ▪ *A
   Checklist for Successful Telemarketing* ▪ *Incentives*

3. **Economics of Telemarketing**   *27*

   In-House versus Outside Service Bureau ▪ *Advantages of
   Outside Service Bureaus* ▪ *Advantages of In-House
   Operations* ▪ *Drawbacks of an In-House Telemarketing
   Operation* ▪ *Compensation Procedures* ▪ *Quotas* ▪ *Cost Sales
   Ratios* ▪ *Costs and Pricing of Outside Vendors* ▪ *The
   "Communicator Hour"* ▪ *Consulting Costs* ▪ *Amortization of
   Expenses*

4. **Understanding the Maze**   *36*

   The Birth of the "Baby Bells" ▪ *Electronic Yellow Pages* ▪
   Electronic Mail ▪ *Voice Mail* ▪ *Touch Tone* ▪ *Automatic Call
   Director (ACD)* ▪ *Headsets* ▪ *Monitoring* ▪ *Automatic Dial
   Recorded Message Players (ADRMPs)* ▪ *Long Distance*

Calling ▪ Local Calls ▪ Foreign Exchange Service ▪ Tie-Lines ▪ Conference Call ▪ Credit Card Calls ▪ Zenith/Enterprise ▪ Call Forwarding ▪ Call Waiting ▪ WATS Lines ▪ 800 Service ▪ 800 Readyline ▪ Two-Way WATS ▪ 900 Service ▪ AT&T Megacom ▪ Reach Out—In-State ▪ Reach Out America ▪ AT&T PRO In-State ▪ AT&T PRO America ▪ The Emergence of the Other Common Carrier (OCC) ▪ MCI ▪ SPRINT ▪ Advantages and Disadvantages of Other Common Carriers ▪ Calling Outside the United States ▪ Be a Clock Watcher ▪ Out of This World by Satellite ▪ Teleports ▪ Resellers ▪ Teleconferencing ▪ Things to Come—Interactive Television ▪ Airline Telemarketing ▪ Automated Telemarketing ▪ Computerized Call Processors ▪ Power Dialer with Answer Recognition ▪ Integrated Voice-Data Terminals ▪ The Professional Telemarketing Work Station ▪ The Future Is Now

5. An Introduction to Success
Organizing Your Calling Strategy   **77**

Know Where You Are Going ▪ Why People Buy ▪ Getting by the Secretary ▪ The Sequence Requires Control ▪ Prospective Characters ▪ Sequence of Success in Booking Appointments

6. The Telephone Script
Preparing Your Sales Presentation   **86**

Base the Script on the Sequence

7. Opening New Accounts
Your Road to Greater Wealth   **97**

Features, Advantages, Benefits ▪ Sell the Sizzle ▪ Specials ▪ Call-Mail-Call ▪ Train Your Customers

8. Hiring and Training
the Telecommunicator   **105**

Job Descriptions ▪ What Is a Telephone Sales Professional? ▪ The Interview ▪ Training and Keeping Your Employees ▪ Sales Account Executive Evaluation ▪ The Telemarketing Voice ▪ "Burnout"

9. Telephone Language and Etiquette   *124*

Buzz Words for Winners ▪ *"Hear" What Isn't Said* ▪
Enthusiasm Gets Action ▪ *Smile, Darn It, Smile* ▪ *Dead
Line—Dead Prospect* ▪ *Screening Calls* ▪ *ABCs and 1-2-3s
of Taking Messages* ▪ *Common Courtesies to Callers* ▪
Techniques of Answering the Telephone ▪ *Best Times and Best
Days for Calling*

10. Prospecting
How and Where to Find Your Customers   *140*

Demographics and Psychographics ▪ *The Endless
Chain* ▪ *Qualified Cold-Calling* ▪ *Buying or Renting
Lists* ▪ *Getting Their Numbers* ▪ *List Testing* ▪ *Lead
Generation* ▪ *Call-Mail-Call* ▪ *Once You Choose . . .*

11. A Unique Approach to Closing
How to Overcome Objections   *152*

Reasons "Why Not" ▪ *Open-Ended and Closed-Ended
Questions* ▪ *Be Honest—Play It Straight* ▪ *How to Close the
Sale*

12. Selling Existing Accounts
Telephone Cycling Increases Your Sales   *169*

Hold on to Existing Accounts—Know Your Customer ▪
Records, Yes—Complicated, No ▪ *Turn Payments into
Additional Sales*

13. Surveys
Increasing Sales with Fact-Finding Questions   *181*

Fact-Finding Questions ▪ *Find the Overlooked Prospects* ▪
Select Questions Carefully ▪ *Information Is Gold*

14. The Art of Inbound Telemarketing   *189*

Sequence to Success ▪ *Know Your Prospect* ▪ *They Are
Calling for Your Help* ▪ *"On Hold" Technique*

15. **How to Handle Complaints**
In a No-Win Situation, Don't Be a Loser   *201*

Procedures for Handling Complaints ▪ *"Don't You Think
That's Reasonable?"* ▪ *Sell Your Polite "No"* ▪ *Common
Traps to Avoid*

16. **The Telephone and the Law**   *208*

Call Monitoring Regulations ▪ *Asterisk Bills* ▪ *Automated
Machines Legislation* ▪ *Scams* ▪ *Registration* ▪ *Profit
Disclosures* ▪ *900 and 976 Number Controversy* ▪ *Lotteries* ▪
Solicitation Hours ▪ *Home Solicitation Laws* ▪ *Strict Rules to
Avoid Trouble* ▪ *Credit Collections* ▪ *Obey Rules of Courtesy
and the Law in Making Collection Calls* ▪ *Sequence of
Successful Collections* ▪ *Timing of Collection Calls* ▪ *Precall
Planning* ▪ *Harassment Prohibited* ▪ *Sales Tax Problems* ▪
Check Local Laws

17. **The Ethics of Telemarketing**   *223*

18. **Success Stories**   *225*

Success . . . Winning . . . Profits . . . ▪ *New England Shrimp
Company (NESCO)* ▪ *Westinghouse Furniture Systems* ▪
Century 21 Real Estate Brokers ▪ *Continental Marketing* ▪
Fingerhut ▪ The New York Times ▪ *Overseas* ▪ *Joanne's
Fudge* ▪ *Spencer Enterprises* ▪ *Rug Doctor* ▪ *Windsor
Vineyards* ▪ *Hadra* ▪ *Thrifty Best Rubbish* ▪ *Walt Disney
Educational Media* ▪ *Union Oil of California* ▪ *Alza* ▪ *DHL
Air Courier* ▪ *Holland Farms* ▪ *Graphic Concepts* ▪
Duddy's ▪ *Correctional Telemarketing* ▪ *A Personal Insight*

Appendixes

A. **Telemarketing Organizations**   *233*

B. **Periodicals on Telemarketing**   *234*

C. **Glossary of Telemarketing Terms**   *236*

Index   *241*

Chapter 1

Dialing for Success

An Introduction to Telemarketing

Man is a tool-using animal.
Carlyle

Give me a lever long enough
And a prop strong enough,
I can single-handed
move the world.
Archimedes

Throughout all eras of history, humankind has learned to use the tools at hand to their very highest and greatest possible utility. This was true when the tool was fire, an ax, an engine, or even the atom.

Today, we are learning to take the telephone, probably the most familiar tool we have, and fine-tune its usage from one of basic utility for communication to a much more spectacular instrument for commerce.

The advent of Alexander Graham Bell's telephone in the 1860s helped ignite the great revolution of technology that transformed our world into today's computerized, colorized, mass-communicative society.

With all innovations, the business sector usually attempts to develop new ways to advance, speed up, or expand markets, but in economically and efficient ways.

As the costs of travel continue to skyrocket, more and more of today's successful business executives and salespeople are finding the telephone an effective medium to present their product or service, using it to replace travel and drawn-out exchanges by mail. In 1985, the average cost of a business-to-business in-person sales call reached $229.70. By comparison, the average cost of a business telephone sale was less than $8.

By using the telephone, these people are accomplishing in a matter of minutes what was once accomplished only by costly personal contacts and lengthy business meetings. The telephone is rapidly becoming our nation's, and the world's, primary marketing tool, and its Number One energy saver.

In 1986, sales by telemarketing were estimated to be over $100 billion, with three-quarters of that figure earned in the business-to-business market. Growth in this new industry can be primarily attributable to its cost efficiency. In 1980, the value of an average business-to-business telemarketing sale was $250. In 1985, it rose to $1,000. In the consumer market, the average went from $19 to $53. It is evident that this trend will continue.

The telemarketing industry growth represents a new trend in our society toward "tele-living." Today, we use the telephone in all facets of life. We shop by phone, learn by phone, see by phone, communicate with friends, businesses, and government by phone, praise by phone, hate by phone, vote in polls by phone, and let our computers talk by phone. Using the telephone in combination with our televisions and computers enables us to do our banking, corresponding, conferencing, and shopping without ever leaving our homes.

At the present time, the telephone is the fastest-growing medium in marketing goods and services. Used correctly and by professionals, the telephone is the most cost-efficient, flexible, and statistically accountable medium available. At the same time, the telephone is still very intimate and personal.

It is individual-to-individual, allowing both parties to create a two-way dialogue that is personal, instantaneous, and flexible.

With the proliferation of telephone technology, a new and demanding need for highly trained and proficient professionals has developed. Every businessperson in every industry has come to realize the importance of telemarketing, but it has been proven that this success is predetermined by the expertise of its implementation.

American businessmen and women know that the telephone,

used alone or in combination with other supporting programs, is the single most cost-effective and time-efficient marketing tool available. When corporate managers first begin pondering a telemarketing program, they ask such questions as, "Why the decision to do business over the telephone?" "Won't we begin to lose business?" "Won't our competition decimate our sales efforts?"

Sooner or later their questions become "What can I do in person that I can't do over the telephone?" If they approach that last question with a totally open mind, in almost all cases they have to conclude, "Nothing!"

"Corporate cowards" are those managers who are content with the status quo, who accept their field representatives continuing to go up one street and down the other, knocking on doors, as they have since their companies were founded. They are satisfied with the results. Such managers should remember that their companies were established in a different era. Since then quill pens have been replaced with computers, the outhouse has been replaced with modern-day plumbing, and the horse and buggy have been replaced with trucks and automobiles. The time has come for the door-to-door peddler to replace his or her sample pack with a telephone line.

In the past five years, the number of companies involved in telemarketing increased from 1,000 to over 90,000. In 1986, telemarketing sales reached over $100 billion utilizing over one million telemarketers. In New York City alone, there were nearly 13,000 telemarketers employed in 1986. *Business Week* has projected that over eight million new jobs will be created in the telemarketing industry by the year 2000.

Getting Preferential Acceptance

The telephone commands attention. When it rings, it cannot be ignored. There isn't one of us who, during an eyeball meeting, hasn't had our sales presentation interrupted by a telephone call. There are few, if any, of us who haven't seen our prospect order something over the telephone while we sat dutifully, waiting to talk to him in his place of business. Just suppose that the salesperson talking to your prospect on the telephone was your competitor. You would have traveled, perhaps a great distance, in harsh weather, to meet with your prospect, only to wait while your competitor sold him!

If you're not prone to change, or if you believe telemarketing is only for the light bulb and photography salespeople of this world, then break out your sales costs by the type of activity. If your company is like most of the Fortune 500 companies, you'll find you can no longer afford to continue to cold-call for new business with field sales reps unless they have appointments with prequalified prospects.

When the cost of obtaining new business with eyeball-to-eyeball selling approaches or exceeds the list price of your product/service, then a new way of doing business must be found and implemented. Very sophisticated and well-executed telemarketing programs have been known to actually increase sales productivity far in excess of 100 percent, while examples of sales productivity increases ranging from 10 to 40 percent are in abundance.

IBM predicts that over 30 percent of its sales will be through telemarketing and catalog sales by 1988. Chrysler attributed a 32 percent increase in fleet sales in 1982 to telemarketing. Datacorp experienced a 60 percent increase in business from just one year of telemarketing use. Time/Life Books, which just celebrated the sale of its 500 millionth book, has 13 branches and a separate division established solely for telemarketing. The list goes on and on with success stories.

Eyeball-to-eyeball sales reps have found that effective use of the telephone can significantly increase their total field selling time. When field sales reps use the telephone to qualify their prospects and set appointments in advance, it stands to reason that they waste less time calling on "nonprospects" and devote more time to making sales presentations to those prospects most likely to buy. Effective use of the telephone actually helps the field sales rep to "extend" the day by increasing productivity, thus reducing the cost and need for additional field sales coverage.

Aggressive sales managers with national accounts are finding the telephone an effective tool in expanding both their prospects and their penetration of major accounts. All too often, field sales reps calling on major accounts get "locked in" to doing business with only one or two individuals or divisions of a large multi-faceted corporation, leaving many prime selling opportunities un-challenged. Usually, all it takes to get an appointment with buyers in other divisions is a copy of a corporate telephone book and a phone call introducing yourself as a vendor who has already been approved by the prospect's company.

Coordinating Uses Pays Off

Telephone marketing is a vital component of the multimedia advertising mix. When used in combination with other advertising media, the telephone compounds effectiveness, often generating four or five times the normal response of one medium alone.

While it can be used to enhance or support other media, no other single marketing tool offers the immediate impact or the precise cost accountability of a well-executed telephone marketing program.

Normal expected response rates, according to recent studies, are shown in Figure 1.1.

With telemarketing, variables such as advertising and sales easily can be controlled and preplanned, and costs can be analyzed. Also, with no other marketing tool can a sales message be delivered to so many potential customers in so little time, while offering one of the major benefits of direct sales—the ability of the salesperson to read a prospect's mood and true feelings and adjust the sales presentation to meet such needs and desires.

Telemarketing provides the unique quality of *speed* in determining results. With direct mail, it might take three or four weeks before you would be able to test the success or failure of a marketing plan.

There is no marketing or sales function that cannot be totally or partially performed over the telephone. Telemarketing can:

1. Prospect for qualified sales leads.
2. Develop qualified sales leads.
3. Set appointments for eyeball-to-eyeball sales presentations.

Figure 1.1 **Expected Response Rates for Different Marketing Methods**

Bill insert alone	2.0%
Telemarketing contact alone	5.3%
Direct mail alone	7.9%
Bill insert followed by telemarketing	9.0%
Bill insert followed by direct mail	9.2%
Direct mail followed by telemarketing	16.4%
Bill insert & direct mail & telemarketing	29.3%

4. Take orders for everything from jelly beans to tank periscopes, computer software to heavy construction equipment, dog food to wine, pens to cowboy hats, cosmetics to bookkeeping services, for items from $1 to $1 million.
5. Cycle distant customers.
6. Upgrade marginal accounts into highly profitable outlets.
7. Convert inquiries and responses from advertising media such as television, radio, print, and billboard into sales.
8. Reinforce other media promotions.
9. Reactivate old customers.
10. Qualify new accounts.
11. Obtain credit applications.
12. Introduce present distribution networks to new products.
13. Develop new nationwide distribution networks.
14. Promote special merchandise.
15. Dispose of surplus inventories.
16. Generate traffic for both retail and wholesale outlets.
17. Solicit donations for fund raisers.
18. Survey for market data.
19. Determine brand penetration.
20. Inform the public on ballot issues and timely products.
21. Help remind voters to get to the polls in key elections.
22. Test the validity and effectiveness of mailing lists.
23. Cover large territories economically.
24. Deliver tape messages to preselected markets.
25. Convert inquiries into qualified sales.
26. Cross-sell other services/products to current customers.
27. Sell tickets to seminars/trade shows/fund raisers.
28. Stimulate cash flow by waking up slow accounts.
29. Recruit volunteers.
30. Collect feedback.
31. Increase average order size, price per item, profit per order.
32. Educate your employees or customers via teleconferencing.
33. Sell subscriptions and renewals.
34. Acquire instant market intelligence.
35. Increase your customer service credibility.
36. Increase competitiveness and lower cost per order.
37. Evaluate weak markets.
38. Standardize your presentations for consistency.
39. Lower loss of sales presentations.
40. Increase market share.
41. Result in a more personal relationship with customers.

42. Stop misconceptions by customers before they snowball.
43. Remind customers of merchandise deliveries.
44. Create better centralized management controls.
45. Handle bank transactions via telebanking.
46. Reinforce field reps.
47. Reinforce name recognition by customers and competitors.
48. Create two-way dialogue between the marketer and the prospect.
49. Enable evaluation of customer mood, allowing adjustment by the marketer.
50. Permit the marketer to choose the time of sale presentation.
51. Allow an earlier release for new products/services due to less necessary lead time.
52. Train employees more economically.
53. Handle sales overloads.
54. Increase the number of accounts per salesperson.
55. Give personal service to accounts regardless of the size of the account or the distance from the home office.
56. Reduce nonproductive selling time.
57. Allow flexibility in credit policies due to lower collection expenses.
58. Create the ability to time sales to customers' buying cycles.
59. Allow preplanning of most costs-per-sale.

Telemarketing is to selling what the production line is to the modern factory. It can be directed either toward business-to-business sales or toward the end-users or consumers. It allows managers always to be able to quickly calculate their selling costs per sale. By maintaining its sales force in one place, a company can completely monitor its selling activities and make it possible for the salesperson to have immediate access to the company's credit department, shipping department, computer bank, and inventory data. Commissioned salespeople can be motivated constantly to maximize their results while hourly employees can be encouraged to meet performance norms.

Many of today's Fortune 500 companies are now jumping feet first onto the telemarketing bandwagon, some in very creative and aggressive ways. In Minnesota, the author was instrumental in the development of one of the nation's first outbound prison telemarketing programs. In 1987, HBO planned to make up to 300,000 telemarketing sales calls per month. *The New York Times* uses telemarketing to sell 75 percent of its subscriptions. In 1970, there were only 10 telemarketing bureaus in the United States. In 1980, the number jumped to 80, and in 1986 it was over 500. Telemarketing truly is the world's fastest-growing industry. Even AT&T plans to start its own telemarketing service bureau, causing quite a bit of nervousness in many companies that dislike the idea of Ma Bell competing with her own customers.

In one 30-hour period in 1985, nearly $40 million was pledged in the most successful telethon of all time—the "Live Aid Concert"—wherein calls poured into an improvised telephone network at the rate of over 6,000 per hour. This rate was maintained even when the concert ended, nearly four days later.

Today's most effective communications tool is 100 years old and the success stories abound, but in reality only a very few marketers really know how to use the telephone effectively.

"Canned" or Taped Calls

Many successful telemarketing programs use "canned" or prepared sales messages. Telemarketers who favor this approach generally feel that inexperienced and inexpensive salespeople can be used effectively to deliver a message in a controlled time period. The canned pitch eliminates the possibility of enticing a prospect with exaggerated statements or false promises.

Today, a new professional has been created, the "communicator," or professional prescripted reader. These men and women have been trained to present scripted presentations with proven techniques of professionalism.

Under optimum circumstances, the highly trained telemarketing professional will produce astonishing results, but many times situations require using communicators to present the message with prepared scripts.

Whenever communicators are utilized, it has been found that more consistency can be attained if prepared presentations are used. In order to give the salesperson or communicator complete organization and still allow for flexibility and spontaneity, several tools of the trade have been created, including flip-charts with one side for objections and the other side for benefits, features, and advantages. More detail on these tools is provided later in this book.

Such tools allow the telephone sales representative to be flexible and appear knowledgeable but not "canned" in the presentation. It also allows the company to feel comfortable that the presentations are standardized and consistent among the entire sales force.

Another technological machine that is being used to an increasing degree is the Automated Dialing-Recorded Message Players (ADRMPs). These machines automatically dial predetermined telephone numbers and play prerecorded messages to prospects or whoever answers the phone. Currently, these machines are quite controversial but have been found very successful in certain applications.

Both the canned presentations and the ADRMPs are successful in producing astonishing results, especially in areas such as collections, fundraising, subscription solicitations, and direct sales of single products to the end-user. Both assure delivery of a sales message without deviation; the use of such a taped message has the advantage of creating third-party credibility.

When presenting a taped message, the most effective results will be obtained by using a recognizable voice, that of a well-known personality or an expert on the subject matter being presented. Such a voice will add credibility to the stated facts and will create an implied, if not stated, endorsement of a product or service.

Currently ADRMPs are being used by many firms (such as Sears, Roebuck) to notify customers that catalog orders have arrived and can be picked up. Many school systems are also using the ADRMPs to notify parents that their children are tardy or absent.

In the 1986 Pennsylvania senatorial campaign, incumbent Arlen Spector spent a reported $350,000 on lists that were marketed using ADRMPs playing recorded messages from President Reagan to millions of Pennsylvania voters. The opponent, Robert Edgar, tried desperately to combat this with his own telemarketing staff of over 400. Obviously, telemarketing is becoming an important tool in today's stormy political arena.

ADRMPs are under attack in many states. In some localities it is illegal to dial a number and begin playing a tape when the phone is answered. In such areas, the consent of the person being called must be obtained before a recorded message is played; the nature of the call must be stated, as well as the name, address, and telephone number of the business or organization being represented before asking for permission to play a prerecorded message.

As the technological hardware improves, so will the state of the art. Forward-looking marketers have made automatic telephone systems workable and respectable, but their application is still limited in scope. Speed, accuracy, and predictable results are the inherent advantages of such systems, making them particularly useful in fundraising, political persuasion, collections, and research surveys.

Recognizing that the common telephone is a computer terminal at home or business, many marketers have harnessed the significance of oral communication to the resourcefulness of the computer. This synergism reflects an important new dimension in mass communication. Business forecasts clearly show that dramatic growth will occur in the use of this communication medium.

The future of ADRMPs is uncertain with numerous legislation currently being inked, but the future of the human element in telemarketing is assured. The human element is one of the primary characteristics that makes telemarketing so unique and so successful. It is personal, intimate, and interactive.

Common Marketing Mistakes

Although the telephone is the only person-to-person mass marketing tool available to business today, until recently little was done to improve the overall methods and techniques of its use as a marketing tool.

Perhaps because we have been using the telephone all of our lives, our familiarity and comfort with our present methods have created roadblocks that prevent us from exploring and developing new techniques for its use. Actually, the uses of the telephone as a marketing tool are as varied as your imagination.

There are as many telemarketing styles and methods as there are telemarketing operations. Likewise, there are many mistakes that are repeated with a great deal of frequency from one telemarketing sales operation to the other.

These mistakes wait to lure your telemarketing program to unqualified failure. They appear everywhere, from the programs of low-budget operations run by relative newcomers to the state-of-the-art operations managed by those experienced pros who should know better. Some of the common mistakes are:

1. Using the telephone for the wrong purpose. You should never attempt to sell a complicated proposal or service by the telephone. Avoid presenting something that requires a visual aid, such as a chart, graph, or blueprint.

2. Choosing the wrong list or marketplace. You must determine what target audience is most likely to respond to your solicitation.

3. Not getting through to the right person. All too often telephone salespeople are willing to settle for the "assistant" rather than finding out when the person who has the real buying authority will be available.

4. Failure to ascertain the prospect's availability. Courtesy and good business acumen require that you clear the way before pitching. If your prospect is in the middle of doing something, call back or you'll destroy your chances for a sale.

5. Using the wrong tone of voice. Because the person to whom you are speaking cannot see you, the telephone focuses full attention on the tone of your voice. Unless you are already known by the person on the other end of the line, you can easily give a distorted and negative picture of you and your company, based solely on how you sound.

6. Using an improper rate of speech. If you speak too rapidly, it's hard for the other person to understand what you are saying. This can easily lead to distrust. Speaking too slowly usually leads to impatience on the part of the listener.

7. Not offering the buyer a provocative reason for listening. When you first call strangers, you face built-in resistance. They don't know you. They might not know your company. They don't know much about what you have to offer, and they cannot see what you look like. You have to offer your prospects a reason for listening: *a benefit*. Don't merely ask for time. It's precious. Instead, offer something in return. It's pretty difficult to turn down a benefit.

8. Failure to listen. Not probing for needs is probably the biggest single failure of telephone salespeople, who too often forget that they learn nothing when they are talking.

9. Assuming you understood correctly. Understanding exactly what your prospect is saying is essential to your being able to serve that prospect. When your prospect has a question, repeat it back in your own words. It is this feedback that assures your prospect of your correct understanding.

10. Assuming your prospect heard you correctly. Use test questions frequently to determine if your prospect really understands you.

11. Not taking advantage of the opportunity to sell up. The telephone is an interactive medium that offers the opportunity to sell up, add on, and switch to an alternative on out-of-stock items. Use it!

12. Failing to provide a forum for customer feedback. The salesperson on the telephone knows! Unless you provide a systematic means for your salespeople to pass along valuable information they receive, you may never use it, resulting in useless and wasted market evaluating opportunities.

No Quickie Experts

It is impossible to develop the sophistication necessary to manage a successful telemarketing program simply by experiencing a one- or two-day seminar. Many organizations, such as the American Management Association, the American Telemarketing Association, the Telemarketing Managers Association, and the Direct Marketing Association, sponsor public seminars, offer instructional videotapes, and provide forums for informational research. The names, addresses, and phone numbers of these and other pertinent organizations can be found in the back of this book.

Many local telephone companies and AT&T also provide fact-finding seminars on telemarketing.

Improper execution, unrealistically high expectancy over a very short period of time, and oversimplification, especially without the involvement of top management, have caused the ultimate failure of more telephone sales programs than can be imagined.

These are the basic reasons that cause many managers to say, "We tried phone sales and they didn't work." On the other hand, forward-looking companies, many in the Fortune 500, realize the necessity of changing their marketing methods and have opened up new marketing channels with effective telephone sales programs.

The shortest distance between a buyer and a seller is a telephone line.

Dollars and Sense of Telemarketing

Today, increasing the productivity of salespeople is a costly problem. Most companies expect their salespeople to make four to six on-premise contacts a day, with the national average cost for each contact amounting to approximately $230. Although the statistics vary from company to company, it is a general axiom that 75 percent of all orders are written by 25 percent of the salespeople. More astounding, perhaps, is the widely accepted belief that on the first go-round, 65 percent of all personal sales calls are made to the wrong people.

Recently McGraw-Hill Research reported that average salespeople spend only 40 percent of their working days selling. The balance of their time is spent traveling and doing clerical work required by management. It has also been revealed that 80 percent of a salesperson's accounts produce only 20 percent of the total orders. In other words, only 20 percent of a salesperson's accounts produce 80 percent of his or her sales. These statistics only prove what all business managers know—the average salesperson spends too much time traveling, filling out reports, and developing small-yield accounts, and too little time selling.

The Research Institute of America reports the average business experiences a 15 percent yearly attrition of customers. Therefore, it can be assumed that even a company that is utopian and operating at capacity has a constant need to increase both its market penetration and its customer base.

But the average on-the-road salespeople are not spending enough productive time selling. Salespeople and the companies they represent would like to convert their nonproductive time into sales, because sales mean money. But the high cost of travel (about $230 a visit) and the amount of time spent traveling and doing clerical work (60 percent) seriously curtail a salesperson's full potential.

There is an alternative. Serious salespeople can increase their contacts and reduce costs through telemarketing. Once a salesperson establishes and masters the use of a well-organized telephone marketing program, the road ahead will be clear. By using telemarketing as the primary tool, average salespeople can become super salespeople, increasing their overall volume and enhancing their companies' market penetration in assigned sales territories.

Using telemarketing, salespeople can contact more prospective customers in one day than they could traveling on the road for one week. At their desks, armed only with a telephone and working only 30 hours per week, they should make between 175 and 250 complete presentations.

Using a "canned" pitch, not deviating from the text, and working the same 30-hour week, the number of prospects they can contact on the telephone would more than double. On the road and working a minimum of 40 hours a week, this same salesperson could perhaps see 20 to 30 prospects, and, if cold-calling, approximately 65 percent of those would not be the decision makers!

Another important point to keep in mind is that the existing customer base is probably the single most important asset to any business. It is the bread-and-butter base upon which you will continue to build your business, expand your product line and cash flow, and maintain your inventory turnover. Some of your present bread-and-butter accounts are probably marginally profitable. Others may not be profitable at all, yet to give them up could result in an overall drop in purchasing or in manufacturing power, creating another set of problems.

In all too many instances, the salesperson who originally opened such accounts now finds the job reduced to that of an order taker. With these accounts, face-to-face visits not only cost you more money than the orders are worth, but such visits are literally stealing the valuable time the salesperson could be using to develop new business. The optimum selling method is, of course, direct contact, but it is physically and economically impossible today for salespeople to call upon accounts as often as they should, and calling on marginal accounts only cuts further into profits.

By using the telephone, rather than in face-to-face meetings, you can regularly contact all of your accounts, marginal and high-yield, as often as you choose and at a much lower cost than eyeball-to-eyeball selling. A telephone salesperson can in a matter of minutes solve problems, chart and cycle inventories, contact the customer at appropriate reorder times, and perform any other in-person contact tasks. Customer cycling programs executed over the phone have definitely proved to be as effective as face-to-face selling. Such programs enable you to reach your customers as often as you wish, at times when they are ready to buy, not just when the schedule permits.

Time, Contacts, and Sales

Telemarketing eliminates the loss of time spent traveling from one account to another. It is impervious to weather and road conditions. With the telephone, there is no time wasted sitting in an office listening to your customer take "important" phone calls, often from your competitors.

With telemarketing, nonselling time can be greatly reduced, while your company's sales volume and bottom line are being increased. The telephone is the fastest cost-effective means of communicating with your clients and customers. Once you master the techniques, watch your sales and bottom line grow!

Another important point to keep in mind is that in today's business climate, increased sales do not necessarily mean greater profits. A sale is not complete until the merchandise has been paid for and the money is in the till. With inflation, each day an account receivable is unpaid means a decrease in its original value.

The U.S. Department of Commerce reports that a $100 receivable has a depreciated value of $90 after only three months, and after six months its value has shrunk to $67. Here, too, the most cost-effective method available for helping your business tighten its credit policies and significantly reduce collection intervals is the systematic use of the telephone.

The successes obtained by a well-executed telemarketing program can be measured easily and the results noticed quickly in four areas. With telemarketing:

1. Your sales volume will increase from those accounts you service by phone.
2. You will realize greater profits from your marginal accounts.
3. Your customer's satisfaction from the added attention and service will increase.
4. Your average cost per order from accounts serviced by telephone will be significantly decreased.

A telephone sales representative should make 90 to 110 or more calls per day and, depending on the product and geographic area, should make between 35 to 50 complete product presentations, or more. This is significantly more product presentations than the average traveling salesperson can handle in a 40-hour week!

Probably the primary reason for the vast growth and success attributed to telemarketing is its basic inherent ability to provide instant quantitative analysis of a marketing program. With the correct and well-designed worksheets, a telemarketing program can provide prompt cost-and-benefit analysis, quantitative figures on number-of-contacts, number-of-presentations, number-of-sales, costs per sale, income per sale, as well as instant analysis of why a call did or did not work.

A telemarketing communicator, using a prepared text to sell a single item (for example, light bulbs or newspaper subscriptions), can make as many as 25 calls and complete as many as 15 presentations or more per hour. Because the number of calls is as apt to decrease as to increase in a six-hour shift, these statistics are based on a six-hour shift. It is recommended that telephone sales reps work three hours, have an hour break, work three hours, and then go home for the day.

Anyone with basic sales instincts can be taught to master the simple techniques necessary to perform well on the telephone. All it takes is training, determination, practice, management, monitoring, and evaluation.

Chapter 2

~~~~~~~~~~~~~~~~~~~~~~~~~~~~~~~~~~~~

Managing the Phone Operation

The first realization that must be made concerning the management of a telephone sales operation is that it requires a specialized blend of expertise and a unique combination of skills.

Because the telephone is so accessible and so familiar to our culture, many marketing managers have jumped into telemarketing head first, and many have drowned. Telemarketing seems so simple. Anyone should be able to do it, right? Don't bet on it.

Telemarketing requires an unparalleled degree of expertise. Much as in the other mass-marketing media of television, radio, print, and direct mail, telemarketing integrates communication devices to *sell* services or products.

Setting Your Goals

The first plateau to establishing a successful telemarketing operation consists of the following:

1. Develop your complete marketing plan with built-in criteria for accounting and systems analysis.
2. Create the call cards, performance tallies, and other record-keeping materials needed.
3. Write scripts, sales outlines, and presentations to be performed.
4. Obtain prospect lists.
5. Establish training and hiring procedures for both supervisors and sales personnel.

6. Establish pretesting before actual implementation of campaigns to analyze scripts, feed back criteria, and target timings.
7. Analyze and evaluate campaigns, personnel, and cost effectiveness and factors of response and feedback.

The goal is management without costly errors and turnover of personnel. Telemarketing can allow adequate controls of these problems via sophisticated record-keeping, monitoring, and motivational interaction.

Factors for Success

Telemarketing can be successful only if the following criteria of management are achieved:

1. Support and commitment by management for the telemarketing center's role in the overall marketing effort
2. Establishment of reachable goals
3. Professionalism in execution and management
4. Interface and continuous interaction between the telemarketing center and other departments
5. Constant emphasis on follow-up
6. Establishment of precise timetables for goals to be achieved

As in all business managing, the successful telemarketing operation requires plenty of care in planning, coordination, and implementation of the overall marketing plan (see Figure 2.1). A good way to understand how a telemarketing operation should work is to envision the smoothly flowing production line of any well-run manufacturing company. A profitable industrial plant requires a frenzied coordination of plant, machinery, personnel, and financial resources to get the most cost-effective and human-productive interplay possible.

Ultimately, management's goal is to direct and manage all of these resources to produce the greatest amount of productivity with the least amount of cost.

A Checklist

The following is a checklist of some of the necessary ingredients toward establishment of a successful telemarketing center:

- Determination of precise management objectives (customer

Figure 2.1 **Direct Marketing Flow Chart**

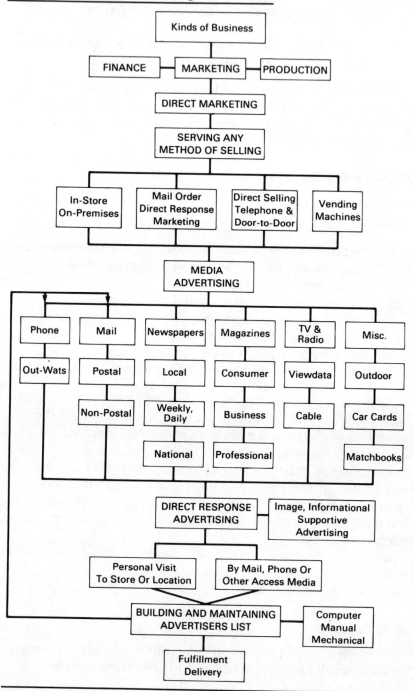

service or outbound selling, surveys or sales presentations, booking appointments or actual selling, etc.)
- Research and development of telemarketing facility, including site selection, facility design, equipment selection, and so on
- Development of training, hiring, compensation, and motivational procedures
- Establishment of productivity standards and objectives
- Development of presentations with input from all pertinent departments, including sales, marketing, research and development, fulfillment, and finance departments
- Establishment of fulfillment and systems coordination to ensure appropriate speed in filling orders and smooth interface between departments

Facility Requirements

One of the first topics that can tremendously affect the success of a telemarketing operation is the actual selection of the facility that will become the new telemarketing home. There are several key ingredients that must be considered when choosing a telemarketing center.

Ever since the establishment of the first telemarketing operation, facility characteristics have played an important role in creating either good or bad impressions, good or bad environments conducive to success or failure, and good or bad motivational surroundings that either spark productivity or hamper it.

Today there are super-sharp telemarketing operations working out of million-dollar skyscrapers, and there are also "boiler rooms" working out of the smoke-filled back rooms of hotel or motel dives. Some telemarketing centers allow their personnel the luxuries of plush carpeting and individual cubicles, with personal headsets, soft music, and personalized coffee mugs. Other operations allow their personnel such "luxuries" as access to a toilet, their own folding chairs, access to the folding table, their own ashtrays, and a fly swatter for defense.

For all practical purposes, the successful telemarketing operation does have some necessary components that can help make a crew more productive, including:

1. A facility with windows
2. Control of a room's temperature, so as to avoid surroundings that are too hot or too cold

3. A facility that has controlled airflow, to help avoid the smoke-filled room
4. Supervision over telephone sales reps
5. A logical procedure for work flows
6. Provision of cubicles, individual desks, or individual work stations
7. Establishment of a monitoring station
8. Enough room so people can feel comfortable
9. Height-adjustable chairs with neck supports and adjustable arm rests
10. A CRT with optional filters and eyehoods
11. Directional lighting that is soft and never too bright or not bright enough
12. Accoustical tiles on the walls and ceilings to help absorb the sounds that can both distract and interfere with a telephone conversation
13. Modern phone systems that can smooth the work flow process and cut down on job nuisance

Obviously, the successful telemarketing operation requires some unique physical essentials to assist in productivity. Some of the reasons for these needs lie in the most common problems found in telemarketing, which include:

- Fatigue
- Eyestrain
- Headaches
- Back complaints
- Neck complaints
- Discomfort complaints
- Stiffness complaints
- Temperature complaints
- Telephone equipment complaints
- Smoky room complaints

Remember, you are dealing with people, and whenever you deal with people there will be complaints. As management, your job is to minimize the problems of your team without spending much money and without affecting productivity.

The motivating manager is many things to many people, but in the end, he or she exerts positive influences to help mold and inspire leadership.

Some of the techniques used by motivational managers in gaining a successful environment from telemarketing operations follow:

1. Individualism. The motivating manager allows the telemarketing crew to bring family pictures, plants, etc. to their work stations to help personalize the work place.

2. Bulletin boards or blackboards. Many successful motivating managers use a blackboard in their phone rooms to help all telemarketing crew members visually see their daily, weekly, and monthly sales performance progress. Normally indicated on these boards also is some form of quota or individual or team results for contests.

3. Snacks. Most motivational managers allow their people to have beverages or light snacks at their work station.

4. Team designations. Many motivational managers use team designations to help ignite productivity in personnel. This uses the natural human competitive spirit as a motivational tool that also helps build group spirit and comradeship.

5. Lighting. The motivational manager takes special precautions to ensure adequate lighting at each work space.

6. Ventilation. Caring motivational managers make sure their people get the best in ventilation and never let the environment become smoky.

7. Thermostat control. The friendly motivational manager locks the thermostat and holds the key to maintaining the correct temperature at all times in the telemarketing center.

8. Humidity control. No one likes to sweat.

9. Noise control. Motivational managers make sure that their crews have carpeting, accoustical ceiling tiles, vinyl desktops, curtains, and cubicles to help control unnecessary noises.

10. Job aids. "Nice guy" managers make sure their people have the necessary job aids and ensure that all tools are within reach of each person. They ask themselves: Are the aisles wide enough? Are the desks high enough? Is there access to rest rooms?

The best way to achieve these goals is to select an adequate facility in the first place, prior to making the initial telephone call.

The ideal chair for a telemarketing center must adjust to the individual sales reps. The chosen room must have unique qualities in sound absorption, temperature control, airflow management, carpets, ceiling tiles, soft but bright lighting, windows, music, and a supervisor for each crew. As far as sound absorption is concerned, the U.S. Occupational Safety and Health Administration has established standards for facilities at levels of 85 decibels for offices. Therefore, always check these ratings before signing any lease, or productivity levels can be affected.

Some Questions

When setting up a telemarketing operation, some questions to ask should include:

- Can the trainers train?
- Who trains the trainers?
- Can the managers manage?
- Who trains the managers?

The telemarketing management has some specific duties that affect the success or failure of the operation.

Qualified managers should be required to prepare and analyze statistical reports, be empathetic and sensitive to personnel problems, demands, and needs, be able to motivate and evaluate personnel, and also have the necessary skills to fix the coffee machine or copy machine on notice, become arbitrator and referee at any given moment, and have the right personality to handle most crises that arise on any given day.

Some of the specialized and unique skills to look for in your management team include:

- Experience in direct marketing campaigns
- Background, experience, and knowledge in motivation and management
- History or knowledge in new high-tech telephone systems
- A personality that lends itself to understanding, teaching, or leadership

In the past several years there has been a substantial tendency to emphasize the quantity of calls as a measure of success in telemarketing. Most pros understand, though, that the true yardstick of success is not in the number of calls made, but in the quality of those calls.

Sales can become a numbers game, but experience has proven that productivity and cost efficiency is more successfully measured by how effectively *each* sales or survey presentation is made, not by how fast it was made.

Therefore, to help ensure the *quality* of each sales or survey presentation, it is recommended that all telemarketing operations implement some sort of monitoring system.

Monitoring is not just listening. It is the key to quality control. Monitoring allows you a check on the sales reps. It can help you keep control and spot-check for unforeseen problems before they snowball.

Monitoring should be a natural characteristic of every telemarketing operation. Some operations look at monitoring only after the trouble signs appear; many times this is too late.

Some of the trouble signs to be on the lookout for include:

1. Slumping sales
2. Customer complaints
3. Low morale
4. Lack of personnel enthusiasm
5. Busy signals on incoming calls
6. Low sales-per-call ratios

Monitoring calls can be a positive force in telemarketing. If personnel are made aware that monitoring is taking place, they should understand they are on notice for *quality* performances.

Monitoring can be utilized as a training tool to show how presentations should and should not be made. Let people listen to themselves and make self-evaluations. Many times people are the best judges of their own work.

Experience has proven the need for monitoring. You must enforce quality control, so remember the golden rule about telemarketing monitoring: *"Always monitor your telephone calls as closely as you do your telephone bills."*

A Checklist for Successful Telemarketing

Good and successful telemarketing operations have many winning concepts and practices in common. The following is a list of some common guidelines to success:

1. Identify purposes or objectives.
2. Use a predetermined script.
3. Pretest scripts and telemarketing campaigns before a full campaign.
4. Hire not a person, face, or appearances but a *voice*.
5. Use precise reports and record-keeping devices.

6. Provide personnel with reinforcement, incentives, and other reasons to succeed.
7. Acquaint the crew with the products or services being sold.
8. Interface all information and coordinate the entire marketing campaign.
9. Know the competition.
10. Be ready; anticipate change.

The telephone sales representatives make up the primary communication tool to your customers. Therefore, you must use these tools to help gain as much information as possible about customers, competitors, and the marketplace. Always provide personnel with the capability to relay any pertinent input to management. It is vital that you keep these sales reps informed about company policies, plans for the future, and objectives at all times. This smooth interaction of information is often the key reason for a telemarketing operation's ability to lead or follow market trends.

Incentives

One of the most controversial topics in management is how to effectively and efficiently motivate personnel. Telemarketing offers many areas for argument in the application of styles of such management.

The first decision you need to make in motivating sales representatives is whether or not to use incentives in the first place. Many managers feel you should not have to "bribe" employees to obtain productivity. Others in the business have found that financial and emotional incentives can be the key and most influential reason for an operation's success or failure.

Experience in telemarketing operations working in all parts of the country, selling all kinds of products and services, and working both consumer and business projects, both inbound and outbound, has indicated a positive link between incentives and sales success.

The primary clue to remember is to link incentives to the performance you wish the crew to achieve. This performance can be evaluated in individual completions per hour, completions per day, completions per week, completions per month, group completions per day, week, hour, or month, by sales, by profits, by formulas, or in some cases with penalties for nonperformance.

The controversy still surrounds incentives, ever so many years since Pavlov's dog, but in telemarketing, a prolific incentive program can make all of the difference.

Other quite popular incentive programs utilize contests with either individual or group winners. Some programs are created to encourage teamwork and some individualism. Some offer competitive romances; others award the individuals who perform.

Here are some traps to avoid when establishing incentives:

1. Try not to make the time or objective period of the contest too short, because the results can be affected by normal day-to-day variations.

2. Don't set the goals too high—telemarketing crews can have a tendency to give up and be unmotivated.

3. Don't set the goals too low—the task will be too easy and the crews won't be challenged. They can therefore lose interest and be appeased with poor performance levels.

4. Always attempt to make the rewards most lucrative or appealing. Therefore, people will care if they win or lose. If the reward is not appealing, no one will care if the performance level is meager.

5. Don't allow the same person to win the contest all of the time—the other personnel might stop trying and again lose performance motivations.

6. Make sure the marketing management is behind the contests, prizes, or incentive program. Otherwise, the personnel might lose interest and enthusiasm for the entire program, thus lowering the performance levels achieved.

7. Allow the personnel to have input as to the incentive programs; otherwise, they may lose interest and you won't have input as to what really will motivate them.

8. Keep your personnel excited and guessing about incentive programs, so they won't tend to get bored or tired of the program and again lose motivation.

The important thing to remember is to establish the performance goals you want people to strive for. Do this both for individual levels and for group goals as well. Psychologists argue both for and against using financial incentives, but in telemarketing, there is usually no better form of motivation.

When establishing incentives, it is good to decide whether you want them to be short- or long-term. Experience has proven that long-term incentives seem to help reduce employee turnover, for they offer rewards for staying at a job.

The best incentive is the one that awards individuals for being both successful and creative in their job. By establishing rewards for being creative, a telemarketing operation can often capitalize on a sales force's input and closeness to customers and the marketplace.

Whichever incentive program you choose (if one is chosen) is predicated on your particular market, product, and management style. The ultimate goal is a happy, enthusiastic, and professional sales team.

Chapter 3

Economics of Telemarketing

Probably the most significant reason for telemarketing's tremendous growth in recent years is pure economics. Bottom-line expenses have pushed the costs of marketing to unprecedented levels in nearly every industry.

It's estimated that as of 1986 the average American business-to-business sales call skyrocketed to over $230 per sale. Much of the problem is cost efficiency and productivity time. The antiquated selling techniques utilized by field representatives just don't hold up when put on an expense sheet.

Look at this example of a field rep's agenda:

Monday, March 12th

8:00	Breakfast with Jerry's Tire	$11.47
10:00	Filled up with gasoline	17.50
10:30	Bob's Service	
11:00	Harry's Wheel	
12:00	Lunch	5.00
1:00	Lenny's Tire	
1:45–3:00	Drove to San Jose	
3:00	Kurt's Mobile Tire	
4:00	Mike's Service	
5:00	Steve's Tire	
6:00	Checked in motel	$30.00
7:00	Dinner with ABC Tire	$37.50

Day's totals: Number of sales presentations: 8
Total expenses: $101.47

Here is an example of a telephone sales rep's agenda:

Monday, March 12th

8:00	ABC Tire	No needs now—sent catalog.
	BCD Service	No answer
	EFG Tire	Sold 16 tires
	HIJ Service	Too busy to talk—call back afternoon.
	KLM Tire	Made presentation—will think about it, call back tomorrow.
	NOP Tire	Line busy.
	QRS Service	Owner not in until 2—call back.
	TUV Tire	Made presentation—needs more info—sent catalog.
9:00		

One hour totals: Number of sales presentations: 4
Total expenses: telephone usage

As you can see, the telemarketing representative made half as many completed sales presentations in *one hour* as the field representative did in an *entire day*, and without spending over $100 in out-of-pocket expenses and putting wear and tear on a company vehicle.

Implemented efficiently, a professionally trained telemarketing campaign can compete with quality presentations.

Telemarketing is the most cost-efficient marketing system ever invented. But there are several economic decisions to consider when attempting an introduction into this growing field.

Some of the budgetary considerations must include:
Set-up
Call card preparation
   Tape conversion to labels
Labor costs
   Salaries
   Incentives
   Bonuses
Telephone installation
Telephone equipment
   Lease
   Purchase
Monitoring equipment
   Lease
   Purchase

General administrative costs
Telephone usage
Script development
Fulfillment
Reporting
Software
Credit verification
Data processing
Creative design
Desks, chairs, blackboards, calculators, cubicles
Technical support
In-house versus outside bureau
Training costs
List acquisition
Phone number look-ups

In order to budget your telemarketing expenses, you must first define your needs and decide whether it would be best for you to hire a telemarketing consultant, establish your own telemarketing center, or employ an outside service bureau of already trained professionals.

In-House versus Outside Service Bureau

Just as with any important business decision, choosing between an in-house telemarketing operation and an outside service bureau involves many pros and cons.

You can find telemarketing consultants on both sides of the fence, some in favor of the in-house operation, some in favor of the outside service vendor. Ultimately, the final decision must be based on your own unique situation.

Advantages of Outside Service Bureaus

Some of the advantages of working with an outside vendor include:

1. Knowledge and background. Most service bureaus are manned by already trained professionals with substantial background in the telemarketing industry. You can capitalize on the fact that these professionals have already learned by other people's mistakes. They can allow you the ability to accurately predict costs and avoid wasted time and money with nonproductive scripts.

2. Lower upfront costs.   Normally, telephone service bureaus can provide you with pretrained telemarketing crews for much less upfront expense money than if you started your own operation. They have already paid the set-up expenses, deposits, and installation charges that can pile up when first starting an operation. This is particularly important when you want to attempt a test campaign.

3. Speedier start-up.   Since a telephone service bureau has a trained and ready work force, the lead time necessary to start up a telemarketing campaign can be significantly shorter and easier than what would be required if you started your own operation. Once a telephone sales rep has learned the basic sales skills and telemarketing techniques, normally it is quite easy to adapt swiftly to any new campaign.

4. Twenty-four–hour service capabilities.   Depending on your needs, most telephone service bureaus have the ability to answer incoming calls on an around-the-clock basis. By incorporating several possible clients together with one crew, they are able to spread the overhead of each telemarketer among several of their clients. Such a service cannot always be economically practical for some companies considering their own telemarketing operation.

5. Campaign testing ease.   Because of the low upfront costs and ready work force, telemarketing bureaus can allow easier flexibility in testing sample marketing campaigns.

6. Handling call overloads.   With the service bureau's work force already in place, it is able to handle any peaks or overloads of calls more efficiently. Often, incoming calls from television media promotions can cause a significant overload in calls that could not be handled effectively by your own operation. Many service bureaus have special phone systems and numerous lines that can route overloads to other trained professionals so as to never lose a sales opportunity.

Advantages of In-House Operations

There are also distinct advantages to using in-house operations, including:

1. Centralized control.   The primary reason for running your telemarketing campaigns from your own facility and organizational structure is control. You have control over the hiring and firing of all personnel, over the scripts and presentations made, over all budgetary expenses, advertising, compensation and incentive policies, and over developmental processes of your marketing effort.

2. Access and interface. Another advantage of the in-house operation over outside bureaus is the ease of accessibility to files, management, and inventory. The easier a sales rep can access information from the home office, the faster he or she can get credit approvals, confirm deliveries, validate inventories, overcome problems, and adjust to management policies. By having close control of your in-house operations, you can gain more flexibility in changing your campaign with fluctuations in the marketplace. Many times this close access to files and management can give the reps a competitive edge.

3. Company and product loyalty. Another great advantage of the in-house operation is that the staff is dedicated and loyal to your company and products exclusively, therefore they have a tendency to fight harder for each sale. Commitment is a unique characteristic, easier to instill in your staff than in the personnel of service bureaus.

4. Complaint and technical control. With an in-house operation you gain access to complaints and technical questions that might not be noticed with service bureaus. Customer service is an ingredient crucial to business success, therefore the in-house operation helps you keep on top of any problems before they snowball.

5. Product line experience. With an in-house operation, employees should have more ready experience and knowledge about the product line than any outside bureau which handles several clients at the same time.

6. Management interface. The in-house operation allows the management team to personally oversee the marketing effort, which also allows you more hands-on exposure to the actual campaign. This can give you more cumulative observation and insight to campaign successes and failures and analysis of results.

Drawbacks of an In-House Telemarketing Operation

Along with the controlled management advantages of an in-house operation, you must recognize that there can be some drawbacks, such as:

1. Capital investment. Probably the most inhibiting drawback to the in-house operation is the amount of initial investment that is required to get the telemarketing program off the ground. Some of the initial expenditures to be considered would include real estate or a building lease, desks or cubicles, telephone lines, telephone equipment, CRTs, training, and script development.

2. Telemarketing requires expertise. To ensure the success of an in-house operation, you must invest heavily in training and management. If management and training supervisors aren't experienced and scripts and campaigns are not organized efficiently, you may have ineffective or unsuccessful results.

When deciding upon the best telemarketing development for your company, you should objectively evaluate and analyze personnel and their capabilities and experience in this specialized but highly successful marketing system. Many firms that wish to start such a program employ a telemarketing consultant to help them ease into it without getting in over their heads.

Some of the considerations to acknowledge are:

- Management experience and capabilities
- Capital resources available
- Anticipated number of responses
- Employee loyalty
- Product knowledge requirements

Compensation Procedures

One key to the success or failure of a telemarketing operation is the formula chosen for compensating the telephone sales representatives and supervisors. Compensation can make the difference between a representative being a profit-maker or an expense item on your balance sheet.

Some of the compensation criteria you must consider include:

- Motivational incentives
  Emotional versus financial
- Draw versus commission
- Percentage of profit incentives
- Exciting versus lukewarm programs
- Spiffs and bonus programs
- Group versus individual incentives

Industry statistics indicate that many types of compensation procedures are in use across the country, so there is no all-encompassing program that is right for every situation. You must adapt a program right for you.

Most companies utilize some form of program that includes salaries or base, commission, and bonus or spiffs.

The human animal has proven itself to need incentives to spark action. In order to help transform crews from order takers, clock-watchers, and losers into salespeople, go-getters, and income-producers, you must integrate some kind of incentive, bonus, spiff, or other motivational program that can ignite them.

Quotas

One of the first details in setting up a telemarketing center is the determination and establishment of reasonable quotas and goals for personnel. Just as, in the writing of a book, an author needs to know where he wants to lead his readers, the telephone sales reps must know your expectations of performance.

The salespeople must have predetermined objectives, goals, and quotas for which they will be held accountable. By knowing what is expected of them, they will be able to have goals to shoot for.

It is vitally important that these quotas be reasonable and achievable. If they are set too high, the salespeople will become frustrated and unmotivated. If the goals are set too low, they can become overconfident and complacent about growth. Either way, you must hold them accountable.

Cost Sales Ratios

When analyzing the productivity of a telemarketing operation, a very effective and valid yardstick is cost per sale, sales per call, sales per presentation, sales per customer reached, customers per hour, sales per hour, sales per 1,000 calls, and so on.

The following is a good example of how to computate productivity levels from call card information:

$$
\begin{array}{rl}
1000 & \text{calls} \\
-420 & \text{no answers} \\
\hline
580 & \text{potential customers reached} \\
-290 & \text{refusals to hear the complete presentation} \\
\hline
190 & \text{actual full presentations}
\end{array}
$$

190 actual full presentations
−157 "no" responses
_____
33 "yes" responses
−2 cancellations of orders
_____
31 actual orders

If the item being sold in this example costs $100, the total amount of sales for this sales campaign would be $3,100. Using these figures, we can analyze the productivity of this campaign and conclude:

Total sales per 1,000 calls is:	$3,100.00
Total sales per call is:	$3.10
Total sales per customer reached is:	$5.34
Total sales per completed presentation:	$16.32

Telemarketing provides you with the capabilities to systematically and statistically analyze your marketing campaign at any time. This allows instant analysis of the effectiveness of scripts, personnel, and targeted markets.

Costs and Pricing of Outside Vendors

The criteria for the contracting of telephone service vendors can be as confusing and varied as the number and services of telemarketing service bureaus available.

Some vendors charge by the hour, by the call, by the sale, at flat rates, labor per hour plus telephone per hour, labor per hour plus commission, labor per hour plus dedicated telephone usage, or per project bids.

If you are interested in securing an arrangement with a telephone service vendor, it is recommended that you obtain at least three different bids and implement a test campaign before committing to any long-term relationship.

The "Communicator Hour"

As you attempt to secure a telemarketing vendor, one very confusing nonsecular term you will encounter is the so-called communicator hour.

Normally, the communicator hour really isn't 60 minutes in length. When service bureaus bill for their "hour," it customarily constitutes only 20 to 30 actual calling minutes, taking into account busy signals, wrong numbers, no answers, and not-homes.

Some of the common usages for the communicator hour are:

- One hour of labor from one person including phone bill
- One hour of labor from one person plus one hour of phone usage
- One hour of actual phone time labor plus phone bill
- One hour of actual phone time labor including phone bill

With these several usages, it is crucial that you spell out the exact definition of time you agree to pay for. Depending on the circumstances of your campaign, there can be financial advantages of paying per-piece (call) rates rather than by the clock, because in the end, no one wants to pay for wasted, nonproductive time.

Consulting Costs

If you plan to integrate telemarketing into the company as an in-house operation, there are numerous telemarketing consultants available to assist you in development of scripts, marketing plans, hiring and training of staff and sales personnel, facility design and set up, as well as systems management designs.

These consultants are available with assorted specializations and varying degrees of expertise; their rates are on a national average of $50–250 per hour.

Amortization of Expenses

Much of telemarketing's growth can be attributed to the low continuing overhead once the initial set-up charges have been covered. Check with your accountant, but the normal operating procedure for most telemarketing operations is to amortize the initial installation and start-up expenditures over longer periods of time.

Telemarketing has proven its economic feasibility in black and white for some 80,000 companies that use it as their primary marketing system. Using common sense and practical applications, it can work for you, too.

Chapter 4

~~~~~~

Understanding the Maze

Telemarketing hardware has come a long way since the old boiler room days. Today, telemarketing is a legitimate profession with a substantial array of available equipment options that can create complete confusion to the person or company desiring to enter this industry.

Telephone equipment is big business, and naturally most of the American superstructure of conglomerates have entered this field, especially with the breakup of Ma Bell.

The best philosophy when entering this maze of equipment and long distance toll options is to remember that the goal is not to purchase the fanciest gadgetry available on the market, but to protect profits by limiting expenses.

In actuality, the only real piece of telephone hardware needed by the telemarketer is the simple, standard, single line, black telephone. This plain instrument of technology hasn't changed much in 50 years, but the application has metamorphosed into a sophisticated tool for triumph and conquest in the instantaneous and economic marketing of goods and services.

This chapter closely analyzes many of the available equipment, hardware, and long distance choices the discriminating telemarketer will encounter when tooling his or her operation. Always remember to determine your primary objectives and wear whatever blinders neccesary to make sure you don't get sidetracked or stuck with purposeless or expensive items you don't need.

The Birth of the "Baby Bells"

For nearly a century, people from all walks of life in America made pet jokes about "Ma Bell." All of that ended on January 1, 1984, when, per a U.S. District Court ruling by Judge Harold H. Greene, American Telephone and Telegraph was ordered to divest its local phone companies. America's most famous monopoly was broken.

Today, the so-called Baby Bells are separate companies in a competitive industry. AT&T still markets long distance services, but now the local telephone company has to compete with private sector companies for business in telephone equipment, long distance, consulting, information services, directory publishing, and other areas of concern for conglomerates.

The seven Baby Bells consist of the following entities:

Company	States Served
Ameritech	Wisconsin, Illinois, Indiana, Ohio, Michigan
Bell Atlantic	Pennsylvania, West Virginia, Virginia, Maryland, New Jersey, Delaware
Bell South	Kentucky, Louisiana, Mississippi, Alabama, Georgia, Florida, South Carolina, North Carolina, Tennessee
NYNEX	New York, Massachusetts, Connecticut, Vermont, New Hampshire, Maine
Pacific Telesis	California, Nevada
Southwestern Bell	Texas, Arkansas, Missouri, Oklahoma, Kansas
US West	Washington, Oregon, Idaho, Montana, Wyoming, Colorado, Utah, Arizona, New Mexico, Nebraska, North Dakota, South Dakota, Minnesota, Iowa

Since the divestiture of AT&T, the Baby Bells have made noticeable efforts to expand into other industries by purchasing other businesses. Today, many of the Baby Bells are in businesses involving insurance, real estate, credit, cellular phones, computers, directories, electronics, and telephone manufacturing.

Some of the other interesting new areas that the Baby Bells have entered include Electronic Yellow Pages, Electronic Mail, and Voice Mail. These new ventures prove the success of the free trade capitalistic marketplace.

Electronic Yellow Pages

One of the most profitable money makers for the Baby Bells has been in the publishing of directories known as the Yellow Pages. Well, with the proliferation of computers in our society, it seems almost natural to put all this information into computer memory banks to allow people to access this wealth of data with their home computers. This product is being called the "Electronic Yellow Pages," and it requires a special operator whose job it is to provide a variety of information about businesses in a caller's vicinity. A caller could ask about dry cleaners and give his or her address. The special operator would then give the names and addresses and phone numbers of all the dry cleaners in the caller's neighborhood. Another program allows private individuals to access this data base with their own personal computers. Customers pay annual or monthly subscriptions and phone usage fees.

Electronic Mail

This is a popular new service that allows several branches of a company to use telephone lines to transmit letters, messages, graphs, pictures, facsimile information, and so on. The service may transform the intercompany memo into the electronic memo.

Voice Mail

This program is designed to turn a telephone into a combination answering machine, message taker, and telephone. Under this system, a main computer at the phone company would answer your phone after so many rings, using your personal voice, just like an answer machine. When you get home, you just dial a personal code number into your Touch Tone phone and the main computer will play your messages.

Touch Tone

An equipment feature that the outbound telemarketer will always find cost effective is the pushbutton or Touch Tone dialing feature.

As you become proficient with a Touch Tone instrument, you begin to use it in much the same way your bookkeeper uses a desktop calculator. You can punch out 11-digit telephone numbers in about 3 seconds, compared to at least five times as long (15 seconds) with the traditional rotary dial. All other factors being equal, the telephone sales representative with Touch Tone dialing can place between 6 and 10 percent more calls per day than his or her counterpart using a rotary dialer.

Automatic Call Director (ACD)

The inbound telemarketing operation that continually receives a high volume of incoming calls, often stimulated by media advertising, truly needs automatic call directors. These machines route incoming calls to the telephone extensions that have been out of service for the longest time. When all extensions are busy, the ACD answers phone calls with a recorded message, stores them, and distributes them, in the order received, to the next available extension.

Headsets

With the breakup of AT&T has come tremendous competition in the telephone equipment business, including the headset market. There are several makes, styles, and prices in this market. The best way to choose a headset, if you decide to use them, is to evaluate each supplier by price, quality, warranty, and comfort. Most professional telephone salespeople prefer to use some form of headset because it allows free use of both hands. Currently, the headset market has models priced from the cheap $19.99 styles all the way up to $200 products designed for professional use. The key is both comfort and utility. If the caller or the prospect cannot hear the conversation, it is not likely a sale will be made. So make sure whatever headset you purchase *works*.

Monitoring

Monitoring is important and necessary for the successful professional telemarketing operation, therefore an effort to establish a suitable monitoring system is required. Monitoring equipment can range from something as simple as a single telephone extension with the speaking end of the headset removed to reduce added noise while listening to a conversation, to something as sophisticated as a computerized silent call monitor which is designed to ease the silent monitoring of several phones with simple pushing of buttons. Remember to check with your attorney as to any local or state regulations that concern the application of monitoring techniques in your area.

Automatic Dial Recorded Message Players (ADRMPs)

One of the most controversial but successful telemarketing tools has been the Automatic Dial Recorded Message Players (ADRMPs), which make telephone presentations of prerecorded messages to either predetermined or randomly selected prospects. These machines are very cost effective for specialized campaigns that need large volumes of calls, and they are used substantially by schools to notify parents of children who are tardy or absent. A new form of computerized ADRMP has been introduced that allows a two-way interaction between the machine and prospect and has been quite effective for governmental information use, census takers, and for survey presentations for qualifying prospect lists. Again, use of these machines is regulated by considerable clouds of new legislation, so be sure to consult your attorney and local law officials before spending any money on one.

Long Distance Calling

When you make a long distance call with AT&T, your call is billed on a per-call and per-minute basis. (See Figure 4.1 for an example of how long distance calls are calculated on an in-state level.) You can make as many calls as you want, to anyone and anywhere in the world. In the telemarketing business, it is not cost effective to use normal long distance calls because of the long dialing time and because of the high cost if you make more than 1,000 calls in a month. Figure 4.2 is one model for tracking long distance calls in a telemarketing operation.

Local Calls

The location of the sales office can often have a greater effect on your operating costs than will the equipment you choose. In addition to the monthly charges, telephone company tariffs for

Figure 4.1 **AT&T/Oregon Long Distance Toll Chart**

Station-to-Station Direct Dial
8 A.M.–5 P.M. Monday–Friday

Rate Schedule (effective October 1, 1985)

Mileage	Initial Minute	Additional Minute per Minute
0–10	$.30	$.15
11–22	.32	.21
23–55	.34	.25
56–70	.42	.30
71–124	.47	.34
125–196	.49	.36
197–440	.50	.37

Rates for Operator-Handled Services, per Call

1. Calling card calls $.50
2. Other operator-handled calls   1.25
3. Person-to-person calls   3.00

Discounts from Basic AT&T Rate Schedule

Evening:	5 P.M.–11 P.M.*	Sunday–Friday	25%
Night:	11 P.M.–8 A.M.*	Daily	40%
Weekend:	8 A.M.–11 P.M.*	Saturday	
	8 A.M.–5 P.M.*	Sunday	40%

Evening rate applies to the following holidays unless a lower rate applies:

New Year's Day	January 1
Independence Day	July 4
Labor Day	Variable date
Thanksgiving Day	Variable date
Christmas Day	December 25

To, but not including.

local calling are based upon message units, the method of billing used to determine the cost of local calls. Message unit charges are usually greater in congested areas, such as downtown, where telephone usage is maximized. In areas where telephone usage is low, message unit fees are generally reduced, sometimes even

Figure 4.2 **Long Distance Telephone Log Form**

DATE	TIME	PERSON MAKING CALL OR RECEIVING CALL	PERSON CALLED OR CALLING	COMPANY CALLED OR CALLING	CITY, STATE	AREA CODE	TELEPHONE NUMBER	PRE-PAID ✓	COLL. ✓	PERS. TO PERS. ✓	STA. TO STA. ✓	TOT. MIN.	CHARGES	CHARGE TO

eliminated entirely. Often just by locating the sales office on the outskirts of a city, as opposed to its central core, you can realize considerable savings in working your local marketing area.

Foreign Exchange Service

This service sounds like the name for overseas calling, but in reality it is a program designed so you can have a telephone number from a service area other than the one designated for the location of your business. This is cost effective when you have a large number of calls going to or from a specific city or area. It provides full 24-hours-a-day, seven-days-a-week telecommunications and can be used for both inbound and outbound calling.

Foreign Exchange allows you to place or receive calls as if you were physically located in the area normally served by the Foreign Exchange number. For example, you may want to use Foreign Exchange Service if your office is in Beverly Hills and a large concentration of your customers are located in Long Beach.

Foreign Exchange is billed on a mileage basis, the distance in mileage between the telephone company's switching facilities in the foreign city and in your city. If you made several calls daily to the Long Beach area from Beverly Hills, you would pay only the flat rate monthly mileage charge between Beverly Hills and Long Beach plus the regular local unit charges for such calls if made from a Long Beach exchange.

Foreign Exchange should be used only when the two areas are close enough so that the mileage charges are not excessive and the total costs will be considerably less than the cost of a WATS line.

Tie-Lines

Tie-lines, which are available through the Baby Bells, and hot-lines, which you can obtain from Western Union, are "leased lines" that run from a distant point to the central switchboard in your office. They are the equivalent of a long distance intercom and are used most effectively by companies with branch offices and switchboard facilities in various cities.

Companies with multiple branch offices often use tie-lines to balance the workload between their various facilities while minimizing long distance costs.

For example, a company based in Los Angeles may have tie-lines to its branch offices in both San Diego and San Francisco. Through the company's Los Angeles switchboard, employees in San Francisco can speak with their counterparts in San Diego. By using a tie-line, employees of all three offices can use the company's WATS lines and Foreign Exchange lines, regardless of which office they are located in.

Conference Call

A conference call enables you to talk with several people in different places at the same time. To do this, simply dial the operator, say you'd like to make a conference call, then provide the operator with the numbers of the people you want to talk to. Often all conference circuits are busy, so it is wise to arrange a calling time in advance with the people involved and then call the conference operator and make an appointment to place the call at an agreed-upon time.

Conference calls can be made on any telephone. The cost varies according to the number of stations, the distance, and the length of time involved in each call. In the very near future, you will be able to direct dial conference calls without operator assistance in most areas of the United States.

Credit Card Calls

Credit card calls can also be placed from any telephone. Telephone credit cards, which allow you to have long distance calls charged to your regular monthly bill, can be obtained from any telephone company business office.

When calling from one number to another, the telephone credit card enables you to charge the call to a third telephone number without the necessity of verification. You can use any Touch Tone telephone to give your credit card number directly to the computer without assistance from an operator. Some very high traffic areas have special credit card pay telephones that will not take coins— only telephone credit cards. The cards have a magnetic stripe on the back, just like any other nationally recognized credit card. When the card is put in the pay phone, it reads the magnetic stripe that communicates the credit card number.

Zenith/Enterprise

This telephone program is designed so incoming calls are billed through one city and answered by another city. Zenith/Enterprise is often used in conjunction with a media or direct mail campaign on local levels. Normally, there is a per-call fee that is higher than regular local or long distance charges, but lower than Foreign Exchange service or WATS.

Zenith/Enterprise is a great way to test a marketing campaign to see if WATS is needed. When customers make a call to your business via an Enterprise or Zenith number, they do not have to say they are calling collect. You are automatically billed for the call. Zenith/Enterprise does have its limitations in that it is limited to only one city per contact.

Call Forwarding

A very popular feature that is becoming more available every day is call forwarding. This feature allows an incoming call to be forwarded to a third phone without operator assistance or hesitation. By punching preselected codes into a Touch Tone phone, the call will automatically be forwarded to another number until another code is punched to stop the forwarding.

This feature is quite effective for a small operation that can't afford to miss important calls.

Call Waiting

This feature allows your phone to avoid giving out a busy signal. The telephone signals a "beep" when a call is coming in while you are on the phone. Simply by pressing the connect button once, you will put the first call on hold, and be talking to the second call. Then by pressing the button again, you are back with the first caller. This feature helps people avoid missing calls due to an annoying busy signal.

WATS Lines

Prior to the breakup of AT&T, Ma Bell had the only game in town for telemarketers, and WATS was the answer. WATS was established by AT&T in 1961. Today WATS, which means "Wide Area Telecommunications Service," is available at varying rates and options with several long distance companies; so, shop around for the best deal and take it. Normally, WATS lines are available either for outbound calls or as 800-number inbound calls. Under the AT&T WATS line program, the lines are rented at flat rates for the particular individual or assortment of zones you choose, and are contracted or billed at by the number of total hours of usage.

WATS traditionally has been a pet program for telemarketers because it provides the advantages of a super-wide footprint of coverage at rates substantially lower than regular long distance.

WATS used to be billed a flat rate by how many hours of toll usage were spent, but today many new programs have been introduced, most of which utilize a billing by the minute of usage.

Under the current program, WATS provides discounts on time of day and day of week calling, volume usage discounts on a per-call basis, and flexibility. WATS requires a one-time installation charge, a monthly charge, and a per-call-by-the-minute usage fee. The overall WATS expense is determined by the amount of usage entailed, with a greater discount for more usage.

The monthly hours of usage are divided into blocks of time that can be discounted at special increments or plateaus as the usage increases. For example, under the current program the first plateau is at 15 hours of usage. The second plateau is from 15.1 hours to 40 hours of monthly usage. Plateau three is over 40 hours of monthly usage. As the volume increases past the plateaus, the usage fees reduce per minute.

Even with the tremendous competition in the phone business, WATS is secure because of its good, clear transmission, availability in all locations in the United States, billing only for actual conversation time (meaning no charges for no answers or busy signals like some of the other common carriers), credit for misdials and wrong numbers, and no minimum usage requirements.

A disadvantage of WATS is the lack of billing information, such as the individual numbers called, that could be quite useful for the telemarketing operation in the re-billing of expenses and analysis of each campaign. With the proliferation of computers in our society, AT&T has created access for WATS users to receive this billing information via interlocking computers.

Other disadvantages of WATS lines include the high installation costs and the need for more than one line for more WATS lines, which means additional installation costs.

Figure 4.3 is an example of how an out-of-state WATS service might be billed. The WATS program is established in "bands" (SA1, SA2, etc.). Each band provides coverage of a specific zone of states. The higher the number of bands, the greater the coverage.

Depending on the area of the country in question, a single WATS

Figure 4.3 **AT&T/Oregon Service Areas and Bands**

SA1—California—North
    Idaho
    Nevada
    Utah
    Washington

SA2—Arizona
    California—South
    Montana
    Wyoming

SA3—Colorado	New Mexico
Iowa	North Dakota
Kansas	Oklahoma
Minnesota	South Dakota
Nebraska	Texas

SA4—Arkansas	Michigan
Illinois	Mississippi
Indiana	Missouri
Louisiana	Wisconsin

SA5—Alabama	New York
Connecticut	North Carolina
Delaware	Ohio
District of Columbia	Pennsylvania
Florida	Puerto Rico
Georgia	Rhode Island
Hawaii	South Carolina
Kentucky	Tennessee
Maine	Vermont
Maryland	Virgin Islands
Massachusetts	Virginia
New Hampshire	West Virginia
New Jersey	

SA6—Alaska

Notes: 1. *Service to higher band includes all lower bands.*
      2. *Home state not included.*

band will give coverage of the five closest states in your area. A five band will give you coverage of the continental United States and Hawaii.

Figure 4.4 represents the breakdown of AT&T's Oregon WATS rates.

800 Service

Inbound telemarketing has taken over America. With the explosion of television media commercials using 800 numbers, television shopping networks, mail order, and increased emphasis on customer service in many industries, the inbound telemarketing operation is transforming itself from a small element for customer service into a major marketing phenomenon (see Chapter 14).

800 number toll-free service was initiated by AT&T in 1967. It is available in many formats. You can choose the geographical areas you want to cover, whether they be one state (intrastate), groups of states (interstate), international, or all three.

AT&T has designed the service in a three-rate structure that employs discounts for the more volume used. Normally, a company would get the 800 service for 24-hour coverage, but when utilized sensibly and with insight as to calling times, substantial amounts can be saved. An example of how AT&T bills for 800 service is shown in Figure 4.5.

Toll-free inbound telemarketing with 800 numbers offers many advantages, including larger market coverage, better customer service, and low costs.

AT&T has introduced a new version of the 800 number service, called the AT&T Advanced 800 Service. This program offers a company many options in the types of service available, such as:

1. 800 single number service. This program gives you one 800 number you can advertise and for people to remember.

2. 800 customized call routing. This program gives you the option to divide your incoming calls into coverage by area codes or territories, so you can have your West Coast call-ins go to your California branch and the East Coast call-ins go to your New York branch. This allows more flexibility and speed in handling incoming calls.

3. 800 routing control service. This program is designed to allow you to control your 800 number much in the same way a call forwarding feature controls your incoming home calls. You are allowed access to the 800 user network to modify your rout-

Figure 4.4 **AT&T/Oregon WATS Rate Chart**

	Day		
Band	*First 25 Hours*	*Next 75 Hours*	*Over 100 Hours*
1	$13.41/.22	$12.74/.21	$12.08/.20
2	14.28/.24	13.55/.23	12.86/.21
3	15.22/.25	14.45/.24	13.69/.23
4	15.56/.26	14.79/.25	14.01/.23
5	15.86/.26	15.07/.25	14.28/.24
6	16.60/.28	15.77/.26	14.94/.25
	Evening		
1	8.99/.15	8.53/.14	8.09/.13
2	9.56/.16	9.09/.15	8.61/.14
3	10.19/.17	9.68/.16	9.17/.15
4	10.42/.17	9.91/.17	9.39/.16
5	10.64/.18	10.10/.17	9.56/.16
6	11.12/.19	10.57/.18	10.01/.17
	Night/Weekend		
1	6.00/.10		
2	6.39/.11		
3	6.83/.11		
4	6.96/.12	Rates effective: 1/1/87	
5	7.11/.12		
6	7.51/.13		

Day: 8 A.M.–5 P.M. Monday through Friday except holidays (New Year's Day, President's Day, Martin Luther King Day, Memorial Day, Independence Day, Labor Day, Columbus Day, Veteran's Day, Thanksgiving Day, and Christmas Day)

Evening: 5 P.M.–11 P.M. Sunday through Friday and the above holidays 8 A.M.–5 P.M.

Night/Weekend: 11 P.M.–8 A.M. all days, 8 A.M.–11 P.M. Saturday, 8 A.M.–5 P.M. Sunday

Monthly Rate: $36.40 per month, per line, plus tax
20.00 per month, per service group
30.05 per month, per line surcharge (if applicable)
5.70 per month, per line inside wire charge (if applicable)

Installation: $99.00 per service order, plus $138.00 per line

Figure 4.5 **AT&T/Oregon 800 Service Rate Chart**

Band	First 25 Hours	Next 75 Hours	Over 100 Hours
	Day		
1	$13.19/.22	$12.53/.21	$11.88/.20
2	13.74/.23	13.06/.22	12.36/.21
3	14.28/.24	13.56/.23	12.85/.21
4	14.48/.24	13.77/.23	13.05/.22
5	14.63/.24	13.91/.23	13.18/.22
6	15.35/.26	14.57/.24	13.82/.23
	Evening		
1	9.90/.17	9.42/.16	8.90/.15
2	10.31/.17	9.79/.16	9.27/.15
3	10.71/.18	10.18/.17	9.63/.16
4	10.87/.18	10.33/.17	9.78/.16
5	10.99/.18	10.43/.17	9.89/.16
6	11.51/.19	10.93/.18	10.36/.17
	Night/Weekend		
1	7.08/.12		
2	7.36/.12		
3	7.67/.13		
4	7.77/.13	Rates effective: 1/1/87	
5	7.87/.13		
6	8.28/.14		

Day: 8 A.M.–5 P.M. Monday through Friday except holidays (New Year's Day, President's Day, Martin Luther King Day, Memorial Day, Independence Day, Labor Day, Columbus Day, Veteran's Day, Thanksgiving Day, and Christmas Day)

Evening: 5 P.M.–11 P.M. Sunday through Friday and the above holidays 8 A.M.–5 P.M.

Night/Weekend: 11 P.M.–8 A.M. all days, 8 A.M.–11 P.M. Saturday, 8 A.M.–5 P.M. Sunday

Monthly Rate: $36.40 per month, per line, plus tax
20.00 per month, per service group
30.05 per month, per line surcharge (if applicable)
5.70 per month, per line inside wire charge (if applicable)

Installation: $99.00 per service order, plus $138.00 per line ing configurations by adding, altering, or erasing current routing instructions, all without having to contact AT&T in writing. You just use your Touch Tone phone.

4. 800 call attempt profile. This program allows you to receive a computer printout of all the call attempts made to your 800 number. The call report allows you information about the area codes, time of day, and other useful information about your incoming calls. It helps you analyze the workload of your inbound telemarketing centers, examine your media campaigns, and adjust for needed marketing strategies.

5. 800 call prompter. This service combines the 800 toll-free number with the computer-automated telemarketing center to allow you to let incoming customers choose from a list of departments or locations by pressing their Touch Tone phone. The system automatically routes the call to that department. This service helps you to prequalify your prospects instantly.

6. 800 call allocator. This service allows you to control where the incoming calls go. It can allocate high volume calls to the more experienced telemarketers, and it is quite useful during peak work periods.

7. 800 courtesy response. This service will provide a prerecorded message when your company is closed.

When used with print media advertising, the 800 number option consistently creates a 25 to 30 percent increase in response. When the broadcast medium is used, giving both a mail-in address and an 800 number option, the 800 number will generally create three times as many responses as the mailing address. When an 800 number is included in a catalog or on a product sheet, response is often doubled or tripled.

800 Readyline^{SM}

Recently, AT&T introduced a new 800 number toll-free service designed for the small business. This program allows you to combine an 800 number with your current in-house telephone lines. Therefore, you can use your current telephone equipment and phone number and just add a toll-free 800 number to help expand your exposure. Dedicated telephone lines are not necessary, because all of your calls—incoming, outgoing, and the 800 number calls—can be handled on the same existing lines you currently use. Your company can have a local phone number and an 800 number and have the best of both worlds at low cost. This service should prove to be very popular due to the lack of high installation costs the regular 800 number creates.

Two-Way WATS

Another new service that AT&T and the Baby Bells have created is designed to give you both outbound WATS and inbound 800 service on the same lines. If you need both services, go for the two-way WATS, if only to save the installation costs.

900 Service

In September 1980, AT&T introduced the DIAL-IT® or "900 number" service. DIAL-IT is an expansion of Ma Bell's Public Announcement Service (PAS), which was available for many years. Historically, PAS was offered by local telephone companies under such names as Sportsphone, Weather, Time, Dow-Jones Report, and so forth.

900 service not only offers PAS type programming, but also provides the ability to initiate mass media-stimulated calling on a nationwide basis. Thousands of callers can now gain access simultaneously, via the public switchboard network, to receive information or express their opinions.

900 is programmed so that some calls may be cut away from the recorded announcement directly to a telephone line at your office. You may designate the regions from which calls should be cut through and the rate of cut-through, for example, one call every minute, one call every other minute, etc. Completed call counts can be delivered either on a cumulative basis every minute to a customer's teleprinting terminal, or daily totals may be sent by mail.

This new service is really an exciting opportunity for stimulating a mass-market response to a promotion, and it has successfully been utilized for everything from Dial a Joke to votes on favorite songs to polls on political issues.

This service can be a cost-effective means for targeting an audience for a product or service. Under the program, anyone can order a 900 number by paying a set-up charge, which can vary according to how well you negotiate your deal. Some of the key considerations in this figure are the length of the message, the types of calls, and so on. The people who call into the 900 number are billed for their own calls at a rate anywhere from $.50 up per call *plus* tolls. For setting up the promotion, your company can receive compensation of varying amounts.

This compensation can add up if you design your marketing promotion well and utilize a real media mix. You can receive call reports on a breakdown of who they were by geographical area or time of day, minute-by-minute call counts, or verbal call counts; there are also options that can make the calls toll-free to the callers.

DIAL-IT 900 numbers can be great for communicating a message when coordinated with other media. It can be used to entertain, inform, or promote—maybe even *sell*.

AT&T Megacom®

AT&T has introduced a new service that combines 800, WATS, and facsimile communications so that with one service you can receive or transmit voice, data, and graphics on an interstate basis anywhere in the 50 states, Puerto Rico, and the Virgin Islands. This service has been very popular with customer service, airline, and inter-company functions.

Reach Out®—In-State

This in-state optional toll calling program is designed for direct dial calls made during the evening and late night/weekends. The program offers the ability to purchase late night/weekend calls in hourly rates. Normally, there is a one-hour minimum usage for the first hour. There is a start-up fee in the $10–20 range and the restriction that it does not apply to any other AT&T service. Figuring in all of the discounts with this program, it usually averages a 15 percent discount on the already 25 percent discount in the evening time slot, and is hourly at $10–15 per hour in late night and weekends.

The Reach Out program supplies the benefits of low rates without spending any money on special equipment or access lines, good Ma Bell sound quality, no distance requirements (as long as it is in-state), and the ability to predetermine phone costs.

Reach Out America

This program is the same type of new service as the in-state program, only with lower monthly hourly rates, and no requirements about distance called.

Figures 4.6 and 4.7 detail how AT&T bills for the Reach Out program.

AT&T PRO^{SM} In-State

Recently, AT&T initiated a program to discount all calls made in-state at all times. During the already discounted time periods, the PRO plan discounts it even more.

Figure 4.6 **AT&T Reach Out Oregon Program Chart**

This optional calling plan offers a discount for direct-dialed calls made between service areas in Oregon during the Evening and Night/Weekend rate periods.

Night/Weekend calls are billed at an hourly rate. A one-hour minimum usage in this period is assumed. Evening rate period calls are given an additional percentage off the existing discount.

There is no minimum usage on "additional hour" Night/Weekend or Evening calls.

Rate Period	Time Effective	% Discount on Reach Out Oregon
Day Rate	Monday–Friday 8 A.M.–5 P.M.	-0-
Evening Rate	Sunday–Friday 5 P.M.–11 P.M.	Save an additional 15% off the regular 25% discount
Night/Week-end Rate	Monday–Friday 11 P.M.–8 A.M. Saturday All day Sunday 8 A.M.– 5 P.M.	First hour $12 Additional hour pro-rated at $10 per hour

Start-up charge: $10

Restrictions: plan does not apply on operator assisted calls, directory assistance, DIAL-IT 900, or automated AT&T card calls.

Rates effective: 3/1/86

Figure 4.7 **AT&T Reach Out America Program Rate Chart**

Plan A

Monthly rate—$8.40. This includes 60 minutes of calling during the Night/Weekend rate period. Each additional hour is billed at $7.55. $10 installation charge.

Plan B

Monthly rate—$9.50. This includes 60 minutes of calling during the Night/Weekend rate period. Also included is an additional 15% discount during the Evening rate period. Each additional hour is billed at $7.55 per hour. $10 installation charge.

Benefits

No special equipment or access lines needed

The same high quality as regular long distance

Improved cost control (rates known upfront)

Not distance-sensitive (valuable if you call longer distances)

Monthly rate includes all local lines billed together for same price

Rate Discount chart

	MON	TUES	WED	THURS	FRI	SAT	SUN
8 A.M. to *5 P.M.	Day Rate Period FULL RATE						
5 P.M. to *11 P.M.	Evening Rate Period 38% Discount						Eve. 38%
11 P.M. to *8 A.M.	Night & Weekend Rate Period 53% Discount						

*To but not including

DISCOUNTS
Discounts apply to the charge for the initial minute occurring within the discount period and to all additional minutes occurring within each discount rate period. Discounts do not apply to the Service Charge.

Effective: 1/1/87

Some of the advantages of this program are:

- Good quality
- No requirement for special equipment
- Low monthly installation
- Monthly charge of only $10 approximately

This program is good for small operations. Here is the breakdown of the discounts:

Evenings, Sunday to Friday	25%
Night	40%
Weekend	40%

As you can see, this program can offer good incentives for the small operator.

AT&T PRO America

This optional discount calling plan offers a 10 percent discount on all direct-dial interstate long distance calls. It applies at all times and is in addition to any existing discounts. Some of the benefits include a billing of all calls, no special equipment, and good AT&T quality; it is good for handling any overflow of WATS lines. There is a low connection charge and a low monthly charge.

Figures 4.8 and 4.9 offer detailed outlines of how AT&T bills the PRO America program.

The Emergence of the Other Common Carrier (OCC)

As the decade of the 1980s progresses, AT&T's dictatorial control of the telecommunications industry in the United States will diminish. Before 1978, when the courts established the right of others to compete with AT&T in the long distance telephone market, virtually all telecommunications decisions emanated from 195 Broadway, American Telephone and Telegraph's long-time headquarters. No longer.

Technology, customer awareness, competitive initiative, and the genius of entrepreneurs in a competitive marketplace have opened all the doors to a full-fledged technological revolution. The excitement, stimulus, and pride of responding to the opportunities made

Figure 4.8 **AT&T PRO Oregon Calling Plan Rate Chart**

PRO Oregon offers a 15% discount on calls between service areas within Oregon. This discount applies at all times. During already discounted periods, such as Evenings and Weekends, the PRO Oregon discount is in addition to the existing one.

PRO Oregon Benefits:

- Detailed billing of all your calls
- Value. You get more and longer calls for the same amount of money.
- No need for special equipment or access lines
- Excellent use for smaller businesses
- A monthly charge that covers all lines billed together
- AT&T quality and service

PRO Oregon has a one-time connection charge of $10. The monthly rate is $10 per month, billed in advance. Minimum service period is one month.

Discount Periods on AT&T Oregon Rate Schedule:

Evening:	5 P.M.–11 P.M.*	Sunday to Friday	25%
Night:	11 P.M.–8 A.M.*	Daily	40%
Weekend:	8 A.M.–11 P.M.*	Saturday	40%
	8 A.M.–5 P.M.*	Sunday	

*To, but not including.

possible by competition is creating a new breed of telecommunications manager, all sharing the gratification inherent in helping to mold any new economic environment.

MCI

One of the largest of the new competitors in the long distance market is MCI Telecommunications Inc. in Washington, DC. The second largest telephone network in the United States, MCI currently has a client base of over 300,000 companies, including over 400 of the Fortune 500. These numbers prove MCI's ability to penetrate the AT&T arena. In addition to low cost long distance, MCI also has its own WATS, direct-dialing international calling, overnight letter service, and a competitive residential service.

Figure 4.9 **AT&T PRO America Calling Plan Rate Chart**

PRO America offers a 10% discount on all direct-dialed AT&T interstate long distance calls. This discount applies at all times. During already discounted periods, such as Evenings and Weekends, the PRO America discount is in addition to the existing one.

PRO America Benefits:

- Detailed billing of all your calls
- Viable option to WATS for smaller businesses
- Value. You get more and longer calls for the same amount of money.
- No need for special equipment or access lines
- A monthly charge that covers all lines billed together
- AT&T quality and service
- Economic option for WATS "overflow"

Charges:

$10 one-time connection charge per service order

$12.75 per month per billing number

Interval:

PRO America can usually be implemented by the second business day following your request.

AT&T Interstate Direct-Dial Discount Schedule:

Evening:	5 P.M.–11 P.M.	Sunday to Friday	38%
Night:	11 P.M.–8 A.M.	Daily	53%
Weekend:	8 A.M.–11 P.M.	Saturday	53%
	8 A.M.–5 P.M.	Sunday	

Rates effective: 1/1/87

SPRINT

The other national figure in long distance is SPRINT. In an attempt to shatter the AT&T sales feature of quality sound, SPRINT has committed to a huge-scale national networking of fiber-optic telecommunications. Its goal is to prove new technology's ability to provide a super-perfect sound quality. It's an expensive gamble, but it appears this could help trigger a new battle for long distance supremacy.

Advantages and Disadvantages of Other Common Carriers

There are thousands of other common carriers on the market today. Often they are seen offering tremendous long distance values, some exceeding 50 percent discounts, and so on. Some specialize in voicegrade, data, alternate voice/data, facsimile, and teleprinter transmission modes. Many are brokers of long distance who lease from MCI, SPRINT, or AT&T.

Probably the best-selling benefit of switching to one of the non-AT&T long distance companies may be the simple 15 percent average discount on long distance. MCI and SPRINT have proven the quality can stay high. They have also eliminated much of the long access-code dialing that was initially required. Other advantages of one of these companies for the telemarketer are the lack of high installation charges, as with WATS, the ability to use the plain old black telephones, and the capabilities to receive a computer printout billing sheet for each call made in a billing period.

Telemarketers like to look at dollars and cents, and these itemized billing reports allow them to re-bill clients for actual telephone usage, to analyze personnel, and to gather additional information to help evaluate market strategies and campaigns.

A disadvantage of using SPRINT, MCI, or other non-Ma Bell entities is the tendency of these companies to bill for calls in six-second increments. AT&T bills a call on the actual "conversation time" of the call, which means only the time of an actual completed call. You are not billed if the call was busy or no answer. This is not the case with SPRINT, MCI, and others. See Figure 4.10 for the anatomy of a telephone call. It might not seem like much, but in a fast-paced professional telemarketing operation, those six seconds can add up.

Calling Outside the United States

It is easy, fast, and inexpensive to dial overseas. Through AT&T, you can now direct dial at least 86 countries in seconds. Just dial

Figure 4.10 **Anatomy of a Telephone Call**

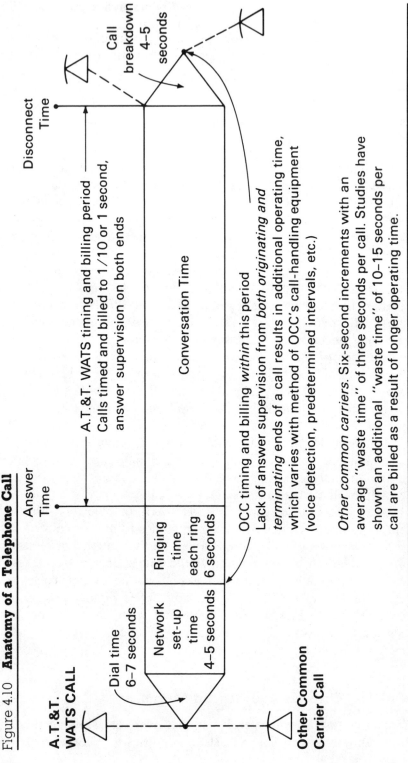

"011," the international access code for station-to-station calls, "01" for operator-assisted calls such as person-to-person calls, collect calls, credit card calls, and so on. Next dial the country code followed by the city code, then the local number you want.

If you don't know the local number, the operator can get it for you. If you're calling from a Touch Tone telephone, press the # button after dialing the entire number. This will speed your call along. If you have any questions about international calling, call toll-free to the International Information Service, (800) 874-4000, in Florida (800) 342-0400. Figure 4.11 shows a guide for international calling.

Calls to certain points outside the continental United States can be dialed in the same manner as long distance calls made within the United States. Simply dial the appropriate area code and then the local number. If you ever have a question regarding the calling of any international, national, or limited area call, dial your "0" operator.

Telephone service to ships equipped with satellite terminals is available in three ocean areas through Communications Satellite Corporation. To direct dial a ship, dial "011" plus the ocean code, then the ship's telephone number. The three oceans where such service is available are the Atlantic (ocean code 871), the Pacific (872), and the Indian (873). For ships located elsewhere and those not equipped with satellite terminals, dial "0" and ask for the Marine or High Seas Operator.

Figure 4.11 **Area Codes for Foreign Countries**

Country Codes		City Codes	Time Differences U.S. Time Zones			
			EST	CST	MST	PST
American Samoa	684	*	−6	−5	−4	−3
Andorra	33	All Points 078	6	7	8	9
Argentina	54	Buenos Aires 1, Cordoba 51, Rosario 41	2	3	4	5
Australia	61	Canberra 62, Melbourne 3, Sydney 2	16	17	18	19
Austria	43	Graz 316, Linz 732, Vienna 222	6	7	8	9
Bahrain	973	*	8	9	10	11
Belgium	32	Antwerp 31, Brussels 2, Ghent 91, Liege 41	6	7	8	9
Belize	501	Belize City*, Belmopan 08, Corozal Town 04	−1	0	1	2
Bolivia	591	Cochabamba 42, La Paz 2, Santa Cruz 33	1	2	3	4

Figure 4.11 (continued)

Country Codes		City Codes	Time Differences U.S. Time Zones			
			EST	CST	MST	PST
Brazil	55	Belo Horizonte 31, Brasilia 61, Sao Paulo 11	2	3	4	5
Chile	56	Concepcion 42, Santiago 2, Valparaiso 31	2	3	4	5
Colombia	57	Bogota*, Cali 3, Medellin 4	0	1	2	3
Costa Rica	506	*	−1	0	1	2
Cyprus	357	Limassol 51, Nicosia 21, Paphos 61	7	8	9	10
Denmark	45	Aarhus 6, Copenhagen 1 or 2, Odense 9	6	7	8	9
Ecuador	593	Ambato 2, Cuenca 4, Guayaquil 4, Quito 2	0	1	2	3
El Salvador	503	*	−1	0	1	2
Fiji	679	*	17	18	19	20
Finland	358	Helsinki 0, Tampere 31, Turku-Abo 21	7	8	9	10
France	33	Bordeaux 56, Lille 20, Lyon 7, Marseille 91, Nice 93, Paris 1, Strasbourg 88, Toulouse 61	6	7	8	9
French Antilles	596	*	1	2	3	4
French Polynesia	689	*	−5	−4	−3	−2
German Dem. Rep.	37	Berlin 2, Dresden 51, Leipzig 41	6	7	8	9
Germany, Fed. Rep. of	49	Berlin 30, Bonn 228, Essen 201, Frankfurt 611, Hamburg 40, Munich 89	6	7	8	9
Greece	30	Athens 1, Iraklion 81, Kavala 51, Larissa 41, Patrai 61, Piraeus 1, Thessaloniki 31, Volos 421	7	8	9	10
Guam	671	*	15	16	17	18
Guatemala	502	Guatemala City 2, Quezaltenango*	−1	0	1	2
Guyana	592	Bartica 05, Georgetown 02	2	3	4	5
Haiti	509	Cap Hatien 3, Gonaive 2, Port Au Prince 1	0	1	2	3
Honduras	504	*	−1	0	1	2
Hong Kong	852	Hong Kong 5, Kowloon 3, Sha Tin 0	13	14	15	16
Iceland	354	Akureyri 6, Hafnarfjorour 1, Reykjavik 1	5	6	7	8
Indonesia	62	Jakarta 21, Medan 61, Semarang 24	12	13	14	15
Iran	98	Estahan 31, Mashad 51, Tabriz 41, Teheran 21	8½	9½	10½	11½
Iraq	964	Baghdad 1, Basra 40, Hilla 30, Mousul 60	8	9	10	11
Ireland	353	Cork 21, Dublin 1, Galway 91, Limerick 61	5	6	7	8

Figure 4.11 *(continued)*

Country Codes		City Codes	Time Differences U.S. Time Zones			
			EST	CST	MST	PST
Israel	972	Haifa 4, Jerusalem 2, Ramat Gan 3, Tel Aviv 3	7	8	9	10
Italy	39	Bologna 51, Florence 55, Genoa 10, Milan 2, Naples 81, Palermo 91, Rome 6, Turin 11	6	7	8	9
Ivory Coast	225	*	5	6	7	8
Japan	81	Kitakyushu 93, Kobe 78, Kyoto 75, Nagoya 52, Osaka 6, Sapporo 11, Tokyo 3, Yokohama 45	14	15	16	17
Kenya	254	Mombasa 11, Nairobi 2, Nakuru 37	8	9	10	11
Korea, Rep. of**	82	Pusan 51, Seoul 2, Taegu 53	14	15	16	17
Kuwait	965	*	8	9	10	11
Liberia	231	*	5	6	7	8
Libya	218	Benghazi 61, Misuratha 51, Tripoli 21	7	8	9	10
Liechtenstein	41	All points 75	6	7	8	9
Luxembourg	352	*	6	7	8	9
Malaysia	60	Ipoh 5, Kelang 3, Kuala Lumpur 3	12½	13½	14½	15½
Mexico	52	Acapulco 748, Mexico City 5, Monterrey 83	−1	0	1	2
Monaco	33	All points 93	6	7	8	9
Netherlands	31	Amsterdam 20, Rotterdam 10	6	7	8	9
Netherlands Antilles	599	Aruba 8, Curacao 9	1	2	3	4
New Caledonia	687	*	16	17	18	19
New Zealand	64	Auckland 9, Wellington 4	18	19	20	21
Nicaragua	505	Chinandega 341, Leon 31, Managua 2	−1	0	1	2
Nigeria	234	Ibadan 22, Kano 64, Lagos 1	6	7	8	9
Norway	47	Bergen 5, Oslo 2, Trondheim 75	6	7	8	9
Panama	507	*	0	1	2	3
Papua New Guinea	675	*	15	16	17	18
Paraguay	595	Asuncion 21, Concepcion 31	2	3	4	5
Peru	51	Arequipa 54, Callao 14, Lima 14, Trujillo 44	0	1	2	3
Philippines	63	Cebu 32, Davao 35, Iloilo 33, Manila 2	13	14	15	16
Portugal	351	Coimbra 39, Lisbon 19, Porto 29	5	6	7	8
Qatar	974	*	8	9	10	11
Romania	40	Bucharest 0, Cluj 51, Constanta 16	7	8	9	10
San Marino	39	All points 541	6	7	8	9
Saudi Arabia	966	Jeddah 2, Makkah (Mecca) 2, Riyadh 1	8	9	10	11

Figure 4.11 *(continued)*

Country Codes		City Codes	Time Differences U.S. Time Zones			
			EST	CST	MST	PST
Senegal	221	*	5	6	7	8
Singapore	65	*	12½	13½	14½	15½
South Africa	27	Cape Town 21, Johannesburg 11	7	8	9	10
Spain	34	Barcelona 3, Madrid 1, Seville 54, Valencia 6	6	7	8	9
Sri Lanka	94	Colombo 1, Kandy 8, Moratuwa 72	10½	11½	12½	13½
Suriname	597	*	1½	2½	3½	4½
Sweden	46	Goteborg 31, Malmo 40, Stockholm 8	6	7	8	9
Switzerland	41	Basel 61, Berne 31, Geneva 22, Zurich 1	6	7	8	9
Taiwan	886	Kaohsiung 7, Tainan 62, Taipei 2	13	14	15	16
Thailand	66	Bangkok 2	12	13	14	15
Tunisia	216	Msel Bourguiba 2, Tunis 1	6	7	8	9
Turkey	90	Adana 711, Ankara 41, Istanbul 11, Izmir 51	7	8	9	10
U.S.S.R.	7	Moscow 095	8	9	10	11
United Arab Emirates	971	Abu Ohabi 2, Ajman 6	9	10	11	12
United Kingdom	44	Birmingham 21, Edinburgh 31, Glasgow 41, Leeds 532, London 1, Sheffield 742	5	6	7	8
Uruguay	598	Canelones 332, Mercedes 532, Montevideo 2	2	3	4	5
Vatican City	39	All points 6	6	7	8	9
Venezuela	58	Caracas 2, Maracaibo 61, Valencia 41	1	2	3	4
Yugoslavia	38	Belgrade 11, Skoplje 91, Zagreb 41	6	7	8	9

For city codes not listed dial "0" (operator)
*City Codes not required
**Military bases cannot be dialed directly

To determine the time in the countries listed above, add the number of hours shown under your time zone to your local time (or subtract, if preceded by a minus sign). Time differences are based on Standard Time (in most states) from the last Sunday in October until the last Sunday in April.

Be a Clock Watcher

Telephone rates are often a factor in timing calls. In the continental United States, for example, there are four time zones, with a three-hour time difference between East and West Coast locations. Between Hawaii and Alaska and the West Coast there is a two-hour difference. The situation is further complicated because

Arizona and Hawaii never change to Daylight Savings Time and parts of Indiana never change to Standard Time.

Telephone rates change three times every day (see Figure 4.12). The weekday, or full, rate is in effect from 8 A.M. to 5 P.M. The evening rate, which is charged at 30 percent off the full rate, is in effect from 5 P.M. to 11 P.M. The night and weekend rate is billed at a 60 percent discount off the weekday rate and is in effect from 11 P.M. to 8 A.M. and all day on Saturdays, Sundays, and some holidays. These discounts may vary from time to time, so check the front of your White Pages for current rate information.

At the present time, telephone charges are based on the time where the call is billed. A collect call to Miami, originated in Los Angeles, is billed based on the time the call is accepted in Miami. All calls that begin in one time billing period but continue into another are billed based on the time the call was originated, no matter how long the conversation.

By placing calls before regular working hours (8 A.M. to 5 P.M.), people on the West Coast can take advantage of night rates when calling people in the Midwest and Eastern states early in the morning. People in the Midwest and East can take advantage of evening rates by calling the West Coast after 5 P.M. local time, when it is still before 5 P.M. in states west of them and people are still in their offices (see Figure 4.13).

Studies show that station-to-station calls are more economical in the long run than person-to-person calls, even when a station-to-station call fails to reach the intended person. If your call is going to be lengthy, you can afford to make several station-to-station calls before you reach your party and still save money.

Figure 4.12 **Rate Application Periods for Toll Calling**

	MON	TUES	WED	THURS	FRI	SAT	SUN
8 A.M. to 5 P.M.	BUSINESS DAY RATE						
5 P.M. to 11 P.M.	EVENING RATE						EVE-NING
11 P.M. to 8 A.M.	NIGHT & WEEKEND RATE						

Figure 4.13 **Area Codes and Time Zones—United States**

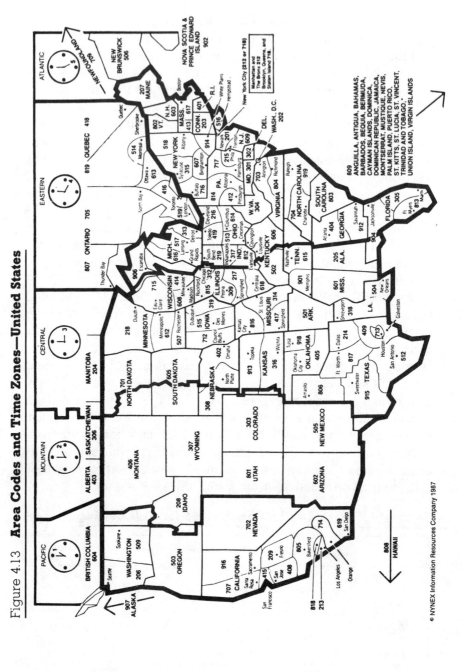

© NYNEX Information Resources Company 1987

If you have trouble when dialing directly, call the "0" operator and explain the problem. The operator will place the call for you, but you will be charged at the direct-dial rate.

A person-to-person call is the most expensive type of long distance call and may be used when you wish to speak only with a specific person or reach a particular extension number. Most businesses, as a matter of policy, do not allow their employees to make person-to-person calls. There are very few businesspeople today who will not return your call, even if it is long distance. When this happens, you end up speaking on their nickel.

When you direct-dial long distance and reach a wrong number, or if you have a poor connection, hang up and call the operator right away. Explain what happened and ask for a credit. The sooner the problem is reported, the easier it will be for you to get the credit on your phone bill. If you have reported your telephone out of order and you have been unable to make or receive calls for more than 24 hours, you are entitled to a credit on your next bill. Call a telephone company service representative and request the credit.

Should you have a dispute with the telephone company, call the business office and speak with a service representative. If you are dissatisfied with the decision or the explanation of the service you received, ask to speak with a supervisor. If the problem is still not resolved, climb the corporate ladder until you find the company official with authority to resolve the dispute.

The telephone company wants you to be satisfied. Sometimes, however, it can be awfully frustrating finding the right person to solve your problems. If everything you tried fails, call the manager of your local telephone company office. Explain the problem briefly and ask whom you can contact in the telephone company to help you. Usually when you do this, the problem is resolved within an hour or two.

As a last resort, contact your local Public Utilities Commission. Be prepared for a long wait. The wheels of government turn very slowly, but eventually they do turn.

Out of This World by Satellite

Microwave and satellite telecommunication transmissions are used by numerous common carriers to bypass many of the land problems created by weather, multiple switching, and electronic interference.

Due to the distance between the microwave, satellite, and transceiver, there is a slight time lapse between transmission and receiving. You have to watch your conversations and be polite. In circumstances in which two parties try to speak at once, their speech can become garbled and chopped.

Satellites can be used for calling from anywhere to everywhere. Companies offering satellite communications can help route your calls by using satellite transmissions in combination with local, Foreign Exchange, WATS, tie-line, or long-line services. Large groups of users can purchase or lease entire Earth stations that will transmit or receive satellite telecommunications in any geographical area.

To place a satellite call, you first must dial an access code, then the area code and telephone number you wish to call. Your call travels over regular telephone lines to the central terminal of the satellite company. From there your voice signal is routed by microwave to a land-based station that is usually located several miles from the center city, to avoid electronic intereference. Then your voice signal is transmitted to the satellite, where it is amplified; it is bounced back down to another ground station, and then travels by land line to the number you've dialed.

It usually takes only a short time for a communications expert to determine if your needs justify using satellite telecommunications. It will take a longer time for a team of experts and a computer to determine your optimum combination of land-based and satellite services. Your company size is not important; the key is its volume of telecommunication traffic. Satellite transmission becomes cost efficient when your company spends 45 minutes a day communicating between two cities that are at least 700 miles apart.

Promoters of satellite communication systems admit they are not always better than any one or all of the various special land-line offerings. Depending on your company needs and which type of land-line service you compare with which type of satellite service, satellite communications can provide you with a number of cost-effective advantages. In addition to cost effectiveness, satellite communications offer these advantages over other phone services:

1. More flexibility in system design
2. Better quality and reliability
3. Better management and control of your own telecommunications system

A privately leased satellite channel provides a direct line between two points for your exclusive use. It essentially offers the same service as a tie-line or a hot-line. You can use it to transmit voice, data, facsimile, teleprinter, or any combination thereof at any time, for a fixed monthly charge, regardless of how much or how little you use it.

The channel can be subdivided to transmit simultaneously two different types of communications, such as voice and data. A privately leased satellite channel is the most cost-effective way to handle a large volume of telecommunication traffic between two points that are at least 700 miles apart.

Teleports

One popular new real estate innovation and development is the so-called teleport. These are specially designed facilities where computer and telecommunications are established with a dedicated satellite channel for a group of companies in one real estate building or complex. These operations are primarily designed for long haul and data transmission, with all costs spread out among the large number of users, all of which are tenants of the complex.

Resellers

As the profile of the telecommunications industry changes, "resellers" are carving out their own separate niche. As the name implies, these firms operate by reselling basic telecommunications services acquired through AT&T, MCI, or other common carriers. For example, a reseller might lease a private line communications channel from MCI, then resell the service to a number of customers on a shared basis.

Teleconferencing

Teleconferencing is a simultaneous one-way video transmission to multiple locations via satellite, supported by a two-way audio hookup through conventional telephone systems. Some business executives think teleconferencing will make live meetings for large numbers of personnel from various parts of the country obsolete, while others look upon this stepchild of the space age as simply an "expensive toy."

Holiday Inns, the Memphis-based lodging chain, is spending $10 million to tie as many as 350 of its domestic hotels together with teleconferencing facilities through HI-Net, a satellite delivery system. It is piggybacking its teleconferencing capabilities on its Home Box Office installations at a cost of about $9,000 per location. Holiday Inns has opted to install a one-way video system. Although two-way video is technically possible, the cost—as high as $750,000 per location—is economically unfeasible.

Atlantic Richfield (ARCO) is investing $20 million in an internal teleconference network designed to link executives at six of its company offices in an attempt to reduce its annual travel costs of more than $50 million.

Picker Corporation, an RCA subsidiary, recently brought together 450 sales representatives in 30 locations for a training teleconference that cost $85,000. A similar conference seven years earlier to which the sales reps were flown to Cleveland cost Picker $550,000.

Excluding the costs of equipment to set up teleconference facilities, direct operational costs make teleconferencing unfeasible to all but large meetings. Satellite time currently costs $400 per hour during nonprime times and up to $2,000 per hour during prime time. A two-way audio hookup through the phone company will cost approximately $20,000 for a three-hour conference in 30 locations. "Uplink" charges, the cost of beaming a signal from the broadcast studio to a satellite during a teleconference, can run as much as $20,000, while "downlink" costs, the costs of getting the signal back down from the satellite to multiple receiving stations, costs about $2,000 per location per teleconference. Package deals are beginning to appear, with companies like HI-Net offering a 10- to 15-location teleconference package at a price of $21,000; however, a ballpark budget forecast for a reasonably sophisticated teleconference is still in the $100,000 range.

Things to Come—Interactive Television

The 1990s will see many changes in the use of the telephone as a marketing tool. Technology is far ahead of our present capability to cope with this electronic marvel on a large scale, but innovative marketers already are successfully conducting limited programs that some of us find mind-boggling.

For example, you can presently purchase, for about $100, the necessary hardware that enables your Touch Tone telephone to interact with your television set. Eventually, you will be able to sit at home and, by dialing your telephone, look through an entire sales catalog, perhaps even the Yellow Pages, on your television screen.

Here's how it works. You turn on your television set and pick up your telephone receiver. You dial an information number for the type of store (drug, department, variety, etc.) you are looking for, and an index of all the stores in that category located in your area will appear on your television screen. If you decide you'd like to do business with the May Company, you simply dial the number beside the name and a complete index of all the company departments will appear on the screen. You then push the number of the department you want, for example, linens, and on your screen will appear a list of every item the May Company has available in that department. You might pick pillowcases; and when you dial in the correct number, you will be presented with color pictures and prices of every pillowcase the May Company has in stock. You make your selection and dial the appropriate number for the item you have selected, punch in your charge code, and hang up. The item you have selected will be charged to your account by the May Company computer and shipped to you overnight by United Parcel Service.

Or, consider a medical emergency. Your daughter just fell off her tricycle, has a bad bruise on her head, and you don't know what to do. You just pick up the telephone, turn on the television set, and dial the emergency index number. On the screen will appear a menu list of all types of medical emergencies that occur around the home. You merely punch the right number into your telephone and your TV screen will instruct you what to do. The state of the art is such that by simply holding your wrist to the mouthpiece of your telephone, a machine can take your pulse and read back the results!

Interactive Television, as it is becoming known, is not without its problems, not the least of which is the individual's right to privacy as far as marketing information is concerned.

There's no end to the different products and services that eventually will be marketed through the combination of telephone and television. You'll be able to buy airline tickets and make vacation plans, compare the prices of tomatoes at your local supermarkets, find the items on special at the drug store, preview the various movies playing in your neighborhood theaters, and, if your local building supply company is inclined to sponsor it, even find out how to repair a leaky faucet.

The remarkable success in television shopping in the mid-1980s might be just a fad, but the incredible numbers don't lie. The Home Shopping Network was marketing over $8 million in goods in services *daily* in 1986. With these kinds of speedometer numbers, television shopping seems to be here to stay. Inbound telemarketing operations must take advantage of this extreme traffic to help sell up, add on, and increase sales. But it requires sales knowledge, management, enthusiasm, and a systematic approach.

During the closing years of the twentieth century, the telephone will introduce more changes in methods of marketing than were brought about by the innovations of plastics during the 1950s and 1960s.

Airline Telemarketing

United Airlines, the leader in testing and evaluating the concept of in-flight telephone service for air travelers, provides air-to-ground telephone service in its 104 widebody aircrafts. Airfone, Inc. handles this communication service for United's passengers at a cost of $7.50 per three-minute call to any destination in the continental United States. United's installations utilize a cordless headset allowing you to direct-dial your calls from the privacy of your seat. In-flight clarity is equal to normal ground telephone installations, and charges may be billed to major credit cards.

Entrepreneur Carl Icahn at TWA currently has plans to begin in-flight marketing of goods and services with a combination mail order–telemarketing operation.

Automated Telemarketing

In 1985, a major pharmaceutical company began an experiment in automated telemarketing that surprised many skeptics. Utilizing a pretested call guide to play prepared messages over the telephone, and integrated with a live telephone sales representative, each completed presentation had built-in responses to objections and was designed to be completed in less than five minutes.

The success rate was impressive. Of 2,500 completed presentations, over 15 percent resulted in sales, which totaled over $200,000. When analyzed on a per-call basis, this campaign achieved an astounding $600 sales per hour.

Computer-assisted telemarketing combines all of the benefits of computer technology with telecommunications. Some of the reasons for automated telemarketing's success can be attributed to the following:

1. Control
2. Increased productivity
3. Increased volume of calls
4. Flexibility
5. Cost accounting
6. Product information access
7. Inventory data base access to ease shipment and fulfillment success
8. Control of back orders
9. Price calculation
10. Customer history access
11. Information as to how to overcome objections
12. Information on competition and marketplace

Automated telemarketing takes many shapes and colors in the modern business community. Some companies use automated tele-marketing as a machine all by itself, to ask the questions and record the answers; they hope that the volume of calls will offset the lack of the human factor in selling techniques.

Other successful companies utilize a more hybrid operation that keys on combining human selling skills with computer terminal access to help have all the questions, answers, and ingredients needed to make a sale, all within the push of a computer keyboard button.

The computer-assisted telemarketing operation has many capa-bilities, including the ability to store and process a large amount of data on prospect profiles with psycho- and demographics, auto-matic control of follow-up calls, call analysis, and record-keeping.

Computerized Call Processors

These machines are very popular for government agencies that receive large volumes of inbound information-seeking calls. These computerized call processors keep several telephone numbers in their memories plus a combination of answering and message-playing abilities.

When a constituent calls the Federal Building, for example, the system answers the phone with a message. This message asks the caller to use his or her Touch Tone phone to qualify the reason for calling. For example, the caller would push 2 for tax forms needed, 3 for tax advice needed, 4 for the county clerk, 5 for the district attorney, and so on. Callers then press the desired number of the office they are calling and the system forwards the call to the right office. This machine replaces a switchboard operator and can record messages if the facility is closed or if someone is only asking for information or to get on a mailing list.

Some companies use these computerized call processors with both inbound and outbound telemarketing to survey and qualify for prospects.

Power Dialer with Answer Recognition

These machines are often used by collection agencies that make many calls but that don't wish to spend expensive time on busy signals and no answers. Here's how it works. The outbound and operator station lines are interconnected to one system. The operators punch in to the system the large volumes of telephone numbers they want the system to start calling. The system then starts dialing numbers. When a busy signal or no answer call is encountered, the system automatically feeds back for another number. When an answer occurs, the system automatically feeds the answered call to an available operator.

These machines are very effective for collection agencies because they can have one operator make high volumes of calls and still be able to make quality presentations. Many of these machines are popular with management because they offer accurate call accounting. They can provide detailed reports on how many calls were made, and how many busy signals and no answers there were. Many have built-in monitoring capabilities as well.

Integrated Voice-Data Terminals

A new tendency in the automated telemarketing industry is the so-called voice-data machines. These machines combine computers, automatic dialers, answer recognition, recording, and voice recognition. Some of the applications for these machines that are successfully being found for telemarketing pros include:

1. Low cost per call
2. Call accounting
3. Electronic mail capabilities

4. Telephone and computer management
5. Integrated data management and control

There can be some problems with machines that are controlled by voices. Accuracy is important and some of these machines have trigger fingers; they either recognize too many sounds as voices, or not enough sounds and cut people off. Other concerns deal with costs, vocabulary, training, programmability, input and output requirements, maintenance, and obsolescence.

The Professional Telemarketing Work Station

Telemarketing has come a long way since the simple black telephone days. That simple instrument still can be the best tool for telemarketing, but as the industry becomes more complex and sophisticated, so do the requirements of marketing and the equipment used.

The telemarketing work station of the professional telemarketer ideally should consist of the following:

1. Desk or cubicle
2. A computer terminal, with these functions:
    Telephone directory
    Directory of clients, prospects, personal friends
    Personal calendar and reminder file
    Log of calls for today
    Electronic scratchpad
    Product knowledge file (features, benefits, advantages)
    Objections file with ways to overcome them
    Modem for access to other computers and data bases
3. Telephone with these features:
    Speakerphone
    Auto-dial
    Auto-redial
    Memory or monitoring accessibility

The telemarketing work station can be as sophisticated or as simple as you can afford, but the foregoing example has been quite successful for the large, professional telemarketing operation.

Today we are on the verge of a new revolution in office facility organization, the so-called electronic office. With advancing technologies gaining in use by general business, only the future will tell if the office becomes a facility for hardware, including computers, electronic digital telephones, CRTs on every desk, word processors, fascimiles, and eventually the picture telephone where both parties see each other.

The Future Is Now

Telemarketing is growing so fast and technology is breaking boundaries so quickly that professional telemarketers really have to stay on their toes and remain aware of the many opportunities in this field.

Even with all of the expensive and sophisticated gadgetry available, an aspiring telemarketing operation can be created with the simple black telephone. Telemarketing success has in the past and is currently being achieved every day with those black telephones.

When entering this field of endeavor, it is best to analyze your personal objectives and spend only what you must to achieve them. Remember, always categorize your telephone expenditures as you would any other financial outlay. Read between the lines and find value for your money. Cut the corners where you can, but still let your prospect be able to hear you.

Chapter 5

~~~~~~

An Introduction
to Success

Organizing Your
Calling Strategy

The shortest distance between a salesperson and a prospect is a telephone line. When prospecting for accounts, the telephone is the greatest tool on-the-road salespeople have at their command. Salespeople who have mastered the techniques of telemarketing and have learned the art of using the telephone as a tool turn cold-calls into "warm" or "certain" calls.

Super salespeople have realized that the telephone helps them to work smart, not hard. The salesperson who has learned to use the telephone as a time- and money-saving device to prospect for customers, whether calling a prospect to introduce a product, make a sale, offer a demonstration, or whatever goal, is the salesperson who gets the benefit of the business from the telephone.

You need to develop a technique in prospecting on the telephone, just as you have developed your technique for selling and demonstrating your products during personal contacts. Most people who are reluctant to use the telephone as a tool feel this way because they do not know how to *use* it. There is no reason to be afraid of the telephone. It doesn't bite you. It can bring you closer to achieving your fantasies and dreams, and bring rewards with no limits.

The techniques discussed herein have been created over the

years by success. Lots of sweat and mistakes went into these words of advice. Study them, experiment with them, modify and adapt them to accommodate your special personality, product, or service, and soon you will join the elite ranks of the super salesperson.

Always organize your telephone calls in a sequence and keep a record of the results. Following a sequence is like following a road map. It keeps you in the fast lane right to business. It will also allow you to plan your conversations in advance, thereby shortening the length of your calls and keeping you in control of the conversation. Most important, if there is any possible way to find and create new business, sequence calling and record-keeping will allow you to discover it. Random, unplanned, and unrehearsed calling does not allow you to discover how or where you are successful and also tends to increase the amount of chatter on every call.

Know Where You Are Going

The first step in organizing your call sequence is to develop a list of the names of the people you plan to contact. Your list should include the name of the person you want to talk to, the name of the company he or she represents, and the phone number. When preparing your list, leave adequate space to write notes to yourself during conversations.

If the situation requires you to make blind or cold-calls and you don't know who it is you should speak with, ask the person who answers for assistance.

Once you have the name of the person you want to speak with at your prospect's place of business, record it on your card and you're ready for the second step of the sequence.

When making cold-calls, never ask for the purchasing agent. Always ask for the person who makes buying decisions. The only time you should talk to a purchasing agent or anyone else is after you have been referred to that person by management. It is much easier and more effective to start where decisions are made and work your way down than it is to start at the bottom and have to climb your way up the organizational ladder.

Why People Buy

The most important requisite in overcoming objections and closing the sale is to know why people buy. People are motivated to buy to satisfy a want, need, craving, or an inner drive. Sometimes people themselves are not aware of these reasons until salespeople arouse their interest and bring the reasons to their attention.

People normally make purchases because they believe that the ownership of a particular product or the advantage of a service will grant them some degree of benefit. This is true even when the motivating force may be pride of ownership rather than use value.

Most buying motives are emotional in nature, and nearly all goods and services are sold through appeal to the customer's basic pride. Most purchases are made to satisfy one or more of the buying reasons found in Figure 5.1.

Getting by the Secretary

In the normal mechanical application of the first call, the initial person encountered is usually either a switchboard operator or a personal secretary. These people are often trained to screen calls, but with practice you can get by them without much difficulty.

To get by these barriers requires special techniques that utilize unique combinations of chutzpah and self-confidence. When first calling the switchboard, ask authoritatively for the name of the secretary associated with the primary prospect or client to whom you desire to speak. Once the switchboard operator has given you the name of the secretary, ask kindly to be connected with him or

Figure 5.1 **Reasons Why People Buy**

To Save	**To Protect**	**To Reduce**
Time	Investment	Risk
Money	Self	Investment
Energy	Employees	Expenses
Space	Property	Competition
	Money	Worry
		Trouble

To Make	**To Improve**	**To Increase**
Money	Customer relations	Profit
Satisfied customers	Employee relations	Satisfaction
Good impressions	Image	Confidence
	Status	Convenience
	Earnings	Pleasure

her. Normally, you will meet with less resistance from a secretary if you already know his or her name.

With a firm, resonant voice, acknowledge the secretary by name and ask to speak to your prospect by his or her first name, forcing the secretary to assume either that it is an internal call from higher up or that you are the prospect's good friend; this technique might cause the secretary to become too nervous to ask for your last name.

If the secretary does ask who is calling, it is best to confidently and without hesitation respond with your full name, quickly adding, "Thank you very much." In almost every case, the combined use of asking for a prospect by his or her first name and the quick addition of a "Thank you very much" will bypass the secretary and minimize any further qualifying.

The primary purpose your prospects have in employing a secretary to screen calls is to save their time by eliminating any calls that can be handled by subordinates. The secretary is employed to filter wasted calls from the boss, but it is also the secretary's job to make certain all calls that should be directed to his or her superior are put through professionally and promptly.

Do not let secretaries feel you are trying to get past them. You can normally get a secretary on your side just by speaking pleasantly and confidently. Always identify yourself and do not forget the "Thank you very much."

When calling long distance or overseas, you can often give your call a sense of importance by adding the name of the city or country from which you are calling. Using a little phrase such as "United States calling for Mr. Jones" can bypass secretary after secretary until within seconds you are talking to your desired prospect. The secretaries never know how important your call may be, or how important you may be, but they won't take chances and normally put you right through.

Sometimes you will run up against a secretary who is trained to ask the nature of the call. You'll almost always get through to your prospect if you are ready for the question and have your answer prepared in advance. The key to an effective answer is to be brief but general in the terms of your response. Don't be too specific, but be firm in how you tone your answer. Portray yourself as an old friend or colleague and again use the "Thank you very much." It will work every time.

If the secretary tells you your prospect is tied up in a meeting or is not available for some other reason, always ask when would be the best time to call back. Often in such situations you may ask if your prospect can call back. When this happens, be sure to spell your last name and make sure the secretary understands your telephone number correctly.

When giving your phone number, always include the area code. Avoid giving your firm's name. A good tip on callbacks is to call the secretary by name. Secretaries are people, too, and they can help ease your foot into your prospect's door. So be sure to establish a relationship with the secretary from your very first call. If your prospect receives a message with only your name and phone number, lacking a firm name, he or she will normally return your call without hesitation. If the prospects receive your firm name, they will recognize you to be a salesperson, and might be more reluctant to return your call.

The Sequence Requires Control

How well you organize your call sequence becomes immediately evident the moment you start talking to your prospect. During the first few seconds of a call, many people make the worst mistake possible in telemarketing—they pass complete control of the conversation to the person on the other end of the line.

Keep yourself in the position of control. If you have preplanned the call and are completely organized with all of the sequences of the sales call, you will by osmosis lead the prospect through your presentation to your final goal, a sale.

Prospective Characters

There are many different types of prospects you will encounter in telemarketing, but many of them do fit into classifications worthy of study. Some prospects are "pushers," people as blunt as can be, who eat nails for breakfast and who don't have the patience for small talk. The best way to handle these people is to be upfront, honest, and right to the point. These prospects might be hard-heads but usually they are this way to put up defenses. No prospect likes to spend money, especially the pusher; but in the end, if you are confident, sincere, and persistent as well as forceful, you will get the sale.

Another type of prospect is the "painter," who enjoys articulately chosen descriptions of your product's features, benefits, and advantages. The painters respond to colorful phrases and buzz words. These prospects can make telemarketing fun, because they force you to find newer and better vocabularies to paint word pictures of your products or services. Every prospect is a painter at heart, so it is vital that emphasis be applied toward spicing up your scripts.

In every crowd there is a "hummer," and telemarketers must learn to recognize one before he or she costs you plenty in wasted time and bad freight. Do you know someone who constantly, returns goods to department stores? When the hummer prospects are called, they always seem to be able to be sold. They use such phrases as "Sure," "OK," "All right," and so on. They seem easy to sell on the first call, but you end up with your goods refused in shipping, or returned, or in the bad debt files. It is important that these prospects be qualified early, either through monitoring, confirmation callbacks, or with returned goods fees. These prospects give "buyer's remorse" a bad name, because they are habitually changing their minds.

The fourth type of prospect you are likely to meet in telemarketing is the "biologist." This type of prospect loves to dissect your entire presentation into its every tiny detail. The biologist most likely will ask to see everything in writing before making decisions. They usually will say, "I don't buy over the telephone." This, again, is a defense mechanism they employ to avoid having to buy anything. Most reputable businesspeople realize that, in today's complex and increasingly competitive marketplace, they must adapt and recognize the efficiency and economics of telemarketing.

The days are gone forever when the biologists can hide their heads in the sand. The best way to handle the biologists is to work with them. Send them your presentation in writing and follow up in a professional manner until you melt down their defense mechanisms and build rapport and credibility. When you are interacting with them on the telephone, always attempt to explain every detail in simple, understandable terms to which the biologist can relate.

Sequence of Success in Booking Appointments

Use this sequence every time you make a business telephone call. When not booking appointments, modify and adapt it to meet your particular needs. It's simple, it's foolproof, and it's perfect. Here, in easy outline form, are the 12 steps to the telemarketing Sequence of Success when booking appointments.

1. Develop a list of names.
2. Verify the prospect's name.
3. Make the prospect commit his or her time.
4. Introduce yourself.
5. State the reason for your call.
6. Qualify the prospect.
7. Make your sales pitch.
8. Overcome objections.
9. Ask for the appointment.
10. Sell your name.
11. Generate additional leads ("bird dog").
12. Smile, confirm, and express thanks.

If you use this sequence enthusiastically and modify it to fit any given sales situation, you can sell anything you want to anyone on the telephone. Be authoritative and never apologize for being a salesperson or looking for business. Selling is your job and people respect you for doing it well and in a professional manner.

Making cold-calls can be exciting if you have the right attitude and have preplanned your presentation. Cold-calls can fail if you use a list that doesn't correspond to the goals you wish to meet. If your survey, sales pitch, or questionnaire is too long in length, it can cause your prospect to become impatient or bored with your phone call. Try to limit your call to important information and make sure you keep the prospect involved in the call. Ask qualifying questions.

When designing your sales presentation, you must ask yourself the following questions:

1. How will I identify the decision makers?
2. How will I reach the decision makers?
3. What is the awareness of my company in the marketplace?
4. What is the awareness of my products?
5. How can I build awareness?
6. How can I develop customer interest in my product and company?
7. What input do I need to determine the customer's needs?
8. What questions can I ask to determine the customer's needs?
9. How can I best explain my product and company?
10. What media support (flyers, samples) can I provide?
11. What objections will I confront?
12. How do I overcome these objections?
13. What do I do if I get the order?
14. Can I give credit terms?

15. What kinds of follow-up are necessary?
16. What additional products/services can I sell up?
17. What are the steps to implement the sale?
18. How often do I call the customer back?

Successful telemarketing requires extensive homework before implementation of your first call. It is vital that telephone sales representatives perform professionally and with confidence; this requires product knowledge, sales skills, and an understanding of the fundamentals in telephone marketing.

Mastering the sequence of a sale can provide you with the foundation on which to build a successful telemarketing program.

The first step in the sequence of success in telemarketing is to develop a quality list of prospects.

The second step is achieved in your first call to the prospect. It is important to verify the prospect's name. This gives you information about the quality of your list, and clarifies that you are speaking to the right person.

Once you are speaking to the right person, ask if it is a good time for you to call, if he or she is free to talk with you, and, more importantly, if the prospect can commit time to the call. It is vital for the prospect to give integrity to your call, because you are wasting your time if the customer does not give you full attention. The prospect might have a client in the office, six other phones on hold waiting for his or her attention, or be late for a meeting. In such cases the prospect cannot give you adequate attention or be receptive to your presentation.

Now that the prospect has committed full attention to your call, introduce yourself and your company. This is common telephone etiquette and is important in establishing your credibility as a professional.

Once the prospect knows who you are, the firm you represent, and has committed to the call, your next move is to state the reason for your call upfront. Always have a good reason for your calls. The customer must know where you are leading, and that you are not wasting time. There should be a real reason for every call. It can be to inform the prospect of a special sales price; it can be to conduct a survey or to introduce the firm.

After the prospect understands your reason for calling, it is time to qualify that you are speaking to the right person. It is not very effective to try selling a person with no purchasing authority. Every time a prospect is called, the qualifying process must be attempted.

Many times we have been jilted into wasted phone calls that could easily have been avoided if the call was qualified at the outset.

At this time, make your sales pitch. Timing is everything in life, especially for salespeople. So make your presentation, and make it well.

Normally, now is when you will be confronted with objections. The successful salesperson looks at objections as opportunities for sales. Learn your objections and learn how to overcome them.

Once you have made your pitch and overcome the obstacles, ask for the sale or the appointment. The prospect expects it, and you have earned the right to make this request. Earlier in your call you gave the prospect the reason for your call, now you are making your presentation.

Continually sell yourself. Your name must generate positive images in your prospect's mind. Keep selling your name until you get the order.

After you have acquired your sale, ask your customer to provide you with additional leads. Also called "bird dogging," this is the secret to many future sales.

Now that all of the steps of the successful sale have been achieved, smile, reconfirm all of the details of your presentation and sale, and express thanks for the order. Every customer appreciates the salesperson who offers thanks for the order.

Chapter 6

~~~~~~

The Telephone Script

Preparing Your Sales Presentation

A picture is a poem without words.
                              Horace

*Noise proves nothing. Often a hen who has merely laid
an egg cackles as if she laid an asteroid.*
                              Mark Twain

Have you ever gone to a movie, and after sitting through two-
and-a-half hours, come out asking yourself, "What was happening
here?" "Where was the script?" "Did they make it up as they
went?" "Were they improvising, ad-libbing?" "They sure don't
make 'em like they used to!"

Well, these are the same questions that prospects and customers
ask themselves after receiving a telephone sales presentation from
an unprofessional or amateur, or a salesperson who doesn't care.

In order to avoid such fiascoes, the professional telemarketer
must prepare a manufactured, adaptable script that the telephone
sales representative can use either as an outline of topics to cover,
or as a verbatim, word-for-word scenario to be used uniformly on
every call.

Both the outline and the word-for-word format allow the telemarketer to measure the success or failure of a call, as well as provide a blueprint for consistency and success.

The outline normally consists of a conceptual skeleton of the 25 to 50 critical elements necessary to frame a quality presentation for the telephone sales reps, but it allows the reps the flexibility and room to add their own vocabularies, styles, and fingerprints to their pitch.

The verbatim script is normally used by the more inexperienced telemarketer, who needs to have the rigid discipline and a roadmap to follow. The verbatim script has some key benefits, including a greater devotion to the guidelines set by sales management, more uniformity in the presentations, higher standards of quality, more accuracy in data collection, lower training expenses, and the allotment of less time for analysis and more time for the actual writing of sales invoices.

The verbatim script allows a higher volume of calls to be made, in a more identical manner, with greater control, and with higher staff morale, leading to lessened customer dissatisfaction and the ability to increasingly target presentations to more specialized prospect lists.

People who read verbatim scripts are commonly called "telephone communicators." Many situations require the hiring of less-trained sales personnel, part-timers, and so on. The new field of communicators provides the perfect way for these people (for example, actors, college students, housewives, retirees) to enter the telecommunications industry. These positions also allow the telemarketers room for lower training costs and lower per-hour costs.

The telephone communicator plays a numbers game based on the law of averages. Unlike the sales account executive, whose success is directly dependent on sales techniques, the ability to close, and personality, the telephone communicator relies on the number of calls to produce a predetermined sales volume because the sales presentation and close is built into the script.

When a telephone communicator makes enough calls, he or she can make a good living. When they make even more calls, they can make an even better living. Their success relates directly to the volume of calls made, the quality of the script used, and their ability to enthusiastically communicate a written message without the listener feeling it is being read.

A well-written script can be tailored to any list of prospects. It controls the fairness of your offer, how effectively the sales message is delivered, and how many times it can be presented in any given period of time. It enables the telephone communicator to sell a product with a minimum of customer dissatisfaction, just a fair amount of actual product knowledge, and predictable results. After only a few hundred calls, you can begin to accurately predict the results of the entire campaign, because most scripts will produce a consistent amount of results from a given list over any volume of calls. Of course, if the quality of the list deteriorates, so will the ratio of calls to sales.

Base the Script on the Sequence

As in all aspects of telemarketing, the written script has its own version of the Sequence of Success.

When working from a prepared script, very often crew leaders will not allow follow-up calls. The communicator must either produce a sale on the first contact or forget the prospect entirely. Following the Sequence of Success in preparing and delivering a script will allow the communicator to eliminate superfluous discussion and develop a justifiable and predictable calls-placed-to-sales-made ratio. The Sequence of Success in presenting a written sales message follows:

1. **Start by verifying your prospect's name.**
2. **Identify yourself and your company.** By immediately identifying yourself and your company, you often prevent your prospect from subconsciously setting up a defense or simply hanging up.
3. **Tell the prospect why you are calling.** Be specific; do not make your prospect guess why you are calling. Do not hint at vague offers. Give the prospect a good reason, a benefit, that he or she can expect to receive from listening to your message.
4. **Ask fact-finding or "test" questions to determine if your prospect has an interest in your offer.** If the prospect shows no interest, thank him or her for the time and say goodbye.
5. **Make your sales presentation.** Your message must be clear, appealing, and precise. Use descriptive words and phrases to describe the features and advantages of your product or service. Do not say too much. Then tell your prospects what's in it for them. Tell them the benefits they will receive from buying your product or service. Limit your presentation to include only the one or two advantages and benefits that will most likely appeal to the largest number of your prospects. If your product or service has several

advantages and benefits and you don't know which ones of them will be most appealing to the largest number of prospects, then experiment with a "split-run." Make several hundred calls using substantially the same format, except every 200 calls vary the advantages and benefits. Your ratio of completed calls to sales made will soon tell you which of your product's advantages and benefits appeal to the largest number of prospects.

6. Overcome objections and ask for the order. When working with a script, you must assume the prospect will buy and you should always follow your answer to an objection with an attempt to close. Ask for the order by giving the prospect a choice. "Would you like to charge your order on Mastercard or VISA, or would you prefer we shipped it COD?" or "Would you like us to ship our product to you in red or blue?" If you have tried twice for a close and your prospect raises a third objection, simply thank your prospect for listening to you and hang up.

7. When you receive an order, **verify** the customer's name, address, and credit information, **read** the order back to be sure the customer understands what merchandise you will be sending, **thank** the customer, and **hang up.**

In preparing your script, write out all the objections you can expect to encounter, and prepare the best possible answer for each of them, including the attempt to close. By using a clipboard and various lengths of paper, you can easily tabulate the responses to various objections. Put your script on top, your answers to objections and attempts to close underneath. It's simple, and very easy to use. (See Figure 6.1.) When working with a script, time is limited, so whenever possible, answer every objection with good old "yes, but. . . ." Agree with the prospect, then give him or her a reason to buy in spite of the objection.

In writing your script, use short, easily understood words. Use as many single syllable words as is practical. After you've written the first draft of your script, count the words, putting a checkmark above every hundredth word. Go back through your script and count the total syllables in every group. If you have more than 150 syllables in any single grouping of 100 words, rewrite and simplify your script. Do not use any of those words that could be subject to different interpretations because they have more than one meaning.

Qualifying or test questions should be close-ended, those questions that are designed to be answered "yes." They are also called "tie-downs," and utilize endings such as "isn't it," "aren't they," "wasn't it," and so on. Properly written, your questions should

Figure 6.1 **Example of a Telemarketing Clipboard**

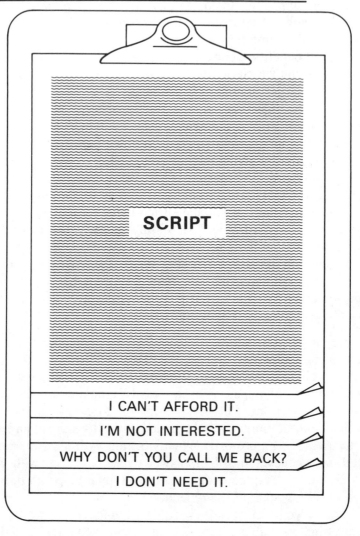

SCRIPT

I CAN'T AFFORD IT.

I'M NOT INTERESTED.

WHY DON'T YOU CALL ME BACK?

I DON'T NEED IT.

"demand" a positive answer from your prospect, which in turn will often trigger a defensive mechanism, the defensive objection. Defensive objections at this point of your presentation are usually the easiest to handle and more often than not will lead to a sale. Answer the objection and go for the close. If, on the other hand, your test questions trigger a negative response, then you must present the "alternative choice." The alternative choice gives the prospect the choice of two positives, both closing questions.

"Would you prefer red or blue?"

"Is ten o'clock OK, or would twelve be better?"

"Would you be making a 5 or 10 percent deposit?"

These questions give the prospect the choice between two *sold* situations. Either way the prospect is saying *yes* to the sale.

The alternative choice question should be a fundamental tool in every salesperson's toolbox, but one must understand that when you use such techniques you must emphasize to crews and to customers that they do not necessarily mean the customer is agreeing to the purchase.

One of the sales tactics that has given the telemarketer a bad name over the years is an unscrupulous use of the alternative choice. Yes, this technique is quite effective in selling, but it should only be used to assist in getting the early "yeses" that can help lead the conversation.

Always reinforce your negotiation to ensure that your customer completely understands what he or she has or hasn't bought. For this reason, it is a customary practice for most professional telemarketing operations to have a "verifying desk," which calls customers of written invoices to verify or confirm complete understanding of all prices, products sold, and terms. This practice can often eliminate misunderstandings.

For some of the really tough objections a prospect might ask you, another successful selling technique is called the "throw-back." This technique is characterized by the salesperson throwing back questions to the prospect.

If a prospect asks if a coat is available in red, the best way to respond would be, "Do you want it in red?" This automatically ties the customer down. It is also called a "porcupine" closing technique, because it is similar to a situation where someone throws you a porcupine. What would you instinctively do? Throw it back, of course. Whenever encountering leading questions about specific colors, styles, or sizes, always use the porcupine.

Another successful close is called the "assumptive close" because the salesperson assumes having the sale.

Here are some pointers for script writing:

1. Keep your scripts to 300 to 500 words/90 seconds.
2. Don't rush your presentation.
3. Talk "to" the customers and prospects, not "at" them.
4. Always attempt to gain the prospect's attention early with a strong opening statement.

5. Keep the prospect involved with questions.
6. Keep it simple, stupid (KISS).
7. Write it from the prospect's point of view.
8. Have a reason to call.
9. Use trial closes.
10. Get the communicators to believe what they are saying.
11. Make sure your offer is good.
12. Sell the sizzle—not the steak.
13. Sell benefits—not the product.
14. Don't write—telegraph.
15. Use descriptions.
16. Use testimonials and success stories.
17. Use an action closer. Get the prospect to do it *now*.

Once you have written your script and trained your crew on how to use it, do it. Use it. Normally you should test your script as suggested earlier. After this testing, you must analyze its success or failure with the following questions:

1. What was the percentage of positive responses?
2. What percentage responded negatively?
3. What percentage showed no interest either way?
4. What percentage refused to listen at all?
5. Why did they hang up?
6. What percentage raised objections?
7. What objections were raised?
8. What percentage wanted more information?
9. Was the call too long?
10. Are the trial closes and final closes in the right spot?

Figure 6.2 shows an evaluation sheet that is quite useful in analyzing each telemarketing call attempted. It forces the sales account executive to evaluate him or herself.

A successful telephone sales presentation must sound relaxed and natural. When a script is used, test it under actual working conditions using samples from your list and taping the calls. Practice, rewrite, and modify it until it works most of the time. No script is 100 percent successful, but if you incorporate the fundamentals discussed in this chapter, with the voice training necessary, your telemarketing can achieve the goals and rewards for which you search. You will find after a time that your sales presentation will flow easily and appeal to the prospect's ear. This is when you will start taking orders.

Figure 6.2 **Evaluation Sheet—For Analysis of Each Call**

Oral communication skills
Effectively presented ideas	1	2	3	4	5
Listened effectively	1	2	3	4	5
Obtained customer participation	1	2	3	4	5

Notes:

Ability to influence others
Gained customer interest	1	2	3	4	5
Displayed positive attitude	1	2	3	4	5
Offered convincing argument	1	2	3	4	5

Notes:

Fact-finding
Used available information	1	2	3	4	5
Probed for new information	1	2	3	4	5
Used open- and closed-ended questions effectively	1	2	3	4	5

Notes:

Behavior flexibility
Adjusted to customer need	1	2	3	4	5
"Tuned-in" to customer	1	2	3	4	5
Aggressive or passive as needed	1	2	3	4	5
Ability to adjust strategy	1	2	3	4	5

Notes:

Persistence
Level of determination	1	2	3	4	5
Ability to overcome objections	1	2	3	4	5
Convincing without being offensive	1	2	3	4	5

Notes:

Personal qualities
Voice tone	1	2	3	4	5
Voice inflection	1	2	3	4	5

Circle one number for each line: 1 is low and 5 is high. Totals become rating.

Three sample scripts are shown in Figures 6.3, 6.4, and 6.5.

Figure 6.3 **Sample Script—Booking an Appointment**

Hello. Can I speak with the manager or owner, please? Thank you. Hello, Mr./Ms. _____, my name is _____ with _____ and the reason I am contacting you today is to introduce you to our new line of _____ in our _____ line. Do you have a minute to talk? No?—oh, I can call you back. Is this afternoon at three all right, or would tomorrow morning at ten be better? _____

Yes?—great! The reason I am calling you is that _____ is having a super special on their standard _____ mufflers. What brands are you using now? _____ What prices are you paying currently? _____ Well, our standard muffler is a super, high quality muffler. It is two-tubed, galvanized, rust-resistant, and designed to give you super customer satisfaction at the lowest possible price. What we would like to do is get our foot in your door and let you see this muffler in person and also show you samples of our other lines of quality products, including turbos, glass packs, imports, and especially our super specials on clamps. Let me tell you what I'm going to do. One of my field representatives will be in your area this Wednesday and I will have him stop by to see you. Would ten in the morning be all right, or would two in the afternoon be better? Great! Let me confirm this. I will send my representative to meet with you this Wednesday at ____ o'clock. Well, it was great talking with you today; I'm looking forward to talking with you again. Thanks for your time. Have a nice day.

Figure 6.4 **Sample Script—Selling Safety Patrol Hats**

Good morning/afternoon. This is _____. May I please ask the name of the individual who handles purchasing supplies for your school safety patrol? _____

Mr./Ms. _____, this is _____ with _____ Company of Cloquet, Minnesota.

We manufacture custom knit products for many schools, clubs, and corporations.

Mr./Ms. _____, how many children are on your school safety patrol? ____

The purpose of my call today is to make you aware of our unique, new knit hat that is made especially for the "School Patrol."

Everyone has voiced a strong positive response once seeing this hat.

Our School Patrol Hat is 100% acrylic, a domestic brand. It's an easy care hat that is washable and one size fits all.

Most important, the School Patrol Hat has a half-inch reflective band that is manufactured by 3M. The body color is blaze orange, the stripe is white, and the words School Patrol are on the hat in black letters. The pom-pom is black.

Mr./Ms. _____, the hat is very attractive, yet it stands out and identifies the wearer as a member of the school patrol.

I'm sure you will agree that this hat will add to the safety of the child on the school patrol. Right?

There are 24 hats in a box. Each School Patrol Hat is $6.95 and there is a $6 UPS delivery charge on each case.

I would like your approval to send you one case of School Patrol Hats. Would you want delivery now or would you prefer to wait for the new school year and have them arrive the first week of September? Naturally, you don't have to pay for them until after you receive them.

Do you require purchase orders?

(If yes)   Please send us a purchase order. Let me give you our company name & address.
(Confirm order quantity, price, and delivery date)
Thank you—have a good day.

(If no)   Let me check the spelling of your name. What is your job title?
(Confirm order quantity, price, and delivery date)
Thank you—have a good day.

Figure 6.5 **Sample Script—Lead Generation: Bar Code Labels**

Unable to contact: Company: _____
_____

Phone: _____
Spoke with: _____   Contact: _____

Good morning/afternoon. This is _____ calling on behalf of _____ Commodities in _____. May I please ask the name of the owner/manager? _____ Thank you. May I please speak with Mr./Ms. _____? Thank you.

Mr./Ms. _____, this is _____ for _____ Commodities in _____. The reason I have called you today is to alert you to the fact that within the next six months to two years all shipments to major companies will require the use of bar codes! Are you aware that most major companies are, or soon will be, insisting on bar code markings on all incoming shipments from vendors for inventory controls? ____

What is a bar code? I am sure you have seen bar code labels when you go to the grocery store, right? ____ A bar code is a machine readable symbol, consisting of alpha, numeric, or alphanumeric characters. Bar codes use a series of wide and narrow bars and spaces to represent the preassigned number.

Mr./Ms. _____, are you currently using bar codes as part of your labeling? ____ Have you planned to use bar codes in the future? ____

To what market/type of customer do you ship? _____
Do you make shipments on government contracts? _____
Do you make shipments to the automotive industry? _____
What is your present method of labeling? _____
If now using labels, how are they prepared? _____
What type of label: pressure-sensitive: ____; dry gummed: ____
Are these labels preprinted? ____ Approximate use per month: __

Mr./Ms. _____, would there be an advantage if you could add variable information in-house?

May I suggest that we have a _____ Commodities field rep call on you to explain the advantages of the in-house pre-pared bar code labels? ____. Who should the rep contact?
    Mr./Ms. _____
    Title: _____
    Phone: _____

If not, would you like to see our literature? _____
Thanks for your time, and have a good day.

Chapter 7

Opening New Accounts

Your Road to Greater Wealth

All aspects of a salesperson's job are challenging, but opening a new account unquestionably offers the greatest degree of excitement and personal satisfaction. The basic principles of acquiring a new account by telephone are much like those you would use in eyeball-to-eyeball selling. There are some exceptions, of course. On the telephone, you must deliver your presentation in capsule form, relying on your voice to create an impression and cause your prospect to form mental pictures of your product or service.

Features, Advantages, Benefits

When attempting to open a new account, always stress the benefits of your product or service over its features or advantages. Features and advantages do not change very often, and certainly will remain the same whether the prospect buys or not. Benefits, on the other hand, are more flexible, and can be "changed" to suit the needs of your sales pitch. Also, benefits are usually your prospect's ultimate concern, and for this reason should be what your sales pitch focuses on. Every buyer wonders, "What's in it for me?"

Benefits save time or money, they make something possible, give customer or consumer satisfaction, promote self-esteem, or just plain appeal to your prospect's ego or greed. Once your prospects know how they will be benefitted by your product or service, they are easily converted into buyers. Although features and advantages may be important to your pitch, always stress the benefits.

Many professional salespeople don't understand the difference between a feature, an advantage, and a benefit. A feature is inherently built into and is part of the product. The advantage answers the question of why a feature is built into a product. The benefit is what the user will gain because of a specific advantage (see Figure 7.1).

For example, consider the Touch Tone telephone. The feature is the Touch Tone dialing mechanism. One advantage is that Touch Tone enables you to dial a number in one-fifth the time it takes to dial the same number on a rotary. The benefits are that you are connected to your party faster and spend less overall time completing each call. If you are a telephone salesperson making

Figure 7.1 **Sample Diagram of Features, Benefits, and Advantages—A Checklist**

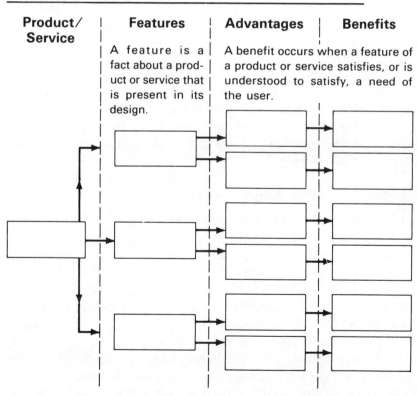

100 calls a day, Touch Tone will reduce the time you spend dialing by up to 20 minutes a day! Another advantage of Touch Tone is that it has the capability of "talking" to a computer. The benefit, depending on the application, may be that it eliminates the cost, expense, and space of a computer terminal in your office.

Let's look at an automobile tire with raised white lettering. The feature, of course, is the white lettering. The advantage is that it looks good and makes your car look better. The benefit is the pride you feel in knowing that your car, or at least its tires, look as good as they can. To many Americans, their car is an extension of themselves. They will buy tires with raised white lettering just for their appearance. To others, the raised white lettering only serves as an advertisement for the tire manufacturer and such lettering can be seen as a disadvantage, depending on who is evaluating this benefit. If a prospect is planning to sell his or her car in the foreseeable future, he or she could be sold tires with raised white lettering if convinced by the salesperson that the car's resale value would be enhanced with such tires. As you can see, features never change, advantages can change depending on the application, and benefits are strictly in the eye of the beholder.

Sell the Sizzle

It is a generally accepted axiom that people will not act unless they are prodded. If people didn't usually dread making decisions, the world would not have a need for professional salespeople. Many salespeople are deluded into believing that once they convince their prospect of the logic of their sales offer, the prospect will buy. Not so. People will not usually buy solely because an offer is sound and logical. Unless you appeal to your prospect's emotions, your chances of closing the sale are somewhere between slim and none.

Elmer Wheeler, often referred to as America's Number One salesperson, emphasized the importance of emotional appeal in selling when he said, "Don't sell the steak. Sell the sizzle." People who are not willing to accept an appeal on benefits or on logic may accept an appeal to their emotions. So if your sales pitch using benefits or logic seems to be failing, make a pitch to your customer's emotions, either a straight emotional pitch, or a combined appeal using emotions and benefits.

When your primary object is to open a new account, never try to sell the prospect more than a single item. Stress the benefits of your company and your products or services. It is unrealistic to go after a major order on the first call. Use the call-mail-call program. Attempt to get your literature into the hands of the prospect, and then offer a "special" on a single item, suggesting the customer buy a sample order.

Once you have succeeded in putting your prospect "on the books," you can build your volume of sales in future calls. The way to build an account is to help the customer buy. Never use "pressure selling" to "jam" this or that "down their throats."

Specials

The "special" you offer your customer must be just that—special! It may be a price concession, an add-on feature, a unique assortment, a discontinued item, or whatever. Don't tell your customer that if you sell so many of this or that, that you, the salesperson, will receive a bonus or a prize. The customer is interested only in the bonus or prize—the benefits—to be obtained from buying your product. For example, don't talk about the trip you're going to win to the Super Bowl; tell your customers how they'll enjoy watching the Super Bowl on the new big-screen television set they are going to buy with all the money they are going to save by using your product or service.

Call–Mail–Call

It's simple. It works. An average rate of response to a successful direct mail program is approximately 1 to 2 percent, including the many people who respond only to obtain additional information. When your direct mail projects interact with your telemarketing program, you can increase your rate of response from 2 to 20, 30, or even 40 percent!

Here is one way you can handle a call-mail-call program and achieve a high brochure-to-sales ratio. (See Figure 7.2 for a sales performance report form.) Before you begin, set an objective for yourself. Your primary objective during your initial telephone contact should be to inform your customer of an offer, or to obtain permission from your prospect to mail your company's literature. If you do obtain a minimum order, take it.

Working with a qualified prospect list, telephone your prospect and introduce yourself, your company, and the products or services

Figure 7.2 **Sample Performance Form**

Performance Report

OFFICE: _____

Date						
Hours						
Gross sales						
Verified sales						
V.S.P.H.						
Cancels						
Cancellation %						
Refusals						
Completed calls						
C.C.P.H.						
Wrong numbers						
Duplications						
No answer						
Total leads used						
Total conversion %						

Hours = Total Rep Hours for this project
C.C.P.H. = Completed Calls Per Hour
Total Conversion % = Verified Sales ÷ Total Leads Used
Completed Calls = #3 + #8
Total Leads = #9 + #11

you are offering (see Figure 7.3). Tell your prospects what they want to hear, namely, the benefits they and their companies will receive and how they personally will benefit from your offer. Ask permission to mail some additional information for review.

Figure 7.3 **A Checklist—Opening New Accounts**

The Telephone Call

1. Identify yourself and your firm.
2. Establish rapport.
3. Make an interest-creating comment.
4. Ask fact-finding questions.
     Confirm information you have.
     Obtain new information.
5. Deliver the sales message.
     Stress benefits over features.
     Use a sales vocabulary.
6. Overcome objections.
     Confirm understanding of the objection.
     Prepare the prospect for your answer.
     Answer the objection.
     Stress a benefit.
7. Close the sale.
     Use forced-choice questions.
8. Wrap up the sale.
     Confirm the order.
     Arrange for your next call.
     Thank your customer for the order.

Follow Up

1. Place the order.
2. Record the date of your next call.

Pre-Call Planning

1. Build a list of potential customers.
     Telephone books
     Trade journals
     Membership lists of trade associations
     The local Chamber of Commerce
2. Determine each prospect's ability to buy.
     Dun and Bradstreet
     Local credit rating bureaus
     Your own credit department
3. Set specific objectives for your call.
     Prepare fact-finding questions.
     Plan to sell a limited order.

4. Prepare your sales message.
  Stress benefits over features.
  Use a sales vocabulary.

5. Prepare your opening statement.
  Identify yourself and your firm.
  Establish rapport.
  Make an interest-creating comment.
  Fact-find to qualify the prospect.

Offer customers your special and tell them how they will benefit. If the prospect wants to give you a minimum order, take it. If not, do not pressure him or her. Verify the prospect's name and address, thank him or her, and promise to have the literature out in three or four days. Then hang up and address the information you promised to send. Finally, put the prospect's name and telephone number on your call schedule for three business days from the day your mail goes out, or four to five days if your prospect lives farther away than three days' mail.

When you make your first follow-up call three or four days later, tell your prospects the reason you are calling—to make certain they have received the promised material as well as to ask if they have any questions or need any additional information about your product line. Your primary objective here is to obtain a minimum order. It is unrealistic to set a goal of obtaining more than a minimum order on the first go-round. Try to sell your prospect a single item, not the entire line. Offer a special on this single item, just to get the prospect on your books and used to buying from you. Be sure to put a time limit on the availability of your special offer, and make that limit clear.

If you get that first order, cycle your new customer for periodic follow-up calls. If you do not get an order, place your prospect's name and number on your call schedule for a follow-up call in one week. Keep calling back each week until you get your first order. You may need to make several calls to interest your prospect and obtain a minimum order. You cannot call your prospect too many times, providing each time you do, you have something interesting or useful to say, either about his or her business or how your product can help him or her earn or save money. Do not call your prospect, however, just to ask for an order. If you have nothing interesting or useful to say, and you only call weekly for an order, you probably will get nothing but an irritated prospect.

Train Your Customers

Train your customers to buy when you call. If you made a cold-call to a prospect or a special call (one that wasn't regularly scheduled) to one of your customers to offer a special deal or closeout, don't be put off. If he or she needs an hour or two, sometimes a day or two, to check inventory or whatever, give it, but make him or her understand your offer is subject to prior sale. If the prospect hasn't called you back by the end of the time period asked for, then call again. If at that time you don't get the order, don't phone again until your next regularly scheduled call. If the prospect calls you later and wants to take advantage of your special offer, say you're sorry, it's been sold or it's no longer available. It may hurt to pass up the order, but after your customer has been disappointed once or twice, he or she will react promptly whenever you call again with a special offer.

When you are selling consumer goods directly to consumers, the foregoing selling techniques remain the same, with one exception. Selling consumer products demands you should mail first, three or four days before your first phone call.

If the product being sold to the customer is a one-time purchase with no anticipated future sales, there are successful telemarketers who never make more than one telephone call to a prospect. These people believe that callbacks will produce sales, but the same amount of time spent on new calls will generate even more. This is especially true for sales based on offers with premiums usually attached.

Statistics vary between studies, but it is reasonably safe to say approximately one-half of all salespeople quit after a single non-productive call to a prospect. Another 30 percent make between two and four calls before giving up. The remaining 20 percent of the salespeople write 80 percent of the business!! This point is stressed because without perseverance, there can be no success in sales.

Buyers are human beings, too. Like you, they have their good days and their bad days. They have their victories and their failures. Most of them comb salespeople out of their hair, so they set up defenses to make it difficult for you to approach them. Those defenses are the tools they use to conserve their time by eliminating the quitters as quickly as they can. It is a form of filtration. Filter out the bad and leave the good. The salesperson who calls on a prospect again and again and again is the salesperson who will eventually get the order.

Chapter 8

Hiring and Training the Telecommunicator

Hiring a telephone salesperson is not a matter of trial and error, although it sometimes seems that way. Proven salespeople don't always fit into the telephone sales mold. Just because the applicant can sell refrigerators to Eskimos in eyeball-to-eyeball selling is no assurance that he or she will successfully make the transition to the telephone.

The eyeball-to-eyeball salesperson uses visual clues to gain information, clues that are not available from the person at the other end of a telephone line. Another difference between eyeball-to-eyeball and telephone selling is the use of space. When selling in person, you can stand, sit, walk around the corner, move closer, and so forth; but on the telephone, the use of space is more ultimate and you can't use gestures or movements to present your message.

The limitations of time create another problem. On the telephone, time prohibits you from selling strictly "off the top of your head." You must stick closely to your sales pitch and get your sales message across in a relatively short period.

To be a successful telephone salesperson, one must have the basic instinct to sell. Experience is always helpful, but should not be a basic requirement. There are many people who have the basic sales instinct but are just too self-conscious to be successful in eyeball-to-eyeball selling; yet, when a telephone line is placed between them and a prospect, they develop the self-confidence and skills necessary to become superstars.

Back in the late 1920s when the first talking motion pictures made silent films obsolete, a very curious situation occurred when the highly paid stars of the silent screen tried to adapt to the new "talkie" industry. Many of them were found to possess shrill or strange voices and either had to take voice lessons, become character actors, or retire.

This same adaptation will be required of many of today's highly paid on-the-road salespeople who will be confronted with the new telemarketing technologies changing the way they do their jobs. It is estimated that there will be eight million new jobs in telemarketing by the year 2000. These new jobs will mean new job descriptions and new necessary skills for those wishing to enter this job market, either in sales, management, or accounting.

Before you interview anybody, you must develop a profile of the salesperson for whom you are looking. First you must identify your market, then match the salesperson to the market you consider your best prospects. You wouldn't, for example, want to put someone with a typical New England accent on an assignment selling pecans in Georgia, unless you want that person to stand out in a crowd. You must watch out for inherent personal biases on the part of the prospects. They might enjoy a strange voice or they might discriminate because of its strangeness.

Determine what kinds of tasks, other than selling, your salespeople will be expected to perform. What equipment will they be using? How complex are the forms they will have to maintain? What writing skills are needed? How "strong" must their arithmetic ability be? By developing a salesperson profile before you begin the interviewing process, you can determine exactly the type of individuals you should be looking to hire.

Before attempting to interview and hire anyone, adequate and precise job descriptions must be formulated to understand what type of people you require.

Job Descriptions

According to Connie Caroli, president of Telemarketing Recruiters, Inc. of New York City, here is a basic list of job descriptions and national 1987 base salary ranges and averages (in thousands of dollars) for employment opportunities in the current telemarketing industry. You can adapt them in various ways to your own situation, finances, and industry.

CORPORATE POSITIONS:

1. Telemarketing Director—Outbound. Complete marketing, strategic, and operations responsibility for the telemarketing division. Including: integrating the telemarketing function into the total company marketing mix, coordinating the telemarketing functions with other methods of sales and/or distribution, bottom line profits and loss responsibility for the division, monitoring the overall effectiveness of the telemarketing department and reporting performance to upper management, establishment of overall personnel policies, directing the sales and service activities of the telemarketing area toward meeting established goals, equipment selection, facility planning, systems design, and cost control. Average national pay for the consumer sector is $35–75, with a national average of $58 per year, and for the business-to-business sector is $41–82, with a national average of $62 per year.

2. Telemarketing Manager—Outbound. Responsible for planning, implementing, and managing the telemarketing department and its programs. Including: hiring and training staff in sales and phone techniques and product awareness, structuring telephone sales representative (TSR) incentive and motivation programs, developing operational procedures and directing the administrative functions, developing the fiscal budget and determining and monitoring productivity standards and individual sales quotas, list selection and data base analysis, and developing direct mail campaigns to support the telemarketing sales effort. Pay: consumer is $25–45, with a national average of $37 per year, business-to-business is $28–53, with a national average of $42 per year.

3. Telemarketing Supervisor—Outbound. Supervisory management responsibility for a group of TSRs within the telemarketing area. Including: recruiting, evaluating, and motivating the sales force, developing and implementing TSR training programs, scheduling TSR staff, administrating payroll, and preparing progress and productivity reports. Pay: consumer is $19–24, with a national average of $21 per year, business-to-business is $21–26, with a national average of $23 per year.

4. Telemarketing Manager—Inbound. Management responsibility for the order taking and/or customer service functions of the corporation. Including: responsibility for orders and inquiries, hiring and training staff in phone techniques and product knowledge, designing and implementing telephone customer service training programs, implementing and monitoring the telemarketing order entry system, developing policies pertaining to fulfillment of orders placed by phone and notification of back-ordered merchandise and cancellations, preparing and implementing the budget, monitoring sales records and designing productivity reports, designing programs for upselling and cross-selling of products, and monitoring price quotation activity. Pay: consumer is $22-40, with a national average of $30 per year, business-to-business is $25-43, with a national average of $32 per year.

5. Telemarketing Supervisor—Inbound. Management and supervisory responsibility for a group of TSRs within the order taking, customer service area. Including: administrating payroll, supervising clerical and administrative support staff, transmitting sales orders between the TSRs and the order processing and shipping-fulfillment area, and keeping TSRs updated on product features and pricing. Pay: consumer is $18-22, with a national average of $20 per year, business-to-business is $19-24, with a national average of $22 per year.

SERVICE AGENCY POSITIONS:

6. Telemarketing Director. Full responsibility for the marketing operations and administration of the telemarketing service center. Including: planning, developing, and executing individualized telemarketing programs for accounts, analyzing billing and program performance to determine center profitability, formulating and controlling budgeting and pricing, client relations and development of client reporting systems, sales forecasting and analysis, facility design, and telecommunications equipment selection. Pay: $38-65, with an average of $48 per year.

7. Telemarketing Manager. Responsible for the operations of the telemarketing service center, including client relations for ongoing programs. Including: managing ongoing accounts through liaison with clients and overseeing individual project development, job estimating, billing, and scheduling of projects and employees, developing and issuing reports illustrating project activity and trends and changes in projects that affect center operations, and monitoring and reporting program progress to clients and service center management. Pay: $25-38, with an average of $32 per year.

8. Telemarketing Supervisor. Day-to-day supervisory responsibility for a group of TSRs within the service center. Including: testing, training, monitoring, and evaluating TSRs, interviewing and selecting TSRs to work on specific accounts, writing specific account descriptions and objectives, summaries and daily account reports, and scheduling and managing staff and work flow. Pay: $17-23, with an average of $20 per year.

9. Sales Director. Responsibility for hiring and administrating the sales executives (account executives) who market and sell telemarketing services. Including: evaluating the marketplace and developing effective sales and marketing strategies, implementing lead generation programs and developing trade advertising and promotional literature, preparing marketing plans for current and prospective clients, creating and designing customized programs for client companies, and working with major clients and assisting in closing other accounts. Pay: $38-75, with an average of $54 per year.

10. Account Executive. Sales and marketing of telemarketing services to client corporations. Including: prospecting, cold-calling, and following up leads, communicating client needs to service center management staff for evaluation, feasibility, and eventual implementation, developing telemarketing campaigns for clients including marketing plans, direct mail analysis, and recommendations for telemarketing support, telemarketing project implementation and administration, maximizing client billings by initiating new projects and expansion of ongoing programs, and billing invoices for payment and maintaining all corresponding records. Pay: $27-42, with an average of $36 per year.

11. Telemarketing Training Manager. Responsibility for interviewing, hiring, indoctrination, and the initial and ongoing training of TSRs. Including: maintaining complete personnel records, researching and creating a telephone sales training manual, monitoring and critiquing TSRs, assigning personnel to programs through assessment of strengths, conducting sales meetings and workshop training seminars, and establishing call standards and implementing tracking programs to maintain call quality. Pay: $24-40, with an average of $35 per year.

12. Telemarketing Services Manager. Responsibility for developing programs and procedures to ensure the success of the telemarketing project. Including: gathering product and project information and goals, developing a workable and effective script, testing and monitoring script success and analyzing call data, and making specific product and project recommendations to management. Pay: $22-34, with an average of $28 per year.

13. Telephone Sales Representative. Responsibility to communicate and sell the presentation to clients, prospects, and customers. Including: enthusiastically presenting scripts without deviation, maintaining accurate call records, maintaining and contributing to ethics and integrity of employer, acquiring all possible product knowledge to accurately describe benefits, features, and advantages, acting as forum for information flow between management and customers/prospects. Pay: $4–15 per year.

What Is a Telephone Sales Professional?

Beyond the basic sales instinct, there are several things you will need to keep in mind when looking for successful telephone sales professionals.

1. A telephone salesperson must have a pleasant voice, not necessarily a beautiful voice, just one that is easy to listen to. A great deal of emphasis must be put on voice tone and control. Your successful applicants should speak clearly and distinctly, not sounding young or old. We know that to most salespeople, this sounds absurd, but there are fairly reliable statistics that show the majority of sales are made by salespeople that are within five years of the age of the buyer. This has not been proven to be true in telephone sales, but it is important to remember.

2. Telephone selling is not an easy job and one can expect to be rejected at least 90 percent of the time. Consequently, a telephone salesperson must have objectivity and realize the law of averages predicts many failures for each successful sale.

3. Successful telephone salespeople must have positive attitudes, and cheerful and happy dispositions.

4. Look for persistence in your applicant. The salesperson who works a little harder will consistently experience the sweet smell of success.

5. The telephone sales rep must be a good listener, sensitive, and responsive to tone of voice, hesitations, and pauses. They must rely on their listening skills to detect buying signals.

6. Sincerity and integrity go hand in hand. You do not want your people to make the sale at any cost. They don't have to lie, cheat, or misrepresent to sell your product or service. By their words, your salespeople must protect your good name.

7. You must look for thoughtfulness. Any good salesperson must be considerate of his or her customers' needs and capable of understanding their problems, motivations, and desires.

8. The salesperson must have superior organizational skills. This job is characterized by a machine-gun–like pace, and to keep up, the professional telephone salesperson must know every objection, every feature and benefit, every product-specific piece of information, pricing, and credit policy. And everything must be organized and ready at a split-second's notice. It takes special reflexes.

9. The salesperson must be able to work long hours at steady paces in very small, confined environments that have one special characteristic—solitude. The successful telephone sales representative must be capable of being alone and not go stir-crazy.

10. The professional must also be a team player, one who enjoys and accepts competition and who is willing to work and help other employees.

To restate the primary characteristics of an ideal telecommunicator, he or she must have great listening skills, a positive attitude, the ability to be objective, some sales ability, and most of all, a special, pleasant, enthusiastic voice. Other important attributes that characterize many successful telephone sales reps include assertiveness, persuasiveness, responsiveness, thoroughness, stability, and honesty.

There are really only two ways to generate a flow of applicants for your sales position:

1. Put an ad in the newspaper.
2. Enlist the assistance of an employment agency.

Newspaper ads should be short, specifying that you are hiring telephone salespeople, the hours successful applicants will work, and offering a realistic earnings figure. The ad should also state when and where to call for an interview. It is very important that applicants make their first impression to you over the phone. This allows you to instantly gain a customer's or prospect's perspective as to how the applicant's voice either stimulates or provides negative reactions. This telephone interview also allows you to filter and screen out the terrible, strange, or negative voice, both saving you from wasting your time interviewing known losers and freeing you to spend more time working with qualified and positively potential employees.

In order to be of use to you, an employment agency must screen your applicants first. To do this, they must fully understand your salesperson's profile and have a list of any specific questions you want to ask. Confer with the agency personnel beforehand so they fully understand your parameters and guidelines. Otherwise, you'll end up paying for a service you won't receive. One positive trend in employment agencies is the newly introduced specialized agencies working strictly with professional telemarketers.

In New York City and Chicago, an important employment agency is Telemarketing Recruiters, Inc., which credits itself with specializing in telemarketers who know it is a profession. As the telemarketing industry expands in the coming years, it will be necessary to use more and more of such agencies in filling our needs. Training and employee turnover are both very expensive propositions for management. But whether you do the hiring yourself or through an agency, it all begins with the interview.

The Interview

As previously stated, no matter which way you handle the interviewing, you must have your qualified applicants make their first contact to you via the telephone. The interviewer must now begin to think like a customer or prospect. You must role-play to gain the all-important first impression of this applicant's voice.

When the potential telemarketer calls you, you must at this time evaluate the voice for clarity, diction, modularity, and the attitude communicated. You must ask yourself if it is possible to detect a smile in the applicant's voice. Does his or her voice generate enthusiasm, is it persuasive, is it believable?

Other important questions that you must answer include whether the applicant is articulate, how strongly he or she controls volume and rate of speech, builds rapport, and sounds confident and experienced. Does the applicant seem to believe what he or she is saying? Does he or she seem relaxed? Use the telephone as your personnel office.

Once the applicant has proved to have the potential attributes needed to be a successful telemarketing sales rep, invite him or her in for an in-person interview. It is here that you evaluate the ability to be a good co-worker. As in all business relationships, telemarketing succeeds through teamwork.

The applicants must prove to be capable of generating confidence, respect, and rapport from their peers. Can they work in a relatively small space without going stir-crazy? Do they seem capable of thinking quickly on their feet? How well do they seem to be at organizing themselves?

It is a very useful idea to begin your in-person interview by asking the applicants to give you a verbal life history. This will allow you to evaluate their ability to think quickly, organize their thoughts in an orderly fashion, create word pictures in your mind, generate favorable mental images with their voice control, and help you gain an insight to their personal goals and ambitions.

Once they have provided answers to the foregoing questions, then you must determine the whys and wheres and hows in their reasons for wanting a job at your firm. Why are they interested in the job? Do they have any previous experience in telemarketing? Was it a positive or negative experience? What do they feel their strong points and weaknesses to be in terms of telemarketing?

In order to provide the most efficient means of conducting such interviews, it is most important that you have all of your criteria and questions preplanned and written down.

Once you are satisfied with the scope of your prospects' answers, describe to them all of the characteristics about your operation and job details that give them incentives for wanting to work for your firm. Include information about working conditions and the kind of equipment used, and explain how you determine salaries, commissions, and bonus plans.

If you haven't disqualified the applicant at this point, it probably is the time to hire him or her, for the applicants who can prove themselves through this type of screening probably will serve you well.

Using these guidelines and your own instinct, you can now evaluate and select your new salespeople with a reasonable degree of confidence and success. In telemarketing, experienced and enthusiastic people are a company's greatest asset, and well-managed companies watch their people flow as closely as they watch their cash flow.

Your competitors know who your "Superstars" are just as well as you do, and a bidding war is expensive. The way to prevent people from considering offers from competitors is to recognize the problems before they become facts.

Recent studies conclude that although the size of a salary and the depth of the benefit package are usually enough to retain journeyman talent, they have little effect in keeping truly gifted people stationary.

When hiring the telemarketer, though, there is often a temptation to glamorize and oversell a position to get a truly talented person. Be realistic, but don't undersell the job, either. Let the candidate know the range of experience necessary to get the job done, the responsibilities of the position, and the possibilities for advancement.

If you don't do this, and you hire the candidate, before very long you will find him or her using your telephone and photocopier to look for another job.

Training and Keeping Your Employees

The first few days on the job are the most important in developing a favorable picture of your company in the mind of your new recruit. Spend the time and expend the effort to get him or her acquainted and involved in the mainstream of your operation as quickly as possible. The degree of orientation will determine how quickly you will start "getting a return on your investment" and will encourage the new employee to develop a sense of loyalty and belonging. The more you can do, the more your new employee will know that you really are interested in his or her development and that you consider him or her a valuable addition to your staff.

Encourage all employees to develop communications with department heads. Let promising employees know that you seek and value their opinion. Without access to management, an employee cannot truly feel a sense of belonging. As a manager, you can't allow everyone to just "drop in," but neither is it wise for you to make your subordinates run the gauntlet to gain access to your ear.

The training process has several steps, including:

1. Role-playing
2. Trainer-TSR, and trainee-prospect
3. Demonstration calls
4. Question-and-answer sessions
5. Word and vocabulary selection
6. Learning the script

It is important that in your training you allow for adequate input to enable your new employees to understand the fundamentals of your operations. This should be both oral and written input. There must be substantial questioning sessions that allow the trainees to learn all stages of training. But this has to be a two-way street, allowing extensive responses by you and your trainees to their own questions.

Reinforcement must be provided to show through practical examples how and why everything is done the way it is. You should provide hands-on testimonies by experienced professionals. This allows trainees to pick their brains and provide real-life examples of the right ways to do tasks.

You must also provide special stimulation to the trainees via simulated calls, which allow them to make mistakes, but also to learn by these hands-on experiences. You must also encourage trainees to reach for the sky. These motives are best triggered through incentives and quotas, which enable trainees to know what is expected, and help them to understand the fantastic successes they can achieve.

To have an effective telemarketing training program, you must do the following.

1. Define the procedure to be learned. This must include all elements of education in the fundamentals of what constitutes a sales call. The trainee must learn to recognize the steps to a sale, as well as learn the script he or she will be using. Just as a waiter or waitress must learn the menu in a restaurant, telemarketing sales reps must learn their products and their scripts until they are reflexive notions in their minds.

2. Give a sample presentation of a quality performance. The next step in the telemarketing training process is to show the trainees an example of what a truly successful and quality presentation looks and sounds like. The best way to accomplish this is either to have the trainees listen or watch sample video and/or audio tapes of successful calls or actually have a professional telemarketing sales rep make a quality call in their presence. Much as in an acting class, the trainees experience a special kind of exhilaration and intensity unique to witnessing an actual call.

3. Give the trainees their turn. Once the trainees have seen and heard what a quality call entails, and they have learned the necessary product knowledge and sales skills, it is time for them to take their first dive into the pool of telemarketing success. The best way to let them get their feet wet is to have the trainees perform sample calls on tape and then play the calls back for them. During the playback sessions, the trainees learn to recognize the simple mistakes they are too nervous to hear during the actual call. They will begin to recognize the verbal and mental signals that prospects and customers give the telemarketing rep on every call.

4. Be sure the trainees practice, practice, practice. After the trainees have learned the sales and product skills necessary to adequately conduct a quality discussion, and they have seen firsthand how a pro works, and once they have experimented with sample calls, it is finally time to let them make mistakes for themselves. But before you let them make actual calls, it is usually recommended that they have made and listened to at least 20 sample calls.

Sales Account Executive Evaluation

The evaluation form shown in Figure 8.1 should be completed by the sales account executives upon being hired and at least once every few months to get a good pulse of their emotional and motivational morale.

Telemarketing today requires specialized expertise. No longer is it easy for most industries to allow the hiring of inexperienced and untrained sales reps who grab a phone book and start calling. Complexity in product lines and sales technology as well as economics in training forces the influx of a new breed of professional telemarketers.

This is not to say that you cannot adequately train your own telemarketing staff from within. Using the broad techniques outlined in this chapter, even the smallest and most cost-conscious firm can train a new staff of professional and successful telemarketers. Do it, and do it right!

Figure 8.1 **Sales Account Executive Evaluation**

Name _____ Date _____

1. Do you enjoy selling?

On a personal one-to-one basis?	___ yes ___ no
Over the telephone?	___ yes ___ no
At the retail level?	___ yes ___ no
At the wholesale level?	___ yes ___ no
Door to door?	___ yes ___ no
A tangible product?	___ yes ___ no
An intangible product?	___ yes ___ no
A service?	___ yes ___ no

2. Do you procrastinate? ___ never ___ sometimes ___ always

3. Are you personable? ___ yes ___ no

4. Do you have the ability to communicate ideas? ___ yes ___ no

5. Are your sales presentations honest? ___ always ___ sometimes ___ never

6. Can your Sales Manager motivate you? ___ always ___ sometimes ___ never

7. Do you shift responsibilities to your Sales Manager? ___ always ___ sometimes ___ never

8. Can your Sales Manager shift responsibility to you?
   _____ always _____ sometimes _____ never

9. Do you spend too much time making calls instead of sales?
   _____ always _____ sometimes _____ never

10. Are you a perfectionist at making alibis? _____ always
    _____ sometimes _____ never

11. List three things you like about selling on the telephone.

    _____

    _____

    _____

12. List three things you dislike about selling on the phone.

    _____

    _____

    _____

13. Do you buy "hard luck" stories instead of merchandise?
    _____ always _____ sometimes _____ never

14. Do you "sell catalogs" instead of merchandise? _____ always
    _____ sometimes _____ never

15. Are your sales presentations boring? _____ always
    _____ sometimes _____ never

16. Does your company offer you job security? _____ always
    _____ sometimes _____ never

17. Is your income potential attractive? _____ yes _____ no

18. Do you believe there is a future for you selling on the
    telephone? _____ yes _____ no   If no, why not? _____

    _____

19. Do you think our company should add additional product
    lines? _____ yes _____ no   If yes, what type of products? _____

    _____

20. Do you depend on your Sales Manager for leads and
    prospects? _____ always _____ sometimes _____ never

21. Do you plan your day in advance? _____ always
    _____ sometimes _____ never

22. Do you keep records and dates of your calls? _____ always
    _____ sometimes _____ never

23. Do you fear competition? _____ always _____ sometimes
    _____ never

24. Does the word "no" inhibit you? _____ yes _____ no

25. Are you punctual? _____ always _____ sometimes _____ never

26. Do you promise your customers things that you know your company cannot deliver? _____ always _____ sometimes _____ never

27. Do you discuss your personal problems with customers? _____ always _____ sometimes _____ never

28. Do you have adequate product knowledge? _____ yes _____ no

29. Do you have adequate knowledge of competitive products? _____ yes _____ no

30. Do you have adequate knowledge of your competitor's prices? _____ yes _____ no

31. How do you rate your company's training program? _____ excellent _____ good _____ fair _____ poor

32. How long have you been a salesperson? _____ years _____ months

33. How long have you been selling your present or similar products? _____ years _____ months

34. How can you help our company? _____

_____

_____

_____

35. How can our company better help you? _____

_____

_____

_____

36. Write in below the primary responsibilities of your particular job.

_____

_____

_____

_____

_____

37. List below the four types of incoming calls that you process.

_____

_____

_____

_____

38. List below the six rules of telephone etiquette which should be practiced on every telephone call.

_____

_____

_____

_____

_____

_____

39. List below five techniques that ensure effective telephone selling.

_____

_____

_____

_____

_____

40. List below six cardinal steps (rules) of a telephone call.

_____

_____

_____

_____

_____

_____

41. List four of your most common objections (reasons) why the customer does not buy.

_____

_____

_____

_____

42. Describe [Our Product] in 25 words or less, as you would when you are selling a customer this product on the telephone.

_____

_____

_____

_____

_____

43. What do you want out of this training session?

_____

_____

_____

The Telemarketing Voice

Before introducing the crew of telephone communicators to the scripts they will be presenting, it is a good practice to work with them in training their voices to become better "telemarketing voices." Many crew managers specifically hire actors, actresses, and singers because of their already trained voices. Paralinguistics have created a science that is used daily in telemarketing. They study the rhythm and rate of our speech, as well as the tone of the voice, and the amount of distinction and clarity in our speech.

Telemarketers must have happy faces.

A good way to start your training is to have each of the communicators tape record their voices over the telephone. No one ever really recognizes his or her own voice when recorded because the voice sounds so strange.

Train the reps to concentrate on their pitch. Just as in music, each voice has a pitch whether it be soprano, alto, baritone, or tenor. Some voices sound better on the telephone than others. Voices that sound too shrill can turn off a customer. It has been found through the years that the most effective telemarketing voices lie in the baritone range.

Train the reps to concentrate on the volume and projection of their voices. It is not good to talk too loud or too low. You want your customer to at least hear the presentation.

Train the reps to concentrate on the inflection they use in their voices. The best telemarketers vividly use expression, speed of the voice, and rhythm to give their voices flavor and gusto.

Train reps to concentrate on enthusiasm. Enthusiasm is contagious, and customers should catch the disease from telecommunicators. No prospect can forget or fight the exhilarating, the feverish, the zealot. So make the reps enthusiastic and they will sell.

Train the reps to smile. Using your tape recorder, have your people try to distinguish between conversations where the communicator smiled, was standing, sitting straight up, or when the communicator was slouched in his or her chair and in a frowning mood. You can tell the difference, and so can the customer.

Every day, before making a single telephone call, every communicator should engage in a series of simple relaxation exercises to release any tension that can affect the telemarketing voice. These exercises include:

1. Sit comfortably in a chair, with your feet flat on the floor, and your back straight.

2. Close your eyes.
3. Start breathing slowly, deeply, concentrating on relaxing all muscles, especially those in your face, neck, shoulders, and throat.
4. Slowly roll your head in a circular motion from side to side, than back the other way.
5. Squeeze your face tightly as much as possible, moving your nose as close to your ears as is possible.
6. Open your mouth as wide as possible, stretching and squeezing your jaw muscles and your cheeks as much as possible.
7. Keep breathing slowly and deeply.
8. Open your eyes.

These exercises will increase the circulation in your upper body, and at the same time cause you to relax and regenerate your awareness and voice.

A fantastic, proven training exercise for learning how to control rhythm and the speed of the voice, and for adding expression consists of writing the following on a blackboard:

This product is priced right.
This *product* is priced right.
This product *is* priced right.
This product is *priced* right.
This product is priced *right.*

Have the communicators practice speaking the lines, each time expressing the sentences differently, thus changing the meaning of the sentence. This exercise teaches how to use the voice to paint pictures.

Train the reps to concentrate on enunciation. By listening to themselves on the tape recorder, they will discover themselves mumbling, slurring words, or speaking either too fast or too slow. Customers must understand what the telecommunicators are saying. Therefore, it is imperative to communicate at a speed and distinction they can understand.

Have the reps watch television commercials to count the speed of dialogue spoken. The actors and actresses used in television and radio commercials are trained to speak at a speed the average person can adequately and economically comprehend. When selling over the telephone or presenting a script, the communicator must learn to speak at a rate of 150 words per minute. To do this, most people will have to practice with a stop watch, and learn to control their voices and their breathing.

"Burnout"

Have you ever become stale, tired, unenthusiastic, and bored with your job? Well, in the telemarketing business "burnout" can be quite a problem. Much of it is due to the basic characteristic of a job that requires that people sit at a desk or cubicle for hours at a time, using their minds, voices, and spirits instead of circulatory muscles.

There are several causes for burnout in telemarketers, including:

1. Lack of training
2. Lack of product knowledge
3. Frustration from lack of career opportunities
4. Low pay
5. Customer rejection
6. Lack of challenges in the job
7. Poor working conditions
8. Poor management
9. Lack of reinforcement or recognition
10. Frustration from poor performance
11. Poor communication and interface with management
12. Lack of supervision
13. Monotony in the job
14. Boredom

The best way to combat burnout among your employees is to make the job interesting and exciting, with challenges, rewards, and reachable goals.

When you recognize a burnout problem with an employee, you should immediately hold a conference with the person in question. Try to get the person to identify the problem and recognize that a problem does exist in the first place.

Once the problem has been identified, try to develop a game plan to solve it. Get the person in question to agree to the plan and to work with you to solve the problem. You must immediately begin open monitoring of the individual to watch the performance levels achieved.

After a short period of time, hold another meeting with the individual and discuss whatever progress has been made. Keep holding these conferences periodically to stay on top of any recurring problems.

Managing a phone operation can be either a bear or really fun and exciting. It's up to you. If you do your homework and establish a professional workplace that is conducive to success, you are already halfway home.

Here is a brief list of the important management criteria you must master to succeed in telemarketing:

1. Develop your plan and objectives.
2. Prepare an adequate budget.
3. Establish a reachable timetable for your campaigns.
4. Acquire any necessary technical support.
5. Analyze the features, benefits, and advantages of your product line, anticipate the potential objections salespeople might encounter in their presentations, and then determine several ways to capably overcome each objection.
6. Write a first, second, and third draft of your possible script or presentation.
7. Create adequate forms for record-keeping.
8. Establish a work flow between departments.
9. Acquire prospect lists (after targeting your audience).
10. Hire and train the supervisory staff.
11. Hire and train the selling staff.
12. Attempt a sample or test campaign of 100 calls to evaluate scripts and selling strategies.
13. Review sample results.
14. Make the necessary modifications to the selling campaign plan.
15. Proceed full speed on the campaign.
16. Analyze and control selling efforts through precise record-keeping examinations.
17. Monitor campaign progress.
18. Interpret and evaluate campaign results.

By systematically managing the phone operation, you can keep complete control of the selling or marketing campaign.

Telemarketing is a super fast-paced industry with changes happening every day, so the successful manager must work hard to stay in the game and keep abreast of personnel problems, feelings, attitudes, and ambitions.

Telemarketing can be a fun business where everyone—communicator, supervisor, and customer—can win. But success can only come from hard work, honest motivation, and ambition. Managing requires a specialized blend of expertise and a unique combination of skills. You can obtain these requirements, and by reading this book you have made a good head start.

Chapter 9

Telephone Language and Etiquette

The telephone is the most powerful marketing force in business today. Handled properly, the telephone is a tool you can use to sell ideas, handle complaints, make friends, and influence people. Handled poorly, the use of the telephone will lose business, lose friends, and alienate people. Every time you dial or answer a phone you must think of yourself as reaching out through space with a friendly handshake and with the desire to talk things over just as if you were there in person.

Unlike an eyeball-to-eyeball meeting, where impressions can be created by your carriage, your dress, your smile, your mannerisms, and your handshake, the only thing creating an impression on the other end of the telephone line is your voice. Impressions of both you and your company are created solely by your sound, your tone, your use of language, your grammar, your rate of speech, your enunciation, and your attitude.

With a little bit of practice, your voice control and speech habits can be improved. Most people don't realize they slur and mumble when talking. Practice speaking slowly, clearly, and distinctly. Talking too rapidly makes you sound like a hustler. The average rate of speech for most Americans is about 125 words per minute, but speaking at a rate of up to 140 words per minute in telephone sales is comfortable to the listener and acceptable. The best rule of thumb to use is to try to adjust your rate of speech to the same speed as the individual you are talking with.

124

Stress the consonants and let the vowels take care of themselves. Often you can develop a deeper, stronger, and more resonant voice just by speaking with your mouth wide open. Be warm, natural, and friendly. No one will ever bite you over the telephone!

You may want to tape record your end of some of your conversations and play them back so you can listen carefully to how you sound. As you probably know, a tape recorder makes your voice sound different to you than it sounds when you speak aloud. Hearing your voice coming from the recorder will give you some idea of how you sound over the phone. When you listen to your tape, ask yourself these questions: How would I feel about this person if he or she called me? What kind of impression does this voice make: favorable or unfavorable? Did I enunciate clearly and speak distinctly at a rate of speech and tone of voice I could understand? Was my voice friendly, knowledgeable, warm, and inviting?

The telephone salesperson obviously wants to create a favorable impression over the telephone. The salesperson especially wants the person at the other end of the line to feel that he or she is confident, polite, and businesslike. The key ingredients for creating these impressions are outlined below:

1. Call the customer by name.
2. Don't slam the receiver down on your desk or counter if you must leave the phone.
3. Don't make the customer wait over 20 seconds without getting back to him or her.
4. Excuse yourself when leaving the line.
5. Know your company.
6. Know your competition.
7. Know your customer.
8. Know your product or service.
9. Know and understand yourself.
10. Let the customer hang up first.
11. Say please and thank you.

Most people tune in only to a portion of what is being said to them. This is especially true when they are listening to a salesperson on the telephone. They tend to listen for key words and phrases which will tell them the main point of the conversation, and then they fill in the gaps with what they think is going to be said, or with their own thoughts. As psychologists and politicians know, if one who is speaking fills in these gaps with "buzz" words, words that are likely to excite or motivate the listener in a predetermined direction, listeners who are not sympathetic to what is being said can often be persuaded to "buy" an idea or a product they normally would not. Everyone has experienced this at election time, for example, when words like "love" and "country" are used by all parties to convince the electorate they are "right" and the others are "wrong."

Buzz Words for Winners

Believe in the effectiveness of buzz words in telemarketing. Keep a list of them beside your telephone. Their inclusion in telephone marketing conversations increases sales. Use them. You will find they are effective for you.

Some words, of course, have more impact than others. Successful telephone selling depends entirely on your ability to use words that help your prospect see what you are trying to sell. To help create a picture in your prospect's mind, your telephone vocabulary should also contain:

1. Dynamic words that create strong impressions: new, powerful, breakthrough, rugged, miniature, unbelievable

2. Colorful and expressive adjectives that arouse feelings: foolproof, flawless, exquisite, convenient, luxurious, money-making

3. Words and phrases that paint pictures: efficient as a computer, larger than a house, smaller than an ant, strong as an ox

4. Personal words that will involve the prospect: you, yours, us, our, we

Figure 9.1 contains a list of words to supply to your sales account executives.

While it is important to sound successful, use language carefully, and project a positive image. Also, remember that you don't learn anything when you're talking. Experienced telephone salespeople who have developed their listening skills know they can listen themselves into many appointments and sales. Think for just a minute. When was the last time a salesperson had you sold on something, then talked you out of it because he didn't know when to listen to what you wanted to say or ask?

Successful salespeople never interrupt when a prospect is speaking. Not only is it discourteous, but the prospect may often lose his or her train of thought, or become annoyed and irritated. What the prospect has to say is important to him or her. It is also important to the salesperson, for it provides clues as to what will motivate the prospect to buy.

When a prospect hesitates, don't insert a word or finish the sentence. The prospect does not think like you and may have wanted to express a completely different thought. When you speak for your prospect, you hear only your words and are unable to read his or her feelings.

Figure 9.1 **100 Words That Have Sales Appeal**

1. absolutely	35. highest	69. reliable
2. amazing	36. huge	70. revealing
3. approved	37. immediately	71. revolutionary
4. attractive	38. improved	72. scarce
5. authentic	39. informative	73. secrets
6. bargain	40. instructive	74. security
7. beautiful	41. interesting	75. selected
8. better	42. largest	76. sensational
9. big	43. latest	77. simplified
10. colorful	44. lavishly	78. sizeable
11. colossal	45. liberal	79. special
12. complete	46. lifetime	80. startling
13. confidential	47. limited	81. strange
14. crammed	48. lowest	82. strong
15. delivered	49. magic	83. sturdy
16. direct	50. mammoth	84. successful
17. discount	51. miracle	85. superior
18. easily	52. noted	86. surprise
19. endorsed	53. odd	87. terrific
20. enormous	54. outstanding	88. tested
21. excellent	55. personalized	89. tremendous
22. exciting	56. popular	90. unconditional
23. exclusive	57. powerful	91. unique
24. expert	58. practical	92. unlimited
25. famous	59. professional	93. unparalleled
26. fascinating	60. profitable	94. unsurpassed
27. fortune	61. profusely	95. unusual
28. full	62. proven	96. useful
29. genuine	63. quality	97. valuable
30. gift	64. quickly	98. weird
31. gigantic	65. rare	99. wealthy
32. greatest	66. reduced	100. wonderful
33. guaranteed	67. refundable	
34. helpful	68. remarkable	

"Hear" What Isn't Said

Much of the art of listening is just good manners. Successful telephone salespeople develop their skills as listeners just as they sharpen their sales pitches to a fine edge. To begin with, a good listener turns off his or her own worries. This isn't always easy, but when you are preoccupied with personal problems, a kind of "static" develops that blanks out your prospect's message.

Proper advance preparation is another key to good listening. Knowing your product and being prepared to answer objections will give you the confidence it takes to be a good listener. When you are relaxed and confident, you will react to ideas, not to the prospect. A good listener will not become irritated or distracted by anything the prospect may say, or by the way in which it is said. Listen for overtones. You can learn a great deal about your prospect's thought patterns from the way he or she phrases things or reacts to those things you say. Avoid making unwarranted mental assumptions about what your prospect is going to say next.

Listen for ideas, not just to the words. Get the whole picture, not isolated bits and pieces. Your prospect's problems and needs are real and important to him or her. You will understand them better once you learn to look at such problems from the point of view of your prospect. Concentrate on what your prospect is saying, shutting out outside distractions.

Take notes. Write down a few key words that will help you recall everything of importance your prospect may say. Do not make detailed notes, or you'll end up concentrating on writing, not listening. Trying to jot down everything your prospect may say will result in your being buried in irrelevant thoughts. Write your detailed notes after your prospect has hung up, while the key words you wrote down are still fresh in your mind.

The telephone salesperson who develops the ability to listen is better able to establish a friendly relationship and instill confidence in a prospect or customer. By listening more and talking less, a salesperson is better able to command attention and control the conversation. In telephone sales, the difference between mediocrity and success is apparently silence!

Enthusiasm Gets Action

Important as listening is, it is enthusiasm that gets action! Let the person at the other end of the line know you're excited about and believe in your product or service. Give your customer the impression that talking with him or her is the most important thing that you could be doing at the time. Rushing the call and using sarcastic remarks, besides being unprofessional, are guaranteed turn offs.

Many salespeople working today, although lacking polish and a workable knowledge of sales techniques, have sold products. Their enthusiasm about their product was contagious and created an immediate positive response from their customers. Enthusiasm in your voice commands attention, creates interest, and gives vitality to your presentation. You can't tell a prospect you have a great product unless your voice reflects it. A bargain is in the mind of the beholder. In other words, your voice must say you believe that you're offering an excellent product at a fair price. When you talk about that product over the telephone, the person on the other end of the line must hear and "feel" your enthusiasm.

Genuine enthusiasm cannot be faked. Successful, enthusiastic salespeople know they can establish a value-for-value relationship with their customers, offering a good product or service in exchange for a fair amount of money.

The basis for enthusiasm is confidence. All the sales aids in the world won't build genuine enthusiasm unless you believe in yourself. You must talk like a winner, act like a winner, and believe you are a winner. You must *practice* talking and acting like a winner. Make a tape recording of your sales presentation, then listen to it and ask yourself, "Is this the kind of person I would buy from?" Look around the next time you go out. See how many losers you can spot and think how different you are. You are a winner! Believe it!

The key ingredients to confidence are knowledge and attitude. Attend all your sales meetings, go to lectures, go to workshops. Read industry periodicals to keep abreast of current trends in your business. Develop a professional attitude by becoming an expert in both your industry and as a salesperson. Learn all you can about selling techniques. Know all the features, advantages, and benefits of your product lines, too. They sell "the difference," but, all things being equal, the salesperson makes the ultimate difference.

Smile, Darn It, Smile

One way to get your enthusiasm across is to smile on the telephone! Concentrate on making your voice sound positive, warm, and pleasant, not dull, monotonous, and colorless. Give information wholeheartedly. Be willing, glad, and sincere in your desire to inform and help. In conveying your message, how you say something is often more important than what you say. Emphasizing certain words makes their meaning clear and concise. Also, the way your voice rises and falls gives importance to the key points of your message.

You will lose your smile once you begin to sound negative. Worse, you will lose control of the conversation and your prospect. Negative phrasing of a statement destroys any chance for positive feelings later in the conversation. Of course, you cannot always say yes; most prospects do not expect you to. However, when you must deliver some bad news, such as telling a prospect you are out of stock on an item or you cannot deliver when promised, you can usually find some positive point to emphasize at the beginning of your conversation which will start your contact positively and allow you to maintain control even after you say no. When you plan your calls in advance, as we suggest, you should be ready with your good news first when you call.

When you prepare your call schedule, notice which calls demand your giving bad news, and plan to begin them positively. Then minimize the negative while telling your customer the truth, especially avoiding bookish or legal sounding words or phrases that create distance between you and your customer. Remember KISS (Keep It Simple, Stupid).

It often takes between five and seven contacts before a customer feels comfortable with your company and familiar with your product, and is willing to place an order. You do not want to use stuffy, trite, or negative language which will create the kind of distance you worked so hard to overcome.

The exception to burying the bad news by putting the negative at the end of your statement is when you use a negative approach to your presentation. When used properly, the negative approach throws the customer off guard because it is human nature to want what you can't have. When using a negative approach, you start your presentation by inferring to your prospect that you don't believe he can handle or qualify for the great deal you have. In reality, the prospect sells himself, often before he knows what's being offered, then he sells you into letting him buy.

Following are examples of some negative phrases often used in business. They usually create distance, rather than warmth. Next to them are a few possible positive alternatives that deliver the same message but are more likely to bring understanding instead of distance.

Positive Approach	Negative Approach
I can approve your request if I can get . . .	I cannot approve your request, unless I can get . . .
So that I can approve your request, may I get . . .	Before I can approve your request, I will need . . .
Although the bright yellow ribbon you want is out of stock, I have that ribbon in a golden yellow. Would that be suitable?	I'm sorry but we're out of stock in the bright yellow ribbon you need.

Whenever possible, use the pronoun "you." It helps create the spirit and attitude you are striving to attain.

The Positive "You" Approach	The Negative "I" Approach
You will be interested to know that . . .	I wish to point out that . . .
You will discover that . . .	I believe that . . .
You will find that . . .	I think that . . .
You must discover that . . .	I believe that . . .

The English language is full of participles, prepositional phrases, conjunctions, and adverbs that tend to complicate our speech and make it dull. Overusing such words, mostly for emphasis, is self-defeating. Use as few superfluous words as possible. Here are a few examples on ways to cut down on wordiness:

Instead of	Use
from the point of view of	for
for the purpose of	for
in case of	if
in terms of	for, in
in the event of	if
accordingly	and so
consequently	and so
likewise	and
for this reason	so
with the result that	so
inasmuch as	because
for the reason that	because
in order to	to
with a view to	to
with reference to	about

Instead of	Use
with regard to	about
on the basis of	by
in accordance with	by
hence, thus	therefore

Dead Line—Dead Prospect

Have you ever been put on hold and then forgotten while you sat with a dead phone at your ear? Or worse, have you ever asked a question and been shuffled from one person to another, having to repeat your story each time? These are only a couple of the horrors we may be put through when we use the telephone. It is easy to be discourteous without realizing it.

There are some simple rules you can use to help eliminate these and other bad telephone manners. Have a list of the phone numbers that you frequently call, and use it when you do your calling. It is discourteous to have a secretary place business calls. It tells the person being called that you think your time is worth more than his or hers.

By placing your own calls, you eliminate this kind of discourtesy and let your prospect know he or she is important. When the prospect answers, you are on the line already and can immediately begin speaking.

When you answer your business phone, always announce your company name and your name. For example, "Good morning. Widgets International. This is Cindy. How may I help you?" Approximately two-thirds of all business telephone calls are answered by "Hello," which tells the caller nothing. By giving both your company name and your own name, you reinforce those names in the mind of your customers. Additionally, you let them know they have reached the right (or wrong) company and/or person.

Screening Calls

When not handled properly, screening calls is guaranteed to irk the caller. Train people always to ask who is calling before putting a call through. Instruct them not to press the caller if they meet with any resistance, but to put the call through. When it's their nickel, there isn't anyone you shouldn't talk to on the telephone. The purpose of asking who is calling is not to enable someone to decide whether or not to take the call, but simply to determine who is calling. Sometimes the caller is accidentally disconnected in the transfer of the call to the proper extension, and doesn't call back immediately. When that happens, and you know who called, the chances are you have the number on your Rolodex and can return the call.

When a caller learns that the party being called is unavailable, he or she will often decline to leave any message, including a name. By asking the caller's name before informing him or her that the person being called is not available, at least you have the caller's name and three options for handling the call and pleasing the customer:

Option 1. Put the call through.

Option 2. Inform the caller that the party he or she wants to speak with is busy and give the caller the option of waiting or receiving a callback later.

Option 3. Inform the caller that the party he or she wants to speak with is unavailable and give the caller the option of speaking with someone else or receiving a callback later.

When a call is transferred, the party answering should always announce his or her name, and, where appropriate, the department.

Keep in mind the caller's time is valuable. It is very inconsiderate to the person calling to have the individual answering the phone involved in other things that delay answering the phone by more than three rings. Many people will hang up when a telephone isn't answered before the fourth or fifth ring, especially when they have been transferred. When that happens, it is usually your competitor who gets the sale. Learn to answer the phone on the first ring. It sharpens up your own operation and creates the impression that you are "on the ball."

The person answering the phone must write clear, understandable messages that include the caller's name, the name of the person being called, the caller's phone number (including area code), the time the message was taken, the message itself, and the initials of the person taking the call. Depending on the nature of your business, you may also want to have the message include the name of the company the caller represents.

ABCs and 1-2-3s of Taking Messages

Make certain all names are spelled correctly. If in doubt, the person taking the message should ask the caller to spell his or her name.

Many letters, such as "F" and "S," "T" and "D," and "P" and "B," may sound alike on the telephone. The person taking the message should always repeat the spelling and verify doubtful sounding letters, using the phonetic alphabet (for example, "That's D like David"). Two of the generally accepted word alphabets used for this purpose are outlined in Figure 9.2.

Numbers can also be easily confused when they are not pronounced slowly and distinctly over the telephone. Like the spelling of a name, every phone number should be verified by repetition. Use the method in Figure 9.3 to pronounce numbers.

A great many people don't receive their messages. The most accurate message in the world isn't going to do anyone any good if it isn't read. When you're out of your office or away from your desk, the person answering your phone should know where you can be reached. Also, you must have one place where you regularly check for messages, then make sure you do check for them.

Figure 9.2 Examples of the ABCs of Telemarketing

A—Alice	J—John	S—Samuel
B—Bertha	K—Kate	T—Thomas
C—Charles	L—Louis	U—Utah
D—David	M—Mary	V—Victor
E—Edward	N—Nelly	W—William
F—Frank	O—Oliver	X—X-ray
G—George	P—Peter	Y—Young
H—Henry	Q—Quaker	Z—Zebra
I—Ida	R—Robert	

The phonetic alphabet used by the United States government to verify spelling follows:

A—Alpha	J—Juliet	S—Sierra
B—Bravo	K—Kilo	T—Tango
C—Charlie	L—Lima	U—Uniform
D—Delta	M—Mike	V—Victor
E—Echo	N—November	W—Whiskey
F—Foxtrot	O—Oscar	X—X-ray
G—Golf	P—Papa	Y—Yankee
H—Hotel	Q—Quebec	Z—Zulu
I—India	R—Romeo	

Figure 9.3 **Examples of the 123s of Telemarketing**

Number	Pronunciation	Sounds
0	oh	Round and long o
1	wun	Strong w and n
2	too	Strong t and long oo
3	th-r-ee	A single roll of the r, and long ee
4	fo-er	Strong f, long o, and strong final r
5	fi-iv	long i and strong v
6	siks	Strong s and ks
7	sev-en	Strong s and v, and well-sounded en
8	ate	Long a and strong t
9	ni-en	Strong n, long i, and well sounded en
10	ten	Strong t and n

Common Courtesies to Callers

Another rule is never, never, never leave a telephone line open. An open phone on a desk or a counter could prove to be embarrassing to the caller or to you. It could also be disastrous to your company. The telephone is a sensitive instrument and can pick up sound through the sides of the mouthpiece. Even holding your palm over the phone will not ensure privacy. When you must excuse yourself from the conversation for a moment or two, there will be no chance of misunderstanding or embarrassment if you put the caller on "hold."

In most businesses, all inbound calls are transferred at least once. Occasionally, the caller is connected to the wrong person or department and has to be transferred again. Multiple transfers usually result from careless or improperly trained switchboard operators and often irritate the caller.

The person answering your telephone should have an overview of your entire company and take the time to determine the correct department to which every call should be transferred. If the caller doesn't know the department he or she wants, your switchboard operator should know, for instance, whether a call for specific technical information on one of your products should be transferred to your sales department or your engineering department.

When you have to leave the line to obtain information, make sure your caller understands what you are doing. "Just a moment," followed by a dead line, will often cause the caller to wonder what you meant or if he or she has been cut off. "Just a moment, please. I have to locate that invoice" is courteous and lets the caller know what is happening.

When you must interrupt a call, don't leave the line for more than 20 seconds without getting back to the caller with a progress report, or he or she may become annoyed and often antagonistic. If it will take you a minute or two to locate the information you want, make sure the caller understands this. Give the caller the choice of waiting on the line or having you call back after you find the information. This can be accomplished by saying, "I'll have to locate that invoice and it may take me a couple of minutes. May I call you right back or would you prefer to hold?" If the caller elects to wait on the line, be sure to go back on the line with a progress report every 20 seconds. However, it is always better to call customers back than to keep them on hold more than a minute. Besides, by hanging up, you will open up your lines for other calls.

Taking a telephone call while someone is in your office is often embarrassing to the visitor and an imposition on his or her time. However, occasionally there may be important calls you have to take. Whenever possible, anticipate such calls and arrange to have your switchboard operator or secretary put them through.

Tell your guest at the outset of your meeting that you are expecting an important call and, with his or her permission, you'd like to take it. Then, when the call comes in, excuse yourself by saying, "Excuse me. This is the call I've been expecting." Many executives choose to take such calls in another office to prevent their guests from having to listen to a conversation that really doesn't concern them. This will make your guests comfortable and they won't have to pretend they aren't eavesdropping.

Never let your telephone just ring and ring. During usual business hours, and especially after an inbound call has been transferred to your extension, the caller expects you to be available to give him or her attention. Answer all calls before your customer becomes impatient and hangs up. An unanswered telephone and a sign that reads "out of business" say the same thing to the caller.

The majority of business people rely on the telephone for most of their communications. They often spend weeks or months developing a business relationship that will lead to a contract or a sale. Yet they seldom, if ever, spend more than a few minutes instructing their subordinates on the above techniques of answering a telephone. Maybe they assume if their three-year-old child can answer the telephone at home, the new person in the office ought to be able to handle the job all right. Wrong!

Techniques of Answering the Telephone

Nobody knows for sure how much business is actually lost through discourtesy at the switchboard, but "guesstimates" made by various people in telemarketing put the national figure somewhere from $1 to 2 million per day. The customer calling from a hot booth on a street corner or a noisy phone at the airport just won't wait for the call to be screened, transferred, and screened again. Neither will he or she put up with an inconsiderate and untrained switchboard operator. The business transaction that took you months to set up can be demolished in 30 seconds by discourtesy at your switchboard.

Everyone in your company should be trained in the techniques of answering the telephone covered in this chapter. The rules and sequence recommended are:

1. There must always be someone available with the primary responsibility of answering the telephone.

2. There must be a notepad and a pen or pencil by every telephone.

3. The telephone must be answered promptly, preferably by the second ring.

4. Always answer your phone by giving the company name, your name, and your department.

5. Whenever possible, address the caller by name.

6. Place the mouthpiece of the telephone between one-half and one inch away from your lips.

7. Begin talking distinctly in a natural voice as soon as you pick up the telephone.

8. Be polite and tactful. Make "please" and "thank you" a part of your regular telephone vocabulary. Put feeling in your voice, making your responses sound as if you are interested in what the caller has to say.

9. Avoid unnecessary delays when the call must be transferred. Make certain the caller gets reconnected to the person he or she is calling. There is no greater telephone horror than a call going unanswered. When the caller finally hangs up and calls back, *if* he or she calls back, that person is certainly going to be more intense and less reasonable.

Best Times and Best Days for Calling

Finally, you should know there is a "best time" to call almost every trade if you wish to discuss business in the most receptive atmosphere. Many food businesses, like the restaurant trade, refuse calls during their peak time periods just before and during lunch and dinner. Likewise, the worst time to call a firm dealing in complaints or collections is after four o'clock. While calling at a supposed best time is no guarantee you will find someone in a receptive mood, the odds certainly are in your favor that they are least likely to be busy then and consequently more receptive to your call.

Figure 9.4 suggests the "best times" to call various trades. Times may vary somewhat between cities and parts of the United States but should be close enough for you to begin a schedule of your own.

Figure 9.5 offers a checklist of telephone behavior for the professional.

Figure 9.4 **Best Times to Call—By Profession**

Accountants. Usually not between January 1 and April 15. Otherwise, any time during the business day.

Attorneys. Usually not available. Best way to contact is through their office or business manager.

Bankers. Between 9 A.M. and 5 P.M.

Chemists. Between 1 and 3 P.M.

Contractors. Before 9 A.M. or after 5 P.M. or at home in the evening

Clergy. Tuesday, Wednesday, or Thursday, and most evenings

Dentists. Usually not available. Leave word with secretary and hope your call is returned, or speak with office manager.

Druggists. Between 4 and 5 P.M.

Farmers. Between 3 and 5 P.M. or any time on a rainy day

Government officials. Between 8 A.M. and 4 P.M.

Grocers. Before 9 A.M. or 1 to 3 P.M.

Housewives. After breakfast and after dinner

Merchants. Between 9 A.M. and 5 P.M.

Newspaper people. Between 2 and 5 P.M.

Physicians. Usually not available (See "dentist" above)

Printers and publishers. After 3 P.M.

Salespeople. Between 9 and 11 A.M.

Secretaries. Between 2 and 5 P.M.

Stockbrokers. Before 7 A.M. or late afternoon

Figure 9.5 A Checklist—Appraise Your Telephone Habits

1. How quickly do you answer your extensions?
2. How do you identify yourself? Department? Company?
3. Is the acknowledgment of the opening statement appropriate?
4. Do you call the caller by name?
5. Do you interrupt the caller or fail to give way when the caller tries to interrupt?
6. If the call must be interrupted, do you explain why and leave and return to the line in a polite manner?
7. Are you attentive to the caller's statements or do you ask questions that indicate you were not listening?
8. Do you express appreciation, concern, or regret where it is appropriate to do so? Do you apologize, if necessary?
9. Do you express in words, or indicate by manner and tone of voice, a willingness to be of help?
10. Is your attitude friendly, helpful, and interested, or does the caller receive routine treatment instead of individual consideration?
11. When the nature of the contact requires that you provide information or explanation, is it given completely and concisely?
12. Do you use technical terms, slang, or arbitrary phrases?
13. Do you handle calls in a manner that would inspire confidence in the way your company is managed? Will the caller want to remain a customer?
14. Are the final arrangements clear?
15. Do you respond appropriately to the caller's "Thank you" or other closing remarks?
16. Do you let the customer hang up first?

Do your job the smart way, not the hard way.

Chapter 10

Prospecting

How and Where to Find Your Customers

Prospects are potential customers who could benefit from or who are in a position to buy and use the particular product or service you are selling. Prospecting is the salesperson's method of searching out such customers. A good prospecting list is an important timesaver in the search for sales. It is not as difficult to build as it may seem. There are several methods and many sources used by successful salespeople to develop a basic list that leads to completed sales.

Before you can develop a qualified list of prospects, you must define your potential customer and determine exactly what type of company or person you want to reach. To do this, prepare a list containing the type of businesses or individuals most likely to buy and use your product or service in the geographic area your company serves.

Then decide what level of management you should contact to make your sale. Some things to consider are your potential customer's annual sales volume, credit rating, number of employees, type of products manufactured or sold, and so on. If you plan to sell to consumers, you might qualify them by income level, family status, ethnic background, life style, age, value of their home, credit card holdings, and so forth.

Once you have defined your prospect, then you can easily determine what kind of prospecting list will best help you.

Sometimes you have a product, but you are unable to define the customer for it. Start by making a list of the type of buyer

140

you think may be able to use it. For example, your list might include marinas, construction companies, bolt manufacturers, steel fabricators, trailer manufacturers, wholesale hardware outlets, or heavy equipment dealers. Once your list is complete, go to the Yellow Pages for a major city, then start calling every company listed under each category. Once you've made your first sale, you can easily define your buyer. All you have to do then is call every such company in the country until you're sold out. This sounds almost too simple, but it works. Don't be afraid to ask your buyer how he or she uses the product you have just sold. More often than not such information will enable you to define a second type of prospect.

Besides the Yellow Pages, there are numerous other sources for fantastic prospect lists. Your best source for lists to use in telemarketing campaigns is your own company files and records of both inactive and active customers. These will help you determine the nature or type of customers you should concentrate on, the location of similar prospects, and the best time of the day and year to contact for potential sales.

Other sources for prospect lists include your files on inquiries that made no sale, list brokers, business directories, organization membership lists, and reverse street directories for consumers.

Demographics and Psychographics

For years now, the direct mail industry has been the leader in the areas of classifying companies and individuals by demographics and psychographics. To the direct marketer, demography is the study of vital statistics about people and psychographics is the study of the personality and cultural traits of various buyers of products and services.

For example, in the area of population classification, buyers can be classified and lists are readily available based upon income, sex, religion, length of residency, education, age, and similar information. Each year, as demographic studies become more sophisticated and data bases increase, more select factors become available.

In fact, if you had a use for a list with such demographic selections as a male student in his junior year of college, majoring in education, going to a school on an athletic scholarship, you could obtain it.

As data bases expand, the direct marketing industry is beginning to learn more about the psychographic characteristics of potential customers. Interesting patterns are developing and it is believed that the computers will soon be able to discern, based upon club memberships, magazine subscriptions, life style, and so on, whether the student mentioned previously would be more likely to buy a sweater from one telemarketer or a classical recording from another.

It is already known that a person who bought a product or service over the telephone once is an excellent prospect to buy a totally different product at a future time, from another telemarketer. From this it is known that a list made up of people who have previously bought over the telephone is better than any list of solely demographic information.

If a person tends to be a repeat buyer from the same company, the closer a product or service being offered is related to a previous purchase, the greater the chance of a successful sale. The list brokers are continuing toward developing more psychographic data and some day it may be possible to determine who is the best prospect for gourmet cookware based on such correlations as the kind of music they listen to, the books they read, or the brand of television set they bought.

Someone just beginning to sell can develop a prospect list based on his or her "sphere of influence." That is, he or she can call and sell to those people and companies he or she already knows, or those already familiar to his or her employer. Usually, salespeople rapidly exhaust their "sphere of influence," however, and have to look to other methods, such as the "endless chain" method of prospecting.

The Endless Chain

The endless chain or "bird dogging" method of prospecting is also limited, but it can be used quite effectively in conjunction with other methods, including sphere of influence selling. In the endless chain method, you simply ask your existing friends and customers whom they know who may be able to buy, use, or benefit from your product or services. Whenever possible, tell them you want a referral, not just someone's name. The difference is that a referral will lead you to someone who has a personal relationship with your friend or customer. Then your use of the friend's name will automatically open the door.

This bird dogging should be attempted after you close every sale. Always ask if the customer knows of anyone else who might also benefit from your service or product, and if you can say they referred you. A friendly customer can turn more business your way than any other method possible. Building a referral business is every salesperson's goal.

Some salespeople play a numbers game and use the "cold canvassing" method of prospecting. Here the salesperson goes up one street and down the other, or up one page in the phone book and down the next, without qualifying anyone beforehand. Use of the cold canvassing method is time-consuming and usually not very effective. However, if you dial enough telephone numbers, a certain percentage of your calls will lead to sales.

When working with an unqualified list of prospects, don't skip anyone. Behind cold-calling lie sales figures and behind sales figures lies thoroughness. Don't miss any opportunity and don't overlook a single subject. The lucky salesperson just happens to be the man or woman who is completely prepared when he or she meets opportunity.

Qualified Cold-Calling

When you must cold-call, whenever possible use the qualified cold-calling method for prospecting. This simply means you qualify your prospects before you cold-call them. Qualifying can be by credit rating, product pertinence, timeliness of calling, or by many other types of character traits. There are almost as many sources to use in developing a qualified cold-calling list of prospective customers as there are salespeople.

The qualified cold-calling method for building prospecting lists differs from straight cold-calling in that you qualify each prospect's ability to buy or use your product or service before you contact him or her. The quickest way to qualify a prospect's ability to buy is to check his or her company with Dun and Bradstreet, TRW, or any other similar credit rating bureau.

You can look up a company's credit rating as quickly as you can look up a telephone number, and it costs much less than the cost of a wasted phone call. Predetermining the prospect's ability to buy is cost and time effective. More important, such credit checks will tell you not only if the prospect can afford to do business with you, but whether you can afford to do business with the prospect!

A word of caution . . . most credit reporting agencies, including Dun and Bradstreet, do not guarantee the correctness of their reports and cannot be held liable for any loss you may sustain as a result of their neglect or failures in collecting or reporting information. In addition, many financially sound, privately owned companies decline to give financial information to credit reporting agencies, or have not been in business long enough to be rated.

You may not want to disqualify a prospect simply because he or she is "unrated." In most cases credit ratings are a better guide for your sales department in prospecting than a guide for your credit department in establishing a customer's credit line.

It is best to start cold-calling with a qualified list that is restricted to organizations located in a predetermined geographic area or engaged in a specific activity, often further qualifying them by size. When telephone calls are going to be followed up by eyeball-to-eyeball meetings, use reverse directories, thus enabling the field representatives to group their calls to a limited geographic area.

A reverse directory, also called a "street" directory, a cross-reference directory, or a criss-cross directory, is a telephone book alphabetically arranged by community and zip codes. Customers are listed by street address, and apartment or room number, followed by the customer's name and telephone number. Current copies are available from telephone companies, several publishers, and at larger libraries. Most of these reverse directories are available on a lease or rental basis and not normally on a purchase arrangement. Figure 10.1 shows a copy of a typical street directory page.

When prospecting for consumer sales, you can also use criss-cross directories to enable you to zone in on an area where specific common factors exist. For example, you wouldn't want to call apartment dwellers if you were selling home insulation. Neither would you be very successful selling Rolls Royces in a predominantly blue collar neighborhood. These cross-reference directories allow you to use demographic and psychographic data to help prequalify your calls.

Buying or Renting Lists

You may develop or purchase a list containing the names of people who for one reason or another you believe will have both the need and ability to buy your products or services. Such lists are readily available through list brokers, and with computer technology, the lists can be quite sophisticated.

List brokers can best be found by checking with the various direct marketing associations; they vary tremendously by the types

Figure 10.1 **Sample Page from a Cross-Street Directory**

N BRIDGETON RD

205 Manus Eugene	289-1337
Wallace Richard M	285-4290
207 Roe Mark E	289-3404
218 Self Ed F	285-1040
221 Brown James F	283-3807
223 Thorne Russell M	283-5645
229 Whitney M F	285-3296
301-A Sanders Jack L	289-6345
B 304 Batty Tony Pyramid Designs	286-2630
B Pyramid Designs	286-2630
B 310 Argo Plastic Company	283-1613
Peterson Donald L	285-4452
314 Colligan Christopher	289-8954
315 Trusty K	285-5139
315-A Peterson L M	283-3820
B South Channel Brokers & Repair	289-2895
320 Oviatt W	289-1243
412 Egland W Tom	283-2383
422 Allman Donald C	285-4660
429 Brustad Michael	283-3750
Miller R	285-4255
Qvale Knute M	289-0545

NE BRIDGETON RD
Zip 97211

10 Runyon Max	289-0218
28 Runyon Geo W	289-1071
34 Shankles Melvin K	289-5923
55 APARTMENT	
55 Bartlett M J	286-4765
B Lawrence Verne Insurance	289-8774
B Lawrence Verne R	289-8470
Lentz Bernie	286-4765
Long Richard C	289-6051
Manchester Kenneth C	286-3426
Potts Clarence H Jr	289-0439
138 Johnson Robert G & Deborah	286-5308
173 BENNETT MOORAGE	

SW BRIDLEMILE LN

3848 Abraham Janet	223-1972
3868 Southgate Douglas D	222-5276
3875 Corgan Charles F & Associates	
Res	222-4710
3891 Houle R	228-0408
3899 Stutte Robert R	224-9051

SW BRIER LN
Zip 97223

9045 Harguth Mark	245-1912
9050 Kangas Arlie	246-3116
9110 Davis Diana B	245-5673
9125 Garofalo Francis R	245-3588
9140 Martin James F	245-5794

SW BRIER PL
Zip 97219

6930 Beam Ronald D	244-5883
7010 Kuhn Steve & Robin	246-3783
7032 Kriko A W	244-4033
7040 Johnson Jim	246-5707
7100 Herbold Cynda	245-9663
7114 Presley Cynthia & Dennis	245-2332
7136 Harvey Christopher & Scotti	245-0485
7200 Pickell John	246-7475
7211 Rothschild Robert K	246-3031
Sherwood Oriental Theatre	
If No Answer	246-3031
7221 Irelan Robert	246-5885
Lewitt Rachael	245-5822
7222 Arriola Mario & A J	244-8190
7300 Weber Robert J	244-5017
7311 Weller W J	244-8478
7534 Klimas Edward	244-3638
7601 Roberts H J	245-6010

NAME OF BUSINESS · NAME OF RESIDENTS · TELEPHONE NUMBER · NAME OF STREET · STREET NUMBER · ZIP CODE

Reprinted with permission of Pacific NW Bell.

of services they provide. List brokers are knowledgeable professionals, qualified to help you obtain the best lists for any purpose. They do not charge you for their services, but are paid a commission on each rental by the list owner. They can help you obtain the names and addresses of the prospects who best meet your qualifications. Included in their expertise is a knowledge of what lists are currently available, and from whom.

When working with list brokers, give them as much information as you can about the type of prospect you want to reach. They will give you, usually within a couple of days, a number of list cards. Generally, list cards follow a standard format and include such information as:

1. A customer profile
2. The total number of names on the list
3. The minimum number of names you must rent

4. The format in which the list is available:
   "Cheshire" or pressure-sensitive mailing labels (one to four across)
   Address plates used in mailing machines
   Index cards
   Computer printouts
   Computer tape
   Computer diskettes
   On-line computer data base
5. How the list is classified:
   Zip codes
   By city
   By state
   By sales volume
6. The date when the list was last brought up to date
7. List accuracy percentage, sample sizes, methods of selection
8. Information to be furnished with the list
9. Any guarantees for unreachable listings
10. Any specifications for delivery, segmentation, sorting, or distribution
11. The future availability of the list
12. Rental times, restrictions, conditions for usage

Often list cards also will tell how the list was obtained and if the usage is restricted, or what other companies are also using the same list. Sometimes, list owners will not allow their list to be used during specific periods of the year or will insist on time intervals between usages to prevent its becoming overexposed.

If your prospects are limited to a small segment of the market and you are unable to obtain such a list through a list broker or on an exchange basis, then you'll have to have such a list compiled. Here again, list brokers are the most qualified to do the job. You'll have to pay for their services, but you will own the list. Once you own the list you can use it as often as you like and can elect to rent it or exchange it with other businesses.

Historically, people who have once bought products or services offered through direct mail marketing media tend to buy through the mail or over the telephone habitually. Consequently, other direct marketers with noncompetitive products or services are also excellent sources of lists. Search out and find organizations in the direct response industry who will rent their lists to you, or offer them the use of your lists in exchange for the use of theirs.

Before renting any list in its entirety, obtain a small portion, perhaps 2,000 or 3,000 names, then pick 200 to 400 of them at random, and use them for testing. If you find there are too many numbers on the list no longer in service, discontinue using them and do not rent the balance of the list. Your time and telephone costs do not permit you the luxury of using an outdated list, for such a list will reduce your number of completed calls per hour, and thus increase your costs per sale. It is important that you test every list or sample every list to eliminate wasted calls and unproductive time.

List selection is probably the most important factor in a successful telephone marketing campaign. Even the best professional telecommunicators will fail if the list is outdated, incomplete, or off-base. You must properly qualify your prospects to ensure at least a chance at success in telemarketing.

Today, the average telemarketer has over 100,000 lists from which to choose. One of the greatest challenges will be in deciding whether to rent or purchase the list you will use. You have a choice either to compile the list yourself, hire someone to compile a list for you, purchase an already established list, trade or exchange for a list, or rent/lease a list from someone else.

Leasing a list has both advantages and disadvantages that must be considered. By renting, you allow yourself a wider selection of prospect names and sources, you have less out-of-pocket expense, and have a built-in inexpensive means to test a list's effectiveness. There are thousands of list management companies that deal in list rentals. These companies offer a wide selection of lists, provide excellent feedback and assistance in defining your chosen markets, planning, and list preparation, and allow you the flexibility to target your lists to very specialized and unique markets.

Some disadvantages of renting lists include not having the option of buying a list you find successful, that some lists of highly specialized criteria often come from the direct marketing arena without phone numbers, lists from one company may overlap and have many of the same prospects as lists from other companies, that there is some uncertainty as to the accuracy of some lists, and the fact that many of the rented lists are substantially overused and multiple-rented to several firms at the same time.

A great source for finding the right list broker for your particular product or service prospect is the *Standard Rates and Data Service List* (SRDS). This is a fantastic reference guide that lists all of the nation's suppliers of prospect lists, service organizations, list brokers, list managers, list compilers, and more. The SRDS is fast, easy to read, and contains most of the best lists and specific information you might need in deciding which list to go with.

Another good source for lists is the major publishers of magazines and newspapers. These companies provide very specialized lists and are available for most professions, industries, and interests. These lists are great for targeting a specific market but don't usually include phone numbers. One advantage of publishers' lists is that they are rarely used or exploited by telemarketers. They are also usually up to date and include good documentation of list history, ownership, and method of compilation.

When procuring your list, make sure you cover your tracks in the contract with the following items importantly included:

1. Title of the list
2. Quantity of the list names
3. Description of names in list
4. What kinds of information will be included for each name
5. Price
6. Usage restrictions
7. Rental time
8. Any other conditions of usage
9. Future availability (if you need to use it again)
10. History of the list including previous owners and date of last update
11. Guarantees for unreachable listings
12. Specifications for sorting, distribution, etc.
13. Quantities of test sampling, and selection method

Getting Their Numbers

You will not always be able to obtain a list that includes telephone numbers. Consequently, in calculating the effective cost of any list, you must give consideration to the added expense of looking up the numbers. To minimize your look-up costs, obtain only lists that are in alphabetical order and in zip code sequence. This will enable you to look up phone numbers in the white pages or in criss-cross directories.

Depending on the directory available, the geographic spread of your list, and your labor cost, obtaining telephone numbers for the names on most lists will cost you from $.10 to .40 each. By calling your telephone company's directory assistance operator, you can obtain an average of three listings every two minutes, or about 90 numbers per hour. Based on new tariff billings in your area, this may cost as much as $.50 per name, or more, plus the cost of your time.

On the other hand, you can consistently look up approximately 50 numbers per hour, using local directories. There are companies such as Metromail and Telephone Look-Up Service that specialize in looking up and putting telephone numbers on existing lists. If you have trouble locating such a company in your area, or any company providing a specific service in the direct response industry, contact the Direct Marketing Association in New York City (see Appendix A).

List Testing

It is important to test your list, otherwise you might be wasting your time telephoning people who don't need to be called, people who don't want to be called, or people you wish you didn't call. When testing a list for accuracy and quality, determine the answers to the following questions:

1. What percentage of names on the list are reachable?
2. What percentage of names on the list possess the psychographic and demographic traits for which you selected the list?
3. How many names on the list, in percentages, were wrong?
4. When was the last time someone contacted the prospects on the list? By phone?
5. What was the percentage of sales to come from the list?

Lead Generation

Telemarketing is a proven and successful means of generating and qualifying leads, especially as a way of preconditioning prospective leads for promotional campaigns that utilize other media, such as direct mail, space advertising, and so on.

By utilizing a person-to-person follow up by telephone, you can eliminate many dead-end sales and increase effectiveness by three to five times.

Telemarketing is today's professional salesperson's most efficient means of generating quality prospects. It can turn suspects into qualified sales.

The interaction of direct mail and telemarketing is a proven generator of both leads and sales. Do not make a general mailing to an unqualified list when your goal is to develop a prospect list. You should only use a list that has already been qualified by demographics and psychographics. When prospecting for commercial accounts, use the call–mail–call–call–call program. When prospecting for consumer accounts, reverse the program and mail first.

Whenever possible, start with a qualified list when prospecting for consumer sales. Use criss-cross directories to zone in on a specific economic area. Develop or rent a list containing the names of people who you believe have both the need and the ability to buy your product or services.

Call–Mail–Call

When seeking commercial sales, focus in only on those companies that you feel may have an interest in what you are selling, often qualifying them by size.

The tried-and-true tested program of call–mail–call is probably the most effective multi-mixed medium marketing program ever utilized.

Once You Choose . . .

Once you have chosen the prospecting method in which you feel most confident, you have to determine how much time and effort each prospect is worth. Although you can never assume you won't make a sale or appointment on your first call, the first order from a commercial account usually occurs during the fifth, sixth, or even seventh telephone call. It has been statistically proven that the normal person needs six personal interactions or encounters with another person before they actually remember who it was they met. Do not give up on a qualified prospect until after you have had 12 negative contacts. Don't get discouraged if your prospecting efforts don't yield immediate results. Like fishing, successful prospecting takes time, skill, and patience.

Following are some important things to remember when prospecting on the telephone:

1. Make certain you are talking to the person who has the authority to do the buying. If in doubt, ask, "Do you do the buying?" If the voice at the other end of the line says, "No," simply ask, "Please tell me the name of the person who does the buying." Before you "burn off" the person you are speaking to, always ask, "Is there any way I might be able to help you?" In doing so, you may just get someone on your side who actually plays a role in making the buying decisions.

2. Never eliminate a prospect just because he or she is only large enough to buy a minimum order. Enough repetitive small orders can enable you to make a good living. Also, small companies often grow up and become big buyers, those accounts you'd give your eye teeth for if you only could get your foot in the door.

3. Establish a system for keeping a record of all your prospects. Qualified prospects should be cycled, just as if they were a buying account. Develop a system that fits your particular product or service. Many salespeople use 3-by-5 inch cards. Others use printed forms. Some use yellow legal pads. List the prospect's name, address, and telephone number, then skip three lines to leave room for any notations before another name is added.

Many companies are creating data bases of prospects with the new proliferation of computers with mail-merge, word processing, filing, and so on. These new technologies make it even easier to combine telemarketing with direct mail marketing to achieve the greatest amount of efficient professionalism in selling.

Whatever prospecting method you use, remember every successful salesperson devotes a portion of almost every day to prospecting for new accounts. There is no business like growth business, and this isn't possible if you depend solely on selling established accounts.

Remember, there is no account using a product or service similar to yours that sooner or later you can't sell. Conditions change. Possibly a new company policy is initiated, maybe a new manager is appointed, perhaps a regular supplier is temporarily out of stock; or, you may develop a relationship in which the buyer feels guilty for not at least "throwing you a bone." Persistence makes winners out of even the weakest salespeople.

Prospecting is very simply the salesperson's method of finding additional buyers for his or her product or service. The telephone, used alone or in harmony with direct mail or media advertising, is the salesperson's greatest tool in the search for new customers. Master the methods of telephone prospecting and you can reach your objectives and attain your sales goals.

Chapter 11

A Unique Approach to Closing

How to Overcome Objections

It is not very likely you will ever find a prospect who agrees with everything you say. The person spending the money wouldn't be normal if he or she didn't put up roadblocks to your presentation, in the form of objections to your product, to protect against salespeople trying to reach his or her money. More often than not, such objections are not outright rejections, but simply disguised requests for more information. Objections are the common denominator found in every type of telephone sales call.

Your success as a salesperson is directly related to your ability to recognize and overcome objections to the complete satisfaction of your prospect. Objections that are ignored never seem just to go away. Even when you think an objection seems to be illogical and without validity, you must realize it is always logical and valid to your prospect. Somehow, unanswered objections will manage to lurk in the back of your prospect's mind, only to reappear just when you think you've made a sale.

Objections are seldom questions. They are almost always statements. Consequently, when prospects ask a question, it must be assumed that they are looking for additional information to help them make a decision.

Whenever your prospect makes a statement that could stand in the way of your obtaining the sale, it is an objection that must be overcome. You must overcome that objection before going on with your sales presentation or the rest of your selling effort will be wasted.

When your prospects make an objection, never take an opposite position and try to prove them wrong, for that will only encourage disagreement and create a confrontation. When your prospects tell you they can't afford your product, don't become argumentative and try to prove them wrong by saying, "Sure you can afford it."

When your prospects tell you they can't afford your product, you can motivate them to buy just by telling them how easy it is to buy—"We can give you 30-day terms" or "We have a dealer finance program I'd like to tell you about" or "Several of my customers have financed the purchase of my product through their local bank" or "Let me take just a moment to tell you about our extended terms," and so on.

When responding to an objection, confine your conversation to the immediate concern of your prospect. Salespeople lose too much time and effort, and often the confidence of their prospect, when they try to answer the wrong objection. If a prospect were to use the "I can't afford it" objection, he or she is informing you of a money problem that you won't solve by proving that your product is a good buy. If you are to motivate your prospect to buy, you must remember that an objection is a problem, your customer's problem, and you, the telephone sales account executive, must find a solution.

All experienced salespeople know that most objections are simply roadblocks to the sale and are often untrue statements. When you recognize such a roadblock, don't waste time trying to overcome it. Here again, use "yes, but," the salesperson's best friend. "Yes, Ms. Prospect, that may be true, but I believe I can show you how to solve that problem. Is there any other reason you cannot give me an order now?" Often such an approach will "smoke out" the real objection, cause the prospect to forget immediately his or her first objection, and enable you to make the sale.

Reasons "Why Not"

In preparing to answer objections, many salespeople make the mistake of developing and memorizing only one answer to any simple argument that may be presented by a prospect. Then when the prospect is dissatisfied with the standard reply, the salesperson stammers and is left with no place to go.

To be successful at overcoming objections, you must compile a list of every possible argument that a prospect may present, and then list several counterarguments for each. Here is a partial list of common objections you may encounter, with some possible responses that have been utilized successfully by professionals for years:

1. *Too expensive*	Compared to what?
	What you are paying now?
	What types of quantities do you have to buy to get that price?
	Is that freight prepaid or freight collect?
	What type of terms do you get?
	At this price do you get a warranty?
	Yes, but . . .
	Not really when you consider Quality Service Guarantee
2. *Don't want it*	Tell me why you don't want it.
3. *Don't need it*	Tell me why you don't need it.
4. *Don't like it*	Tell me why you don't like it.
	How do you know you don't like it?
	What don't you like about it?
5. *Not now, maybe later*	This is a limited offer, it may not be available later.
	Fine, can I call you back this afternoon, or would tomorrow morning be better?
	When would it be better to call— Wednesday, or would Thursday be better?
6. *Buy local/friends*	What are you currently paying?
	Do they have them at this price?

	Do you understand how much your friendship is costing you in dollars and cents?
	Try a few of ours and continue with your current supplier.
	What happens if your friend is out of stock?
7. *No money*	With your good credit, I'll give you open account terms, or maybe you'd like me to put three dozen on hold till Friday?
8. *Don't buy on the phone*	Have you had a prior bad experience?
	Tell me why you prefer not to do business on the phone.
	Tell me why you don't trust me.
	We're willing to trust you by sending our product to you on open account terms.
	If we didn't think we had a quality product, we wouldn't do this.
	What guarantees do your other suppliers give you?
	Who's trusting whom—we're prepared to offer credit.
	Did you realize that many of the Fortune 500 do their purchasing over the telephone?
9. *Need permission to buy*	Can you tell me who makes the final decision regarding purchases?
	Why don't I give you a call this afternoon after you've received permission?
	Would you like me to call him/her?
10. *Business is bad*	I'm sorry to hear that, perhaps my timing is perfect.
	Let me show you how to

	increase your sales and profits.
	I have a super deal that can change your current business trend.
11. *Can't see the product*	At this low price, why not trust me, you don't need to pay up front, and they do carry a full warranty and guarantee.
	At this low price, why not invest in a few and take a look at them?
12. *Bad mood*	Why are you in a bad mood?
	Would you rather I call you back in an hour?
	I think I have something that can make your day better.
13. *Moving*	Where are you moving?
	I have just the right thing for you to draw customers to your new place of business.
	I have just the right thing for your open house sale.
	It will surely draw many customers to your new location as well as give you a hefty profit.
14. *Under contract*	What do you mean by being under contract?
	Do you purchase everything from them?
	Can you tell me who your current vendor is?
	What types of prices are you paying?
	Can you tell me when your contract is up for renewal?
	Do you mean to tell me that you have to purchase everything from them?

Are you saying that if I am selling twenty dollar bills for ten dollars you cannot buy?

15. *No space or room*

Put your arm out—are you touching anything? No? I can put 15 in that space.

Don't buy to store them at this low price; promote them and make a profit.

Why not put a couple of your key salespeople on them and have them all sold before you receive them?

16. *Not the right season*

Now is the time to load up and have them before your season begins.

At these prices, you can't afford to pass up this deal.

I cannot guarantee that when your season is here we'll be able to offer them at this fantastic price.

17. *I need time to think*

Would you prefer I call you back in 20 minutes or would this afternoon be better?

18. *Just bought*

What brand did you buy?

What price did you pay?

What sizes and styles did you buy?

Are you low in any other sizes?

Maybe you need to fill in your inventory.

At these fantastic prices you could purchase a small amount from me and use them as a promotional item to lure customers into your store.

This will help you move the ones you just purchased.

19. *Can't buy everything*

I wouldn't expect you to, but I have a whole warehouse full of these mufflers, and you can make a profit on them.

I wouldn't expect you to, but how about purchasing a few to try out as a promotional item?

With these prices you can make a handsome profit.

20. *Never heard of . . .*

Length in business . . .

Other customers as referrals . . .

We're Number One

21. *Too many in stock*

You might consider buying this product at this *low* price and setting up a promotion so they'll help move some of your existing inventory.

You might consider buying my product at this low price and price average it with your current stock, so you can lower your entire inventory and make more money.

22. *Service*

We are only as far as your telephone.

This product has been very good for us and our customers, but if you ever have any problems whatsoever, don't hesitate to give me a call.

I am only a split-second away.

This product carries a full warranty.

We know how to give the best service.

23. *Warranty*

Ours is the best warranty in the industry.

Because we use the telephone, if anything goes wrong, just

	grab your phone and I am only a split-second away.
24. *Delivery speed*	How long do you wait currently? Because we use the telephone, your orders are shipped within a super short time of your phone confirmation. We're only a phone call away.
25. *Freight*	Do you need them right away? Do you know what freight deduct is?
26. *Discount*	This is already a discounted price. If I can get you a discount, would you order the entire amount?

Every industry has its own particular common objections to overcome. You can teach anyone how to sell successfully if they have or learn the basic instincts of salesmanship.

Begin by introducing the product and the company the salespeople are selling. Give them information on how the product is made, distributed, and used. Technical data need not be stressed, but do provide answers to all of their questions, and keep the technical particulars available should they need them.

If, during a phone call, salespeople get a technical question they cannot answer, train your people to admit they don't know the answer, but will get it and call back with the correct answer, being sure to let the customer understand when to expect a callback.

Obvious problems in the product or service should be pointed out to the sales crew. Inform the salespeople of the methods your company recommends using to overcome anticipated objections. Beyond the obvious, don't go further than this in discussing how to overcome objections until the salespeople have had a chance to personally work the product on the phone.

There are rarely more than 20 reasons why a person won't buy a product or service. Those reasons may be phrased in a million different ways by thousands of different personalities, but the number will seldom, if ever, exceed 20. You'll find the reasons to be it is too hot, too cold, too wet, or too dry, too cheap or too expensive, I'm overloaded, I don't have any money, and so forth. The reasons may change with the product or service, but the number is limited and each one can be reduced to its basic type of objection.

During those first days of working on a new product or service, have the salespeople list on a yellow legal pad each reason they find that motivates a person to buy. Also list each objection to buying. When the same reason or objection is repeated by different prospects, put a checkmark beside their original notation. By the end of the second or third day, have a sales meeting. This is where the teaching really begins. Everybody reads his or her list and gives a suggestion on how to handle each situation. Explain what worked and what did not work. When a salesperson has encountered an objection that couldn't be overcome, ask suggestions from his or her peers. After the fourth or fifth person has spoken, everyone will realize that the objections are similar from one person to the next.

By the time the sales meeting is completed, the salespeople have become computers. They know the reasons motivating a prospect to buy. They know all the objections any prospect is likely to make, and they have six, eight, or ten different answers to overcome each one. Now your salespeople are ready to sell.

Sometimes in raising an objection, your prospect will simply be wrong, or the objection will be so ludicrous that nothing you say will be able to overcome it. You can't agree with the prospect, and, although you know there are exceptions to every selling rule, you know better than to say he or she is wrong and start an argument. The best thing to do is to *take his or her temperature*—find out if the objection is real or simply a diversionary tactic.

When an objection does not make sense, you have to find out what the prospect is really thinking, because until you do, you have no logical way to answer it. Even if you dream something up, you will not know what the objection is. It's the odd-ball, unreal objections appearing from nowhere that are the hardest to overcome. But, until the prospect's objection is answered, he or she will feel uncomfortable buying from you.

Open-Ended and Closed-Ended Questions

When you meet a difficult objection, start by asking open-ended questions beginning with who, how, when, where, which, or why. Kipling once wrote, "I keep six honest serving men, they taught me all I know. Their names are How and Where and Which and When and also Why and Who." These are the basic questions a good journalist must answer in every story, and these are the questions the professional salesperson uses to lead a prospect to a sale.

Open-ended questions do not give the prospect the ability to answer with a "yes" or a "no."

Another sales tool for the professional salesperson is the "closed-ended" question. These questions force the prospect to answer either with a "yes" or a "no," but in most cases, preferably with a *"yes."* Closed questions utilize words such as "is," "do," "has," "can," "will," and "shall." Some salespeople use the closed-ended questions in a way to force prospects to tie-down their responses in a positive manner, such as using the closed-ended participles at the end of the questions. For example, "This is the best price, isn't it?" "This product has performed the best, hasn't it?" "This product meets your needs the best, doesn't it?" "This will do the job, won't it?"

These closed-ended questions don't give the prospect much of a chance to respond any other way but with a *"yes."*

Salespeople must be tactful, but they must also probe. If you don't know or uncover a prospect's real thoughts, you will never be able to make the prospect see the fallacy of his or her argument.

Once you know and understand your prospect's true reasoning, you can counter it by using a variation of the "yes, but" technique. First, admit your prospects' objections have merit and tell them you understand why they feel the way they do. Then prove their objections invalid by offering them positives that outweigh their negatives.

When overcoming an objection, the key word is "diplomacy." Don't turn your presentation into a debate and never throw your prospect's mistake into his or her face. The successful salesperson is a student of psychology. He or she knows by giving prospects the impression that he or she is agreeing with them, he or she can skillfully prove the prospect's thinking unimportant, overcoming the objection and making the sale.

Be Honest—Play It Straight

Every salesperson has an ego, but you cannot let your pride stand between you and the sale. Utilize your skills to overcome objections. Never use deception. Always play it straight. Otherwise you won't survive in the game of selling. Give your prospect the benefit of the doubt and avoid bluntness. You may be able to win an argument but, when you do, you'll also lose the sale every time.

There are times when an objection need not be answered. Such objections usually take the form of misstatements made by your prospect, often when he or she is delivering a monologue. If the misstatement is unimportant, ignore it. If you feel the misstatement warrants correction, don't interrupt your prospect. Wait for him or her to finish what he or she is saying, then proceed as if you were walking on eggs. Corrections are arguments, and arguments antagonize.

Most prospects will give you several reasons why they won't buy but often they're just laying down a smoke screen. If you feel you've overcome all of your prospect's objections but are turned down when you ask for the order, search for the real objection, the one standing between you and the sale.

There is an old axiom among professional salespeople: "You can't begin to sell until the customer raises an objection." Some sales professionals don't call them objections, but opportunities to close.

In overcoming objections, you must remember that every prospect is different. The prospect's thinking is based upon his or her wants, fears, needs, and desires. No two people are exactly alike and no two prospects will ever react or respond the same way to identical suggestions. The successful salesperson develops closing techniques to direct the prospect's thoughts and actions. He or she does this skillfully, by asking questions and overcoming objections, and also by listening.

The professional telemarketer utilizes his or her listening skills to peak levels. If you don't hear the objections you cannot overcome them. If you don't hear the customer say yes you might forget to write up the order. Listening is a primary key to success in telemarketing.

The following is a list of some key fundamentals in listening training:

1. Prepare. You must free your mind for listening. Make sure you have your presentation prepared in advance, with your objections, features, benefits, and advantages thought out before you make your call.

2. Think like the customer. You must learn to see things through the eyes of your prospect. Don't talk "at" them, talk "to" them.

3. Limit and control how much talking you do. Keep asking yourself to "shut up" and take the order. Sometimes silence can be golden. Too much talking can "unsell" many an order.

4. Listen for ideas and concepts, not words. Always think in terms of the total picture. The big picture.

5. Concentrate. Focus your attention on every word your prospect says, or doesn't say. Don't let distractions or your own talking let you miss a customer's responses, replies, etc.

6. Learn to love pauses. Never interrupt customers when they are trying to say yes. Allow long pauses by customers to continue. Many times it does not mean they are through talking.

7. Ask questions. Keep the prospects involved, and use questions to lead and qualify them.

8. Take notes. Learn your own form of shorthand. You may make over 100 calls a day, and no memory can keep up, so keep notes on every call, every response, every objection (see Figures 11.1 and 11.2). These little details can be the answers you might be looking for later.

9. Repeat questions, statements. Get your prospects to elaborate on all objections so you can learn their real motivations, as well as gain understanding and knowledge about how you must best pursue them.

10. Keep it cool. Don't get angry. Use your head and let the hard stuff pass by you. Be professional and listen to the negatives, but learn by them.

11. Don't jump to conclusions. Never assume anything. Don't answer sentences for your prospects because you really aren't a mind reader.

12. Let the customer know you are still there. Use occasional "uh-huhs" and "yeses" to let the customer know you are listening to his or her voice. This will relax your prospect and allow him or her to continue.

13. Practice. Listening is a skill, just like riding a bicycle. It takes practice to become proficient.

Sales trainers historically have taught that the secret to successful selling lies in overcoming objections. Trainers in telemarketing have learned that to be successful in telephone sales it takes a very specialized mastering of voice skills, preplanning, *and* overcoming objections.

Each industry has its own set of problems and its own set of common objections that sales personnel must learn to overcome.

Figure 11.1 **Importance of Repetition and Memory**

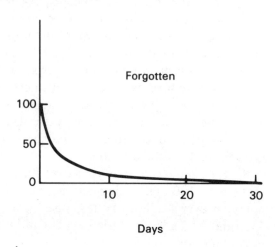

Percent of Memory

A message read or heard only once is 66% forgotten within 24 hours and is practically out of mind in 30 days.

Forgotten

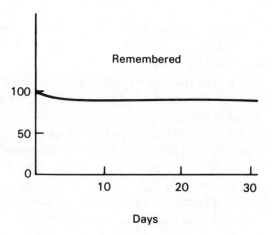

Percent of Memory

A message read or heard several times a day for 8 days is virtually memorized; at the end of 30 days, the memory retains 90% of the message.

Remembered

Only an incubator of ways the telemarketer can use objections as opportunities to successful sales has been presented here.

Objections no longer have to be feared by the sales crews. Utilizing a systematic approach to overcoming the objections you encounter, you will find that objections are nothing but keys on the cash register of success (see Figure 11.3).

Figure 11.2 **Sample Checklist for Determining Ways to Overcome Objections**

Common Objections	Ways of Overcoming Objections
1.	1.
	2.
	3.
2.	1.
	2.
	3.
3.	1.
	2.
	3.
4.	1.
	2.
	3.
5.	1.
	2.
	3.
6.	1.
	2.
	3.
7.	1.
	2.
	3.

8.   1.

                        2.

                        3.

_____

9.   1.

                        2.

                        3.

_____

Figure 11.3 **Overcoming Objections and Closing the Sale**

The Three "F" Technique (Feel, Felt, Found)

1. Feel: "Mr./Ms. _____, I understand how you *feel*."

2. Felt: "Other companies have *felt* the same way."

3. Found: "However, many have *found* they could reduce costs significantly and thereby increase profits through the use of our product.

Closing the Sale

To close a sale means to get an order. It is the time when all selling is over. All of your effort is directed toward one thing in selling—the close. It could occur at any time in the sales message; the sooner the better. For simplicity's sake, let us identify three types of closes:

1. Open-ended: "How many widgets can we send you?"

2. Forced choice: "Would you like us to deliver 12 widgets this week, or would you like to order 24 so as to have some inventory backup in case you have a heavy demand?"

3. Assumed: "Based on the movement of widgets in other parts of the country, we feel you should maintain an inventory of at least 6 at all times. I'll send you an order of 6 immediately. You should receive that order by Thursday."

Summarize the Order

Arrange for the Next Call (Recycling)

Express Thanks

How to Close the Sale

Once a person has gained product knowledge, learned how to overcome objections, and mastered the techniques for handling inquiries and how to organize a sales campaign, it is surprising that many salespeople still fall short of their sales expectations.

The primary reason for most sales failures once the fundamentals have been mastered is an instinctive fear of closing the sales.

As sales account executives, your primary job duties include actual selling. You are paid to sell and that takes learning special techniques in closing.

What is a close? A close is just the natural attempt to achieve your goal in your sales presentation—getting the sale. This means *asking for the order.*

Once you have established your prospect's need and provided the characteristic benefits, advantages, and features of your products to meet those needs, you must ask for the order. By this time, your prospect already expects you to ask for the order. Closing never can be a substitute for a poor sales presentation, but it is necessary to consistently inform your prospect throughout the pitch that you are asking for an order.

In order to close a sale successfully, keep the following points in mind.

1. Have a positive attitude. You must be positive and confident in your sales approach at all times. By expecting a sale and assuming you will be getting a sale, all you really need is a simple "yes" from your customer. By using a positive approach to selling and to your products, you will find your prospects responding on every call.

2. Always be closing. Sales statistics indicate that a normal sale requires at least three attempts on the part of the salesperson to ask for the sale. Therefore, never get disillusioned by simple "no" responses from prospects. Usually your sales success is just around the corner from another "no."

3. Take their temperature. In the normal course of any sales presentation, there comes a time to determine the interests of your prospect in your products. Once you have provided all of the benefits, features, and advantages of your products, you must start asking questions to get feedback as to how your presentation is being received.

Start by asking opinions. Give your prospect an opportunity to interact and participate in the conversation. Using the alternate choices—open and closed-ended, tie-downs, and porcupines—you have already learned, you can begin to lead the conversation to the close.

Never lecture. Always attempt to involve the prospect. Start taking the temperature of your prospects. How are they responding to your presentation? You must know how you stand so you can adjust to the situation. Trial closes are simply trial attempts to asking for the sale. They tell you how the customer wants to be sold. Here are some sample trial closes:

"This is a tremendous guarantee, isn't it?"
"Are you interested in premium or standard quality?"
"You aren't allergic to green are you?"

One of the most effective closing techniques in telemarketing is the so-called assumptive close. If, after you have presented a super sales performance and have overcome all of your prospects' objections, and you know your product will do the best job, then why not assume that you have the order? You have already proven yourself. Used correctly, the assumptive close will lock it up for you.

Always use the assumptive close first. Most of the time, if you have done your job professionally, it will be enough to do the job. Here are some common assumptive closes:

"Where would you prefer this order be shipped; would your office be all right, or would the shop be better?"
"Would you prefer COD, or would you want 30-day billing?"

Chapter 12

Selling Existing Accounts

Telephone Cycling Increases Your Sales

It is amazing how much of our lives is dependent on cycles. There is the cycling of seasons, the cycling of the earth around the sun, the cycling of the moon around the earth, the cycling of good times and bad times, the cycling of money throughout our economy.

Cycling is fundamental to telemarketing success.

Existing accounts represent the bread and butter of any business. They provide the dependable income that keeps your business running. Cycling these existing accounts can make or break many firms.

Most of your time is spent selling and servicing your regular customers, and it is here that your major increases in sales volume should occur. It is always much easier to build volume from existing customers than it is to open or sell new accounts. Therefore, it is fundamental to learn the unique and rewarding techniques of servicing and cycling these existing accounts to their most effective return.

Even though existing accounts are a company's bread and butter, and are the best place to expand sales volume, most field reps do not take advantage of this because of the lack of time. Most reps spend more time traveling, waiting in outer offices, and trying to track down buyers than they do directly relating to their regular customers.

To compound this problem, field reps have to spend valuable time visiting marginal accounts that are barely profitable. Adhering to tight schedules further prohibits the proper handling of existing accounts. Average field reps cannot call on customers when it is to their best advantage—when the customer is ready to buy. Rather, they must call on their customers when it fits into their travel schedule.

You can eliminate these problems in your business by developing a telephone cycling program for your existing accounts. Such a program will save you a great deal of time and money while allowing you to efficiently and profitably contact all of your regular customers, even marginally profitable accounts, when it is most convenient for them and best for you.

Account cycling by telephone increases your company's visibility and minimizes crisis sales management—the necessity to solve those problems that time alone has expanded and blown out of proportion. Telephone cycling affords you more frequent contact with all of your accounts than you could possibly have if you depended on field representatives.

Thus, you gain better control of your sales activities and their costs. You also gain better, more thorough market coverage and increase your exposure through added customer contacts while maintaining your sales force at its present size.

Hold on to Existing Accounts— Know Your Customer

By account cycling, you keep your customers buying, you keep them paying, you keep them owing, and, most importantly, you keep out the competition by keeping their shelves full.

A survey by the Rockefeller Corporation revealed the following facts on why customers stopped buying from their regular suppliers:

1 percent die.
3 percent move away.
5 percent formed other friendships.
9 percent changed for competitive reasons.
14 percent changed due to product dissatisfaction.
68 percent quit because of an attitude of indifference toward the customer by one or more persons representing the supplier!

Granted, we cannot do much about the first two categories in the list, but we *can* do something about the remaining four. We can keep in periodic contact with all our accounts, calling on them by telephone on a regular basis. Here again, we must agree with an old axiom, "It's five times easier to keep an existing account than it is to open up a new one."

Your customers benefit from telephone cycling, too. A telephone call takes up far less of their time than an eyeball-to-eyeball sales meeting. You can schedule your calls much more conveniently than you can schedule road trips, motels, and business luncheons. You can schedule your calls and your selling so your customer never has to worry about running out of the merchandise you provide.

You are able to maintain a regular and orderly schedule that the customer can depend on. This reduces his or her inventory, worries, and the amount of space necessary for storage. It also allows you to better utilize warehouse space for storage of your own products, as you, too, will have a definite idea how much you regularly sell and when you need to resupply.

The best method for cycling by telephone is:

1. **Compile a list of all your regular accounts.**
2. **Establish their buying cycle.** The period between when your customer buys once and then is ready to buy again is the "buying cycle." The period of time it takes you to complete all of your contacts in a particular territory is called the "sales cycle."

While field representatives can seldom make sales cycles coincide with the buying cycle of their customers, if you study your regular customers' buying habits, you can establish their buying cycles and use this to advantage in your telephone sales.

3. **Establish the "optimum reorder point" for your customers.** This is the time when their stock has been depleted by two-thirds of their full, normal inventory. This is also the time most customers will be receptive to competitive bids and buying. You must use this point to schedule your regular telephone calls, and get an order.

4. **Determine fluctuations.** If your customers' buying cycles seem to fluctuate in response to many factors, such as seasonal activity, you must know what the factors are and how they influence their demands. Once this is determined, you will be able to sell efficiently. Also, you will be in a good situation to help your customers while increasing your own sales. You will be able to let dealers who respond to your company's sales programs know in advance of special advertising dealing with the goods they buy, allowing them to plan their ordering accordingly, and save.

5. **Notify customers of price increases.** When you are planning a price increase, all of your accounts should be notified in advance. If you plan special promotions, such as give-aways or tie-in deals,

all customers who historically have participated in such programs should be notified.

6. Be aware of seasonal influences. You should be aware of seasonal influences on your customers' buying habits or needs. Christmas, for example, will usually have a major impact on your customers' buying cycle. Customers who regularly order once a month may order weekly just before a holiday. Constantly be alert to general influences, such as weather, politics, social trends, etc., that may affect each of your customers, causing one to buy much more or less than others.

7. Keep the cycle flexible. Be certain to keep your customers' cycles flexible, so you can exploit unpredictable influences that would open up more selling opportunities.

8. Group accounts. It is important when you set up a cycle schedule that you group accounts with similar buying cycles. This way, high volume accounts can be called once a week or so, and low accounts can be called every other week. By grouping your accounts by volume, you have the added advantage of being able to rehearse one sales pitch for that day's calling. You could contact all the high volume customers on Monday, for example, with your mind set just on dealing with them. This technique greatly simplifies selling by the telephone and gives your sales program impetus, because it is focused on one goal and one group of customers at a time.

Records, Yes—Complicated, No

Record-keeping for your regular accounts is absolutely necessary to good telephone cycling. All of the data required to maintain an account cycling system by telephone can be sustained on a single account card or sales call report. Record-keeping need not be complicated, but it does need to be thorough. Your sales call report card should include:

1. Customer's name, address, and telephone number
2. Name of your contacts within the customer's organization
3. Customer's credit limit established by your company's credit department
4. Information on your customer's regular inventory demands and on the products he or she usually buys
5. Special information, factors, or situations that affect or alter each customer's buying habits, for example, price increases, special sales, contests, give-aways, etc.

6. Best time of the day to call the customer

The body of your sales call report should be divided into four vertical columns, one each for the following:

1. The date you make the call
2. The information you gather about what the customer is ordering; any important details you feel are pertinent to his or her personality and buying habits; follow-up information, such as seasonal items, your customer may find of interest at a later date
3. A list of all invoices and credit memos for easy reference and to help establish buying patterns
4. The date you plan to make your follow-up call

You should allow space on each card for personal notations about each customer. Note the customer's secretary's name and personal interests. Note your customer's personal interests, such as coaching Little League. This allows you to make your conversations more personal than a bare sales call.

When you make your actual sales call, follow the Sequence of Success. Then, after completing the call, record all of your notes on your sales call report card, process the order, and make a notation to call your cutomer in a day or two after the order is scheduled for delivery. This follow-up call is legitimate and is a chance to advertise yourself.

You should call the customer shortly after the order has been received to make certain he or she is pleased with the purchase and that he or she has received everything asked for in good condition. This call often results in fill-in orders, but the main purpose is to let your customers know you are interested in them and their businesses. There is no one more satisfied than a satisfied customer. There is no one easier to sell, either.

Your sales report card functions to:

Create value for each prospect
Provide detailed results of each call
Establish controlled work-flow guides
Establish follow-up procedures
Allow for feedback and analysis of each call

Some call report cards also require even more specific information about each call to be recorded. Sample call report forms are shown in Figures 12.1 and 12.2. A sample callback form is shown in Figure 12.3.

Figure 12.1 **Sample Sales Call Report Form**

Complete Address: _____

_____

Account: _____

Priority: _____

Contact: _____

Title: _____

Phone No. _____

Best Calling Time: _____ A.M. _____ P.M.

	Call Date	Call Detail	Follow Up	Next Call Date
1				
2				
3				
4				
5				
6				
7				
8				

Principal Market(s): _____

Current Buying Pattern: _____

Special Requirements: _____

Financial Data: _____

_____

Credit Rating: _____

_____

Personal Notes: _____

_____

_____

_____

Many telemarketing operations want to know quantitative statistics from each call, including:

1. Date of the call
2. Start time of the call
3. Stop time of the call
4. Whom you spoke with
5. What was discussed
6. Busy signal?
7. Wrong number?
8. Not in?
9. Not interested?
10. Disconnected line?

For one version of a statistical call report form, see Figure 12.4.

In order to standardize their forms, many institutions require standardization even in the abbreviations used by their sales personnel. This allows management to be able to adequately decipher the call cards in case of employee turnover and changes in territories, as well as evaluation of performance.

Some of the key abbreviations currently used on call card reports are as follows:

DIS	Disconnected number
NR	No response
CB	Call back
NI	Not interested
DNA	Decision maker not available
CAT	Requests additional information/catalogs

These abbreviations can be adapted and modified to your particular industry, and are also used extensively by telephone sales communicators reading scripts.

Figure 12.2 **Sample Sales Call Report Form**

| Account _____ Phone _____ |
| Ind. Name _____ Home Phone _____ |
| Bus. Home _____ |
| Address _____ Address _____ |

Follow-Up Date _____

Best Day	Best Time

	Credit
Customer	App'tion
Instructions _____	D&B _____
	Financial
Ship Via _____ Deal # _____	Statement _____
	Personal _____
Territory _____	Guarantee _____
	Bank _____

	High Limit
Sizes & Types Used _____	Approved For T/A's _____
	Account Appr'd By _____

Open	C.O.D.

Remarks

Date	Sold	Quoted	Mail

Figure 12.3 **Sample Callback Form**

CALL-BACKS

Time	Monday	Tuesday	Wednesday	Thursday	Friday

Figure 12.4 **Sample Statistical Call Report Form**

Statistical Report: Week of _____

Date:	Cum	Cum	Cum	Cum	Cum	Cum	Cum	Cum
Calling/Shift hours:								
A. # of sales/yes								
B. # of refusals/no								
C. Completed calls								
D. # of wrong numbers								
E. Total leads used								
F. Hours								
G. Completed calls per hour								
H. Verified sales								
I. Verified sales per hour								
J. Cancellations								
K. Cancellation %								
L. Duplications								
M. No answers								
N. Total conversion %								
Positive response rate								

Key: Hours = total communicator phone hours. Completed calls = addition of A + B. Total leads = addition of C + D. Total conversion % = verified sales ÷ total leads used.

178

Another very effective tool for the telemarketing salesperson is the "sales call-performance checklist" (see Figure 12.5). This checklist is a fantastic outline of each telephone call with the checklist of important required ingredients necessary to insure the success of each call. It is a rule of thumb to require this checklist be used by all rookie sales reps, and most professionals use it casually as a tool for each day.

Figure 12.5 **A Checklist—Selling Existing Accounts**

The Telephone Call

1. Identify yourself and your firm.
2. Establish rapport.
3. Make an interest-creating comment.
4. Deliver your sales message.
    Stress benefits over features.
    Use a sales vo-cabulary.
5. Overcome customer objections.
    Confirm your under-standing of the objection.
    Prepare the customer for your answer.
    Answer the objection.
    Stress a benefit.
6. Close the sale.
    Use forced-choice questions.
7. Wrap up the sale.
    Summarize the order.
    Arrange for the next call.
    Express your thanks.

Pre-Call Planning

1. Set call objectives.
    To sell the regular order
    To sell more than the regular order

Follow Up

1. Record your notes—update customer record form.
2. Record the date of your next contact.
3. Place the order—make sure customer gets it.

    To upgrade the order
    To sell a special item

2. Prepare your opening statement.
   Identify yourself and your firm.
   Establish rapport.
   Make an interest-creating comment.

3. Prepare your sales message.
   Stress benefits over features.
   Use a sales vocabulary.

Turn Payments into Additional Sales

When you cycle your accounts by telephone, a working relationship between your sales department and accounts receivable people is absolutely necessary.

Your accounts receivable department should notify each salesperson *immediately* when any payment is made by a cycled account. This offers the salesperson an opportunity to call and thank the customer for the payment, thus opening another sales opportunity. It also allows the salesperson to check on the customer's use of his or her line of credit. If it has dropped well below the credit limit, the salesperson knows he or she can get approval from the credit department for further purchases, and sell more merchandise.

The simplest method found to keep sales account executives informed of when payments are made is to make a photocopy of every check received. This is done each morning right after the mail is opened, before any check is processed. The photocopies are then transmitted to the sales manager.

The sales manager passes the copies around the sales room, allowing each sales account executive to initial those checks that represent payments received from his or her accounts. After all sales account executives have examined the copies, they are returned to the manager. Any check not initialed by a salesperson is traced back by the sales manager to determine which person sold the account.

If you follow these simple suggestions, you can easily expand your present sales volume with your regular customers. They, after all, account for three-fourths of your business, they are regular buyers, you have credit and buying information on them already, and they have made those important first purchases that establish them as an account. By establishing a telephone cycling system, you will increase sales with your regular and valuable customers and actually help their businesses as well.

Chapter 13

~~~~~~

Surveys

Increasing Sales with Fact-Finding Questions

Conducting a telephone survey is an excellent method to determine whether or not an individual or a company can benefit from or is in a position to buy and use your products or services. The successful telephone survey is short, preferably not more than seven basic questions, and never more than a dozen.

Fact-Finding Questions

KISS—Keep It Simple, Stupid—applies to all aspects of telemarketing, especially the survey. Questions should be easily understood, requiring little or no interpretation. The perfect survey questions can be answered yes or no. If you develop a survey question you think should be answered yes or no and find that more than one out of every ten people asked the question expand on their answer, reword the question. The person taking the survey simply can't afford the time or the telephone expense to ask questions that produce essay-type answers. In other words, the success of any survey depends on your ability to ask closed-ended, fact-finding questions.

To be most effective as a sales tool, a survey should be semi-qualified cold-calling. If you're selling Cadillacs, you don't conduct your survey in an area where you know most of the residents are poor. Criss-cross directories can help you zero in on a specific area. Membership lists can help you reach special interest groups.

Industrial guides that list sales volumes or numbers of employees can save time.

A survey should be designed to qualify a prospect as a potential buyer and to determine his or her basic interest in your product or service. The people conducting the survey should be pleasant and knowledgeable. The quality of the leads generated by a survey program will increase in direct proportion to the ability of the person taking the survey. Many surveys fail to produce their desired results only because they are conducted by inexperienced communicators.

Find the Overlooked Prospects

These overlooked prospects are often located in out-of-the-way places, sometimes in small towns 50 to 100 miles apart. When it is not economically feasible for a field salesperson to flush them out, the telephone should be used. The time and expense of making telephone contact with a prospective customer in Southwest Nowhere is substantially the same as it is to make contact with someone based in New York, Chicago, or Los Angeles. In addition, the Southwest Nowhere prospect seldom hears from salespeople while your major city prospects probably comb salespeople out of their hair.

Select Questions Carefully

People are sometimes reluctant to give specific information about their business and seldom have specific dates at their fingertips.

The keys to using a telephone survey as a successful sales tool are to keep it simple and to ask only those questions the respondent is likely to be able to answer without doing any research. Properly implemented, a telephone survey will result in reducing your overall costs of marketing. Either directly or indirectly, a telephone survey can be used to increase your sales, your marketing area, and your market penetration.

It is very important to clarify one area of real concern for the legitimate telemarketer. In the past, many unscrupulous operators have used the telephone survey as a selling tool. They never intended to survey for information in the classic sense, only to use it to get the foot in the door—get the conversation started, and then go in for the kill.

These practices have contributed to the constant battle to clean up the telemarketing industry.

For the purposes of this telemarketing book, it must be understood that the ethical way to survey over the telephone is to actually *survey*.

Don't claim to be conducting research if your prime objective is to get a sale. Of course, information is a basic step to always getting a sale, but you must be upfront with your customers. Don't mislead them. Many legitimate survey-research firms have complained about the unscrupulous telephone operators who use their good name in misbegotten schemes.

Therefore, always avoid any traps that can cause you grief. The survey telephone call is a very important tool for gaining the information that makes successful sales possible. But always remember to keep the two distinct and clear.

Information Is Gold

The single most elusive and valuable asset a person or company can acquire for success in business today is *information*. It may be product information, updates on competition, qualifying information from prospects, credit background, or even negative feedback from complaints. But information is *gold, money, the edge to success.*

Telemarketing can gather information faster, more efficiently, and more economically than any other tool available today.

Well-written telephone surveys can do all the things a marketing manager always dreamed of—sell, inform, suggest, provide instant market feedback.

Surveys can prospect for new accounts, help ignite existing customers, update clients on new products and services, book appointments for field reps, and nearly every other possible business requirement indicated in Chapter 1.

Figures 13.1 through 13.4 offer a compilation of actual scripts that have been used successfully by professional telemarketers to book appointments, inform customers about new product lines, take credit applications, qualify buying decision makers, and acquire important competitive market knowledge.

Some of these scripts are primitive outlines, others verbatim blueprints, but each was individually designed to meet a unique desired objective.

Figure 13.1 **Sample Survey Script—Lead Generation**

May I please speak with the owner, manager, or director of marketing? ____

Good morning/afternoon. This is _____ with _____ Telemarketing.

Do you have a moment?

We are calling you today to make you aware that we are looking for work.

Have you ever heard of _____ Telemarketing?

_____ Telemarketing is a professional telemarketing organization.

We use WATS telephone lines and specialize in outbound telephone marketing.

Are you presently using telemarketing?

_____ has a joint venture with the State of Minnesota where we have established telemarketing centers in three of the Minnesota Correctional Facilities.

We have taken selected inmates and trained them in outbound telemarketing.

Under a controlled setting with calls monitored they are now making professional calls.

They have worked for companies such as 3M, Burlington Northern Railroad, and many others.

We are doing market research surveys and lead generation programs, and are also selling products over the phone.

Our calls are both productive and cost effective.

Would you be interested in having our Marketing Vice President call you to discuss the details and benefits of the program?

Thank you, have a good day.

Contact Name _____

Company Name _____

City/State _____

Telephone Number (____ *)* _____

Figure 13.2 **Sample Survey Script—Carpet Cleaning Supplies**

Today's date _____

Name of individual _____ Position _____

Name of company _____

Address _____ Telephone No. _____

City _____ Zip _____

	YES	NO

Are you the individual who purchases carpet cleaning equipment? ___ ___

If not, name of the person who does _____

_____

Telephone _____

Do you clean carpets? ___ ___

If not, why? _____

_____

What kind of carpet cleaning equipment do you use?

    Brand name _____

    How old _____

Do you use:

    Steam extraction ____ Shampoo ____

    Combination ____

Condition of existing carpet cleaning equipment:

    Good ____ Fair ____ Poor ____

Are you happy with present methods of cleaning carpets? ___ ___

How much do you charge per square foot for cleaning carpets? _____

How many square feet do you clean per month? ____

Where do you purchase your janitorial and carpet cleaning chemicals? _____

Are you happy with your current supplier? ___ ___

Do you purchase those chemicals at competitive prices? ___ ___

If _____ could provide you with heavy duty, high quality carpet cleaning equipment that would pay for itself, would you like a free demonstration? ___ ___

Who do you know who would be interested in getting into the carpet and upholstery cleaning business?

Name _____

Telephone _____

Mail ___ ___

Survey taken by _____

Figure 13.3 **Sample Survey Script—Real Estate**

Name of business _____

Address of business _____

City _____ Zip code _____

Survey taken from _____

Position _____

Type of business _____

Own or lease space? _____

What year did you move in? _____

How long a lease? _____

How long in business? _____

Approximate size of location (square feet) _____

Do you have warehouse facilities? _____ Approximate size _____

Would you be willing to expand to accommodate a new account?

_____

Are you happy with your facility? _____

Do you need more or less space? _____

Do you plan on any expansion in the near future? _____

Have you spoken about additional space with any real estate broker or builder during the past six months? _____ If yes, who?

_____

If no, would you like to? _____

Comments _____

_____

_____

Survey taken by _____

Phone number _____

Figure 13.4 **Sample Survey Script—Lead Generation**

Company _____

Address _____

City/State/Zip _____

Telephone _____

Survey taken by _____

Date _____

Good morning/afternoon. I'd like to speak to the person in charge of (company name)'s employee medical insurance program.

Who would that be? (Full Name) _____
   (If person is in—continue. If not in—say you will call back. Find out best time.)

Good morning/afternoon ___(name)___ , my name is _____. I'm calling from _____ Services. Since we represent most of the HMOs, PPOs, and traditional group plans we provide a single source for companies of your size. This reduces your time and trouble comparing and evaluating the various group options for you and your organization.

May I ask you a few questions?

(If No Time—Would there be a better time to call? (Record Time) If still Negative—I was calling to learn more about your company to see whether your company could benefit from our services. Would you be interested in getting some information in the mail?

If Yes—I'd like to ask you a few questions about your company to determine which literature we should send.)

1. Does your firm offer any type of health insurance coverage for its employees?
   Yes _____ No _____ (If No, have you considered offering it to your employees Yes No*)
   (*if No, then continue with question #6)

2. How many full-time employees who live in metro area are covered under your firm's health plan? _____

3. Does your company offer HMO, PPO, or standard group insurance or both?
   HMO _____ PPO _____ Group/Major Medical _____

4. Can you tell me who your carrier is for that plan? _____

5. Does your firm currently contribute toward health insurance coverage for its employees? Yes _____ No _____

6. Thank you for your time. As I mentioned before, _____ handles most HMOs, PPOs, and traditional group plans and can present all the options available. When would be a good time for one of our representatives to contact you to set up an introductory meeting? _____

   Comments _____
   _____

Use these samples to help suggest ways you can write your own survey. The survey is the most effective telemarketing tool for almost every task, so *practice, learn, and use them.*

Chapter 14

The Art of Inbound Telemarketing

As in all systematic approaches to marketing, telemarketing is a multi-dimensional concept. A square has four sides, a triangle three, a box has width and height, a cube has width, height, and length. There are dimensions of telemarketing that occur when a person calls another person.

One dimension is the caller's perspective. Another is the perspective of the callee, or person called. Then there is the dimension of the caller in perspective to the people in the room while he or she is calling. The same could be said for the callee, if someone else is in the room when the telephone rings.

The dimension discussed in this chapter concerns telemarketing's finest hour—the inbound telephone call.

Inquiries you receive from potential customers via the telephone are identified as "inbound telemarketing." Just as the name indicates, it is selling via an incoming telephone call.

When a customer calls you, you must recognize that this person has taken time (a very valuable commodity these days) to contact *you*. He or she is your most important prospect.

Inquiries usually reach you by mail or by phone. Their one common denominator is that the person making the inquiry has found something about your company that interests him or her. Behind almost every request for information from you is a person who has a "sell me" attitude.

Of course, every inbound telephone call does not represent a qualified sales prospect. Very seldom, however, will you find people willing to call your company and expend the effort to make an inquiry when they are not looking for information to assist them in making a current or future buying decision. Usually, these people are searching for a source of supply for a product or service they have determined they need. Therefore, you must recognize the inbound telephone call for what it is: a *sales opportunity.* Your primary objective in handling all inquiries is to generate increased sales in the most effective and convenient way possible. The telephone is the most effective tool for qualifying an inquirer's interest expediently, answering his or her questions, and then making a sale or an appointment.

Never let these sales opportunities get away from you. Many firms let these prime selling moments slip through their fingers, and then ask themselves why business is bad.

When you receive an inquiry, analyze it and decide on the best means of response with your present sales message. Often, an inquiry can give clues as to the motives of the inquirer and the extent of interest a person may have in your product or service.

For example, you may want to vary your sales presentation if you know your inbound caller is about to enter a new market or is dissatisfied with a competitive product he or she is currently buying.

Always respond to a mail inquiry in a prompt and concise manner. You must get to hot prospects while the curiosity is still fresh in their minds. Even when you determine that a written inquiry requires a written response, always attempt a telephone call to help learn inquirers' true motivations. This will help you qualify them, determine how detailed a response is required, refresh their memories, and cause them to look for your response among their morning mail within a specified time frame.

Sequence to Success

Like everything else you do on the telephone, there is a simple sequence to follow in handling an inquiry. Through advanced preparation and by following the sequence, you will be able to accomplish skillfully your primary objective of getting either the sale or the appointment. Your precall sequence should be prepared from the following four suggestions:

1. You must have complete knowledge of your product or service. In response to a direct inquiry, you should be prepared to satisfy the request of the inquirer and field all questions asked of you. Thorough knowledge of your company's literature, advertising material, specification sheets, and production schedules will allow the flow of your answers to be smooth, instilling confidence in both your company and your product. However, if you don't know how to answer a question, admit it. Don't bluff. Don't put the caller on hold for more than 20 seconds. It is more courteous to call the inquirer back once you have searched and found the answer to the question than to keep him or her on hold while you look it up.

2. If you have a product that needs a demonstration or if your policy is to shift responsibility for the ultimate sale to a field representative, know within a day or two when your representative will be in the area of the prospect's place of business. You should also know about how long it will take you to contact your field representative so that in addition to telling him or her your prospect's name, you can also tell your prospect when a salesperson will call.

3. If your inquiry was received through the mail, gather as much information about the inquirer as is readily available before you respond. The more you know about the inquirer, the more flattered he or she will be when you contact him or her. Everyone responds positively to flattery and this response will help you sell. In addition, customer information is the clue to whether or not your inquirer is a "live" lead. Check your company files to see if he or she has bought before. Check credit rating sources, such as Dun and Bradstreet, to get an idea of your prospect's size and ability to buy. In addition, get into the habit of reading trade journals directed toward consumers of your product or service. They often are an invaluable source for telling you who's who.

4. Prepare a list of one-liners made up of fact-finding questions, interest-creating comments, and statements designed to overcome objections. Learn as many of these as you can. You should always have a list of one-liners by every telephone extension list. This list will often bail you out when you just can't think of what to say, or have to handle a particularly difficult customer.

After preparing yourself according to these suggestions, you are ready to make your call. The first step in making a telephone call in response to a mail inquiry is to identify yourself and inform the potential customer you are calling regarding his or her request for information. Restate the inquiry to refresh his or her memory and establish for yourself and your prospect that you have an understanding of precisely what he or she wants to know about your product or service. Then answer the inquiry clearly and completely. Unclear or partial answers will not satisfy the inquirer or help you reach your primary objective of making a sale or getting an appointment.

Traditionally, inbound telephone marketing has been used solely for the unadorned order and information-answering functions. Outbound telemarketing was always used for the more complicated tasks of prospecting, qualifying, and actual selling.

Today, the professional telemarketer recognizes the *sales opportunity* an inbound call provides; therefore, marketing plans in today's sophisticated arena must combine both inbound and outbound perspectives to mold each campaign adequately to the unique characteristics of a product, service, or firm being represented.

Many kinds of companies use toll-free 800 numbers to ease access to inquiries and potential inbound sales. No matter what service or product is being marketed, inbound telemarketing can prove to be a very cost-effective tool for success.

But there are some inside and outside influences that can affect the amount of success you can achieve. The following are some factors to consider when deciding on an inbound campaign:

1. Style, type, and features of the products or services being sold. Ultimately, the key characteristics of your products can affect the productivity of an inbound program. The more complex your products are, the greater the need for more expertise and knowledge on the part of your inbound operators. Taking into consideration the skill levels of most inbound representatives, the less product knowledge necessary, the more successful an inbound program will be. For example, it is increasingly easier to market records, books, or tapes via inbound telemarketing, but more difficult to achieve substantial success with selling hi-tech, complex products, such as microchips or aircraft carriers.

It is important not to generalize success rates and take this all as gospel, because there are many exceptions to all rules. Many companies have found remarkable success in inbound telemarketing of complex services such as investment securities. These unique campaigns do require higher skilled and trained operators, though.

2. Levels of selling skills the operators have. The best first step in the transformation of a crew of telephone operators into successful inbound telemarketers is the realization that these trained crews are not "operators" but "sales representatives." Anyone can learn how to answer a telephone and take orders. The truly professional telemarketer understands there is a science to selling that it isn't just percentages, low prices, and good luck. Success in selling, no matter if it is in inbound or outbound telemarketing, door-to-door vacuum cleaner selling, or employment as a clerk in a fast food restaurant, requires training.

Selling is confidence—confidence in knowledge of the fundamentals of sales. If you want to succeed in using inquiries to increase your sales volumes and gross profits, and reach your quotas, your incoming operators must be educated in the basic rules, regulations, and systems to *selling*. The success or failure of any inbound marketing campaign can often be directly attributable to how well the personnel has been exposed to the simple basics of sales. The reps must see themselves not as telephone answering machines, but as *sales account executives*. They must take pride in their sales ability and the opportunities it offers.

3. How much emphasis the company puts in inbound telemarketing. Another increasingly important factor that arises when analyzing the success or failures of marketing campaigns is the amount of in-house support the campaign received. If your company is dedicated to direct mail and only has the inbound forces there as a pacifier to some rising executive's whim, don't expect any miracles. As in any business or team, morale is crucial to winning. If you want to succeed in inbound telemarketing, support it, do your homework, and give the campaign your best shot. Oftentimes a halfhearted campaign brings only halfhearted results.

4. The kinds of payments allowed. The productivity of an inbound telemarketing campaign can be drastically affected by the forms of payment allowed. This is especially true when considering a television advertisement-inbound telemarketing exercise. In nearly every instance, a television ad that indicates that CODs (collect or cash on delivery shipping) are accepted will out-perform the same commercial that indicates credit cards only. Under these circumstances, allowable percentage of returns must be taken into consideration to adjust the profitability of COD acceptance. In all cases, the easier the terms of acceptance, the better the results. Your prospect is already motivated by the significance of using a "toll-free" call; now you must add additional incentives or remove any roadblocks that can cause reluctance or hesitation to act. Keep it as easy and simple as possible.

5. Seasonal fluctuations. Any inbound telemarketing campaign that tries to sell the right product at the wrong time is just wasting a lot of time and effort. Every industry has its good seasons and bad seasons. The tire industry lives for its summers, the auto industry for its falls, the real estate industry for its springs, and the mitten industry for its winters. Don't try to confront the seasonal fluctuations. It simply won't work. Research on your customer's best buying times can be a great help in signaling the time to begin your campaigns.

6. The type of media being targeted to reinforce. Every inbound telemarketing campaign is affected tremendously by the media it reinforces. For example, a campaign that reinforces a television commercial is going to produce different numbers than the same campaign reinforcing a radio or direct mail campaign. The sheer number of potential readers or watchers or listeners can dramatically affect the numbers of inquiries. The effectiveness of the media advertisement itself can alter results, too.

7. Demographics of the target audience. Much of the factoring effect here should be controlled by your advertising director, but there is no denying that the type of people viewing a television commercial definitely affects the success or failure of an inbound telemarketing campaign. It's always hard to sell beer during cooking shows and silk stockings during a boxing match. You must always recognize the importance of demographics in analyzing the success or failure of any marketing effort.

8. The number of previous airings of the commercial. There are certainly times in life where less is better, but not in the marketing game. Here, more is great. We are talking about mental images, memory penetration, and repetition-response rates. Today's mass population receives a vast amount of stimuli every hour of every day, and it is quite an expensive task to challenge this constant maze of media static. Therefore, a proven winning formula used by many marketing firms is: *lots*. They believe that lots of commercials, lots of the time, and lots of money spent hopefully will equal lots of revenue and lots of response. Of course, lots of bad is still bad, so it is vital that the messages being communicated are *good*. Therefore, in inbound telemarketing campaigns that are used to reinforce another medium advertisement, the more times a message is sent out, normally, the better response of incoming calls.

9. The mental image a company may have attained with its audience. As mentioned previously, lots of bad is still bad. No one can overcome extreme adversity. Therefore, the reputation a firm may have can without question alter and either help or hurt a marketing campaign.

10. Quality of the media that is presented. The item in question here is whether or not the actual programming in which a commercial is seen can affect the response to that individual commercial. Will an audience for "M.A.S.H." react in greater numbers than an audience for "The David Letterman Show"? The answer is *yes*, it can have an effect. Some programming is interactive with its audience, others instill a passivity or even anger, depression, anxiety, or sleep. Therefore, an inbound marketing campaign will feel its response rates drastically altered by the actual quality of the programming being sandwiched.

Generally, inquiries can become a substantial medium for sales growth, if the campaign is planned and implemented professionally. The following is a short list of some of the practical applications for which inbound telemarketing has proven successful:

1. Take orders.
2. Gather immediate credit data.
3. Gather demographic and psychographic data.
4. Quote prices, terms, and product features, benefits, and advantages.
5. Book appointments for field reps.
6. Screen and qualify the prospects.
7. Inform the caller as to the nearest dealers.
8. Provide warranty information.
9. Act as customer service department.
10. Offer additional offers (up-sell).
11. Accept reservations.
12. Provide alternatives.
13. Turn suspects into prospects.
14. Suggest additional products, services, options.
15. Minimize delays.
16. Put out any potential problems.

Know Your Prospect

The next step in your call sequence is determining your inquirer's potential as a customer. (See Figure 14.1 for a sample script.) Asking questions to qualify him or her, beginning with who, what, where, how, and when, will elicit information and provide you with an understanding of his or her potential, as well as possible ideas you can use to make a sale. As in cold-calling, you want to maintain control of the conversation. At this point, you should avoid questions that can be answered with a simple yes or no. Depending on your product or service, this can be accomplished by asking such questions as:

1. "Where are you located?" or "What section of town are you in?"
2. "What kind of facilities do you have?"
3. "What type of customer base do you have?" or "For what type of use do you need our product?" or "What kind of problems are you currently experiencing?"
4. "What kind of volume are you doing now?" or "Who are your present suppliers?"

To verify information you have already received as well as any new information you elicit, ask questions that can be answered with yes or no. If you feel you need further information, you can always go back to open-ended questions, which should be designed to inform you what sales approach or what kind of appeal (emotional, logical, ego, etc.) will most interest the inquirer.

Once you have qualified the customer, the next step in your sequence is to decide quickly on a realistic objective. If your product or service requires a field call, your objective should be to make an appointment or pave the way for your territory salesperson. If your product or service does not require a demonstration, your objective should be to obtain a minimum size order. If you go after too large an order, you'll frighten your prospect away. The order you want will be small enough to minimize the customer's risk, yet large enough to carry him or her until your next cycled contact.

You are now ready to convert the inquirer into a customer, the next step in your sequence. Think from the inquirer's point of view, remembering that what is of interest to you may not necessarily be of interest to him or her. Start with an interest-creating and thought-provoking question, using wherever possible someone the inquirer probably knows in the industry as a reference.

Once you have followed your step-by-step, field-tested sequence to this point, you have successfully converted your call from an answer to an inquiry to one where you're about to make either a sales presentation or an appointment. Though each person has a different style, every telephone call effectively handling an inquiry includes these six elements:

1. Accomplish precall preparation.
2. Identify yourself and, if the inquiry was obtained through the mail, indicate you are responding to a mail inquiry.
3. Restate the inquiry and express interest.
4. Determine your inquirer's potential.
5. Decide on your objective.
6. Convert the inquirer to a customer.

Figure 14.1 **Sample Sales Script—Inbound**

Good morning/afternoon/evening.

Thank you for calling _____, this is _____

How may I help you today? _____

_____

I will be happy to assist you, but first I will need your name, address, and telephone number.

Please bear with me, thank you.

Name please _____

Address _____ City _____

Telephone number _____

Thank you, now let me get you the information that you desire.

Using dynamic words, describe the features, advantages, and benefits of the equipment or service that the customer is inquiring about. Use your flip chart.

Ask for the order. Close!

Determine the reason that the customer is not giving you the order. What is the excuse for not buying?

Use your flip chart, which will list common objections and give you suggestions as to how to overcome the objection.

Answer the objections and once again ask for the order. Stress benefits. Close!

Ask questions, actively listen, paint the picture that you want the customer to see by reflecting enthusiasm, using descriptive words and phrases, dynamic words, and colorful adjectives. Try to use personal words that will involve the customer.

Handle the objections and again ask for the order. Close!

Thank the customer for the order or if you did not get the order, then promise to mail additional literature. Alert the customer that you will return a call to him or her in a few days to make sure that he or she understands the literature. Answer any additional questions.

Thank you for calling _____Mr./Ms. _____

We want your business; have a good day.

By following this sequence and systematically applying your own skills and techniques, you will be able to use the telephone successfully to convert inquiries into sales or to qualify leads for an eyeball-to-eyeball visit. A checklist for handling inquiries is shown in Figure 14.2.

Figure 14.2 **A Checklist—Handling Inquiries**

The Telephone Call

1. Identify yourself and your firm.
2. Confirm receipt of inquiry.
3. Restate inquiry.
4. Answer inquiry.
5. Make an interest-creating comment.
6. Ask fact-finding questions.
7. Deliver the sales message.
   Stress benefits over features.
   Use a sales vocabulary.
8. Overcome objections.
   Confirm your understanding of objection.
   Prepare prospect for answer.
   Answer objection.
   Stress a benefit.
9. Close the sale.
   Ask a forced-choice question.
10. Wrap up the sale.
    Confirm the order.
    Arrange for next call.
    Express your thanks.
11. Arrange for an appointment.
    Stress a benefit.
    Ask a forced-choice question.
12. Wrap up the call.
    Confirm appointment.
    Express your thanks.

The Follow Up

After you close a sale:

1. Open a customer's record form.
2. Enter the date for next telephone call.
3. Place the order in correct procedure.

After you arrange for an appointment:

1. Send out material agreed upon.
2. Record date for salesperson visit.
3. Notify field salesperson.

Incoming Inquiry
1. Analyze the written inquiry.
2. Accept the telephone inquiry.
    Identify yourself.
    Express your interest.
    Confirm your inquiry.
    Record inquirer information.
    Answer inquiry/arrange for return call.

Pre-Call Planning
1. Gather information
    About product
    About field responsibility
    About inquirer
2. Set specific call objectives.
    Answer inquiry.
    Determine inquirer's potential.
    Set limited sales objective or arrange for appointment.
3. Prepare an opening statement.
    Identify yourself and your firm.
    Confirm receipt of inquiry.
    Restate inquiry.
    Answer inquiry.
4. Prepare an interest-creating comment.
5. Prepare fact-finding questions.
    To confirm information you have
    To obtain new information
6. Prepare your sales message.
    Stress benefits over features.
    Use sales vocabulary.
7. Prepare for objections.
    Product/service objections
    Price objections
    Postponement objections

They Are Calling for Your Help

Today, sales executives realize that incoming telephone calls must integrate into their overall marketing plan. The customers who can't wait for you to come to them, but instead initiate the contact themselves, create your most obvious selling opportunities. They are calling because they believe you can help them with a purchase they are about to make or are thinking about making in the foreseeable future.

Whether or not you fully capitalize on the opportunities each incoming call presents depends upon the quality and experience of the person receiving the call. A salesperson will look to maximize the invoice and sell all the correct products or services necessary to enable the customer to accomplish his or her goal. On the other hand, an order taker will merely make it possible for the customer to purchase what he or she asks for, hoping it is what the customer actually needs. The key to converting an order taker into a salesperson is product knowledge. The person who handles incoming telephone inquiries must be as knowledgeable as the field representatives if you are to take advantage of those golden opportunities that are present every time a prospect calls you.

A complete catalog of all your products, including up-to-date price lists and specification sheets, should be at every desk or counter where you receive incoming inquiries pertaining to your product or service. Next to that catalog, keep a list of all promotional prices and a list of close-outs. Use your inbound telephone as a means to dispose of your "dogs and cats," those items left over from a promotional campaign, discontinued products, and merchandise that has been cosmetically damaged in your facility. Offering on-the-spot bargains is an excellent way to upgrade an order or convert a prospect into a customer, buying what you want to sell.

You'd be surprised how many people are shy when they're on the telephone. By using the technique of introducing yourself, then immediately asking your prospects for their names, you will usually get their names and help put them at ease. Once you have your prospect's name, use it often in your conversation. People are proud of their names, like the recognition, and will have positive feelings when you care enough to use it.

"On Hold" Technique

Putting someone on hold is a technique used to take the position of control away from the caller and put yourself in control of the conversation. Leave the caller on hold for about 10 seconds, never more than 20 seconds. If you're really looking for something, or have to take care of something else, get back on the phone, apologize, and let the caller know you'll be with him or her in just a few moments; then get back within 20 seconds. If you keep someone on hold for more than 20 seconds before you get back, you'll more often than not find a different party on the other end of the line, one who is tense and upset.

Chapter 15

How to Handle Complaints

In a No-Win Situation, Don't Be a Loser

Mistakes happen. When they do, you're bound to find an irate caller on the other end of a telephone line. The first thing to do is *listen*. Hear these callers out completely. Encourage them to get it all out of their system with questions, such as, "Is there anything else?" or "Are you having any other problems?" You have to understand the entire problem through the callers' eyes before you can begin to get them back on your side.

In most cases, the callers' anxiety levels probably will be up in the clouds somewhere. Let them vent their emotions, even if they choose to call you every name in the book. When your callers raise their voices, you talk *softer*. Nothing can be gained by trying to out-shout them. Do not interrupt, and above all, do not be defensive. The key to success in handling any complaint call is to maintain rapport.

Most of your customers will never make a complaint (at least to your face, or to your attention). Research indicates that many of the few people who do make the effort to complain will tell or advertise their bad experience to at least a dozen or more people. You have to handle complaints before they snowball.

It is extremely bad business to let any ill feelings stay out there in the public. Negativity is unbelievably contagious. But so also are *good feelings*. Every business person hopes for the best form of advertising—*word of mouth*. Happy customers do tell other people. Therefore, it is imperative and a key requisite for success in sales growth to handle each and every complaint immediately, effectively, and to the complete satisfaction of the customer.

Work smart, not hard. If your customer is upset, let him or her unwind and blow off steam. Express concern, and be sympathetic. Something as simple as, "I am sorry you are having difficulty, Mr. Caller. Let's see if we can work this out," is usually all it takes to begin winning the customer back to your side. Make sure you completely understand the problem. In your own words, repeat back to the caller what you think he or she is saying. If you need additional information, such as an invoice or a date, ask for it at this time.

Once you are completely sure you understand your customer's problem, determine whether or not you have the immediate expertise to solve it. You may have to check your file or speak to someone else before you have enough information to conclude the matter to everyone's satisfaction. If that is the case, or if the caller is really angry and you want to give him or her a chance to cool down, explain that the problem is out of your area of expertise and you will have to speak to the service manager or another person with authority. Determine if you can call back with the solution at a specific time, but don't make the customer any promises you cannot keep.

It is very important that you do call back at the agreed time, even if it is just to indicate that you don't have the information yet but want to set the time for another callback. If you want time to work to your advantage, particularly if you receive the complaint late in the day, respond early in the morning before the pressures of the day take their toll on the caller.

In working out your solution to any complaint call, do it as quickly as possible, preferably within an hour. If the solution can be handled immediately, do it before you get off the phone. If the solution requires more time, explain to the caller why, and assure him or her of a prompt answer.

If the caller is complaining about someone else in your company, such as another salesperson, do not get involved. It is a no-win situation for you and you can only compound the problem. Tell the caller you appreciate the call, apologize for the problem, and refer the call either to your manager or to the person being complained about. Of course, track down your manager or the other person and relay the message.

Procedures for Handling Complaints

The procedures you use to handle complaints can either turn a problem into another possible sale and a happy customer, or result in a very messy situation that can damage future business in your territory.

The following procedures are recommended to effectively turn these no-win situations into the best possible environments for happy customers and possible additional sales:

1. Always document all complaints (see Figure 15.1). This provides you with information for the future and eliminates all possible

Figure 15.1 **Sample Customer Complaint Form**

Date of Complaint: _____

Customer Name: _____

Address: _____

City: _____ State: _____ Zip: _____

Tele/salesperson: _____ Field Rep: _____

Major Complaint: _____

_____

_____

_____

_____

_____

_____

Action Taken: _____

_____

_____

Follow Up: _____

_____

_____

Date of Follow Up: _____

misunderstandings from either faulty memories or any accusations that may arise. Documentation also provides a forum for possibly eliminating the reasons for the complaints. It allows quantitative statistics about the complaint that may help overcome any future such situations.

2. Determine whether the product was sold via the telephone, through the mail, or by a field representative. This information will tell you who sold the product and when, and it will let you determine from which shipment or supplier the merchandise came.

3. Gather information about the product. This will help you determine whether the complaint concerns the service provided or if there are actual problems with the product itself.

4. Ask your customer for copies of the invoice or other background documents that will assist you in following up on the complaint.

5. Establish shipping fees. You must have policies for determining who pays for the shipping cost for returned goods. Some firms accept returned goods freight-collect, some only freight-prepaid.

6. Establish returned goods policies. You must establish certain company policies concerning the handling of returned goods. Some firms have handling charges, and others limit the time allowed for returns. Specify other limitations that you might require.

By establishing procedures for complaints, you will find that these no-win situations can many times be avoided or at least turned into positive encounters.

"Don't You Think That's Reasonable?"

In actually solving a problem, you must explain to the caller what you can or cannot do, but never make promises to do something that you cannot reasonably expect to deliver. When you are at fault, admit it, apologize, and explain the error. Make your solution fair and reasonable. If there are any concessions or adjustments to be made, offer them first. If there is nothing you can do, tell the caller your side of the story, let him or her know again that you understand the problem, and explain why you cannot help. Then, stick to your decision.

When the situation warrants a negotiated solution, it will usually work to your advantage to appeal to your caller's sense of fair play. For instance, "Ms. Caller, I appreciate your bringing this situation to my attention. Now, let's see if I can help you. I know you want to be fair and neither of us wants anything we're not entitled to, but have you looked at it this way? . . ." Then, tell your side of the story.

When you are through with your explanation, or have suggested a solution, ask something such as, "Mr. Caller, don't you think that's reasonable?" or "Ms. Caller, I think that will handle it, don't you?" Do not be afraid to ask the caller, "What will it take to make you happy and resolve this situation?" You have already appealed to his or her sense of fair play and you'll often find your caller wants less than you were actually willing to give in concessions or adjustments.

If the caller is not satisfied with your solution and there is someone with more authority he or she can appeal to, outline the procedure he or she must follow, giving names, addresses, and phone numbers where applicable. If the buck stops with you, sometimes it is helpful to ask for time to give the problem more thought or to get additional information. You can say, "Mr. Caller, let me check with my factory and see if there isn't something else I can do for you. It will take me a while to reach all my factory people so, if you don't mind, may I get back to you sometime tomorrow morning?" It is amazing how often a person will find something that is totally unacceptable today totally realistic and acceptable tomorrow.

Once a problem has been solved, it is always a good policy to make a follow-up call. It shows the customers you are interested in them and sincere in your desire to serve them. Such a call also offers you the opportunity to make an additional sale.

Following each complaint call, make a record of who complained about what (see Figure 15.1). Make a note of whether or not the complaint has been satisfied. Test your own effectiveness by writing down how long it took to satisfy the customer, and, as time goes on, make a concerted effort to reduce that time span, by first making a record of all your complaint calls, then analyzing those records. You will quickly discover those specific annoyances or problems that heretofore have been unknown to you but exist inherently in your product or service.

There is usually justification for all complaint calls. Even when there is not, a positive approach and a little tact will enable you to work out a reasonable solution and retain the caller's good will. You cannot always say "yes" to the caller's request, even though that is an easy way out.

Sell Your Polite "No"

There is a technique to denying your customer's request. You can develop the skill to say "no" firmly, yet pleasantly and sympathetically. A cold abrupt denial of a problem will create resentment and the customer will be lost forever. Presented in a positive yet firm way a denial can often turn into a solidifying of your relationship with the customer.

Common Traps to Avoid

When handling a complaint call, always give the customer the same good consideration you would give if you thought he or she were going to place an order. Avoid the following traps:

1. Statements such as "you say" or "you claim" imply doubt and tend to make callers think you are questioning their veracity.
2. Don't act surprised or be at a loss for understanding with the customer. Here, again, customers will think you are questioning their integrity.
3. Do not promise something you cannot deliver.
4. Do not use such words as "problem" or "complaint." Instead, use words like "situation," "experience," "mistake," and "misunderstanding."
5. Once you have stated the nature of the complaint back to the customer, do not rehash it.
6. Do not state that the same problem "will never happen again." It always does!

Handling a complaint call successfully is mostly a matter of attitude. If you handle such calls as if they were just headaches, all you'll end up with is more grief. Start out by putting yourself in your customer's shoes and you will win every time.

Asking for trouble is good business! Sophisticated managers know that when you encourage complaints you gain a tremendous source of information and increase your sales. A recent survey indicated that only one person in 50 customers will go out of the way to make the effort to complain when small problems that cost only a few dollars or result in minor inconvenience are involved. ("It's not worth the hassle." or "Where do I write?" or "How do I write it?" or "They won't do anything anyway so why take the time to tell them?") You have angry customers out there you don't even know about. Therefore, you must attempt to handle those people who do have the energy to bring the problem to your attention.

It is obvious that unless you know about and take care of your customer's problems, you will lose countless thousands and thousands of dollars in revenue and sales.

In today's marketplace, the consumer feels that all companies carry the same merchandise and that all stores look alike. When you listen carefully and act immediately on what you hear, you show your customer that your company is the one that is different— the one that really cares about its customers. If you play your cards right, this customer can turn into your best form of advertising—the happy customer—and your company will prosper with more sales and more happy customers. Yes, even this can be contagious.

Chapter 16

The Telephone and the Law

As with any American growth industry, telemarketing professionals must realize and learn to deal with rules and regulations that form the parameters of their workplace. Unlike some industries, telemarketing must answer to direct regulation on both the state and federal levels.

Interstate telecommunications is regulated by the Federal Communications Commission (FCC), while each individual state has a Public Utilities Commission that regulates intrastate commerce via telecommunications.

It all began when Congress passed the Communications Act of 1934, which established the FCC and rules and regulations for the telecommunicator.

Today, telemarketing is a $100 billion industry. With all of its growth have come many problems and certain natural intricacies that have created a new wave of outcries for legislation. This legislative activity has crystallized into several areas of specific interest:

- Restrictions on telemarketing solicitation hours
- Limits on kinds of telemarketing calls allowed
- Registration of consumer telephone numbers into "nonsolicitation" seclusion
- Call monitoring
- Phony names
- Asterisks in phone directories signalling companies that monitor, use outbound telemarketing, etc.
- Requirement that telemarketers must disclose nonprofit finances

- Restrictions on message and prerecorded machines
- Telemarketing company registration and permits
- Requirements for consumer contract laws
- Home solicitation laws
- Telephone directory copyright lawsuits
- Telemarketing boiler room frauds
- 900 and 976 number lawsuits
- Requirement for telemarketing script approvals
- Teleport regulations
- Informational disclosures by manufacturers of automated dialing machines
- 800 number service number regulations
- Credit laws
- Truth-in-lending laws
- Mail fraud used with telemarketing
- Definitions of lotteries

The professional telemarketing industry has chosen to lobby its side of the story extensively both in the state legislatures and in each lawsuit they have confronted, primarily through actions by the Direct Marketing Association and the American Telemarketing Association.

Call Monitoring Regulations

In a recent telephone survey of state telephone regulatory commissions, it was determined that very few regulations currently exist concerning call monitoring; in the few states that do have regulations, it was primarily for requiring phone companies to place asterisks in telephone directories to identify companies that use monitoring equipment.

Monitoring of employees and telephone sales representatives is authorized under the Federal Wiretap Statute, which permits monitoring for training or internal control reasons if one party to a conversation gives prior consent to the monitoring. Normally, the prior consent is achieved by getting a signed release from every employee or telephone sales rep to be monitored. Therefore, call monitoring should provide few dilemmas except in Georgia, Michigan, West Virginia, or Wyoming (as of the Spring of 1987).

All call monitoring is prohibited in Michigan and Georgia without consent of all parties to the conversation. In West Virginia, telemarketers must put asterisks before their telephone numbers in telephone directories to indicate that their phones will be monitored. Also in West Virginia, these telemarketers must provide a beeping tone on all conversations that are being monitored. In Wyoming, it is against the law to "tap" or monitor any telephone line.

Asterisk Bills

A new form of legislation that has gained popular support in many areas of the country is the so-called no-call or asterisk bills. This legislation would require publishers of telephone directories or prospect lists to place asterisks by the names of consumers or firms not wishing to be solicited over the telephone.

Some of the problems with these bills include:

1. Costs to the directory publishers and list brokers increase.
2. Confusion exists as to what format to use for asterisks.
3. Costs are incurred to delete names from current lists.
4. Would you be able to solicit current customers if they were on the no-call lists?
5. Will customers realize the kinds of calls they might miss if they decide on an asterisk?
6. What will directory assistance operators say to inquiries for phone numbers of asterisk customers?
7. How much would people have to pay for an asterisk?
8. What is the definition of a customer?

Realizing that a problem does exist, with some customers not interested in being solicited over the telephone, the Direct Marketing Association has created the "Telephone Preference List." The Preference List contains a list of corporations and individuals who wish not to be solicited by the telephone. To help maintain the integrity of the telemarketing industry, it is very important that professional telemarketers abide by these people's wishes. Telemarketers everywhere should help to diminish the boiler room image that telemarketing has in many people's eyes. The future of asterisk bills is uncertain, but much of the controversy can be stifled if unscrupulous telephone operations were run out of business.

Automated Machines Legislation

One subgroup in the telemarketing industry that has experienced tremendous growth is the ADRMP, or Auto-Dialed Recorded Message Players. These machines vary in style, use, and operation, but they all allow telemarketers to make previously programmed or random calling with prerecorded messages.

These machines are currently regulated in 13 states, and with several other states following suit, it appears that the machines will find a much more limited scope in telemarketing.

California, Florida, Texas, Michigan, North Carolina, Wisconsin, Arkansas, and Colorado presently prohibit any use of ADRMPs unless the telemarketer has prior approval from the party being called. A prearranged relationship can constitute a prior approval. In these states, this regulation generally limits their use only to previous customers or for inbound sales or offers.

In California, a law recently passed requires that telemarketers use a live operator to get permission to play a prerecorded sales pitch or message. Two exceptions were included in this legislation:

1. Schools may utilize prerecorded messages to notify parents of a child's tardiness or absence.
2. Vendors may use the messages to notify or confirm customers of delivery dates, arrivals, or other detailed information on sales made by live sales personnel.

In California, the state government also has special requirements for the manufacturers of these machines. All manufacturers of prerecorded message machines are required by law to supply written copies of all pertinent laws concerning the machines to any customer who purchases such equipment. By requiring these so-called informational releases, the customers are notified that many states restrict usage before they even purchase them.

Scams

Telemarketing has had a public relations problem since its beginnings, due mostly to many fraudulent and deceitful operators who have swindled millions of dollars from unsuspecting so-called customers. One scam that has been getting headlines has concerned a group of telemarketers who conned people into giving their credit card numbers over the telephone. Numerous unauthorized charges were then made on the accounts whose numbers were fraudulently stolen.

Many of these "boiler rooms" have historically given the telemarketing industry a bad image and much bad press. Many such schemes move from town to town, from one fraudulent product to another, from one name to the next. In most cases the banking industry eats most of the charges, but they often end up in additional interest charges to the customer.

The United States Postal Service has joined forces with the FBI to help fight these operators, especially in the COD market.

The future of telemarketing as a reputable industry depends on a continuing emphasis on integrity, honesty, and ethics.

Registration

In some states, telemarketers are required to register with the government, much the same way as insurance and real estate agencies. In California, a new wave of legislation has been introduced to combat the substantial growth of dishonest boiler rooms working several large metropolitan areas.

Under the new California laws, all scripts must be submitted to the California State Attorney General's Office and all telemarketers must register. Much of this attention is aimed at the dishonest operators selling office supplies and gold and other investment schemes over the phone. Some of the industries that are exempted under this California legislation include real estate brokers, insurance companies, stock brokers, record clubs, book publishers and clubs, and lead generation companies.

Profit Disclosures

One area of particular growth in telemarketing over the past few years has been the nonprofit or charitable organization fundraising telemarketing programs. Yes, telemarketing is quite effective as a fundraising tool. But new legislation is under discussion to require such telemarketers to disclose the percentages of the donations that go to pay the telemarketers and the percentages that actually go to the charity.

The National Association of Charities is working with the National Association of Attorney Generals to draw up new guidelines and potential legislation to quiet the uproars by citizen groups complaining about the marketing overheads. More than 37 states have fundraising regulations. For example, in Maine, telemarketing fundraisers are limited to 30 percent of the revenues after paying their phone bills.

900 and 976 Number Controversy

In the last few years, much excitement on the part of both advertisers and mass consumers has resulted over the introduction of the tolled numbers with prefixes of 900 or 976. The telephone companies have had some problems, including lawsuits that have arisen because people did not know that calls to these numbers were toll calls.

Much of the problem can be traced to children who have been motivated by television commercials and peer pressure to call "joke lines," or "sports lines." Some of these children call these numbers to hear recorded messages time and time again, resulting in $100 phone bills for their parents.

Time will tell of the future of such services, but because they are very profitable for both advertisers and the phone company, it appears likely they are here to stay.

Lotteries

Many scams by unscrupulous telemarketers have used a lottery, gift-promotion, free trips, and so on to help sell their products or induce other sales. Again these bad apples have caused new legislation to be written across the country to stop them in their tracks.

In Hawaii, all telephone solicitors must get a permit from the state, and it is against the law to offer consumers any kind of prizes, gifts, or inducement for a sale.

Some of the topics that must be defined in these new legislations are actual explanations and determinations of the meanings of what a lottery or inducement really is.

Solicitation Hours

One of the great attributes of telephone marketing is its flexibility in allowing the telemarketer to choose the time of the call. When dealing with consumer marketing, this has become a very sore subject. Legislation has been introduced in every state of the union concerning restrictions in calling hours allowed by law.

Texas restricts telemarketing calls to consumers to 9 A.M. to 9 P.M., Monday through Saturday, and 1:30 to 9 P.M. on Sundays. New York has proposed legislation that would make it illegal to make telemarketing calls into its jurisdiction between 5 and 7 P.M., before 10 A.M., and after 8 P.M.

The basic rule is to use common sense. Most reputable and professional telemarketers use the guidelines of sticking to between 9 A.M. and 4 P.M., Monday through Friday for business-to-business customers, and 9 A.M. to 9 P.M. Monday through Friday, and 9 A.M. to 3 P.M. on Saturdays for consumers. Again, a little common sense can go a long way in telemarketing.

Home Solicitation Laws

In addition to all of the specific laws that have been created with the telemarketer in mind, all telemarketers must learn and understand the rules and regulations concerning home solicitations. These laws were enacted to protect the everyday consumer from unscrupulous door-to-door salespeople who were notorious for using high-pressure techniques.

Again, telemarketing has had a hard time protecting its good name because many of these unscrupulous artists have brought their nasty high-pressure techniques with them into this industry.

In 16 states, these home solicitation laws have been altered to include telemarketing in their jurisdiction. These home solicitation rules include requirements concerning contracts, cooling-off periods, and use of high-pressure techniques.

In Oregon, the law prevents a telephone sales agreement from being a binding contract unless the seller receives a written, signed contract from the buyer with all terms of the agreement; the contract must be made pursuant to a telephone solicitation.

Many of these home solicitation rules include credit laws, truth-in-lending regulations, consumer protection guidelines, and even postal regulations.

Title 18, Section 1343 of the United States Code is administered by the United States Department of Justice, and it provides criminal sanctions when a telephone, radio, or television is used for fraud. It prohibits any person from devising a scheme, or intending to devise a scheme, to defraud or obtain money or property by false pretenses, false representations, or false promises when engaged in interstate or foreign commerce. This section also makes it illegal to:

1. Make any comment, request, suggestion, or proposal which is obscene, lewd, filthy, or indecent over the telephone.

2. Cause the telephone number of another person to ring excessively with the intent to harass.
3. Call any person without disclosing your identity when the intent of the call is to annoy, abuse, or harass any person at the number called.

Anyone found guilty under this section of a violation of transmitting, or causing to be transmitted, such a scheme, by wire, radio, or television, is subject to a $1,000 fine or imprisonment for five years or both.

Title 15, Section 52 of the United States Code deals specifically with false, misleading, or deceptive practices. It prohibits the dissemination of false advertising by any means for the purpose of inducing, or which is likely to induce, directly or indirectly, the purchase of food, drugs, devices, or cosmetics, or the use of any unfair or deceptive acts and practices in the dissemination, or causing to be disseminated, any false advertisement or representation that fails to reveal material facts. False advertisement as herein means that which is misleading in a material respect taking into account the following (among other things): all representations, oral or written, designed, devised, sounded, or any combination thereof.

All this legal jargon means but one thing. You cannot lie, cheat, steal, or harass via the telephone without risk of criminal prosecution.

Strict Rules to Avoid Trouble

More will be said in Chapter 17 on ethics, but for now it is wise to avoid falling into a trap, especially when the salespeople you employ are exuberant and/or on commission. Under normal circumstances, any of the following must be grounds for immediate dismissal:

1. Using deceptive trade names or words
2. Not stating name, company name, and reason for call, once the prospect has committed his or her time
3. Misstating the source or manufacturer of a product
4. Making disparaging statements about competitors
5. Making false statements about other companies
6. Misrepresenting the value of free gifts
7. Using testimonials, endorsements, or the truth in any misleading way
8. Exaggerating claims with regard to any product

Title 15, Section 2301 of the United States Code addresses the subject of consumer warranty protection, including service contracts. It defines a consumer product as any tangible personal property which is distributed in commerce and which is normally used for personal, family, or household purposes. Included in that definition is such property intended to be attached or installed. This section is designed to protect purchasers, which it defines as any person to whom the product is transferred or any person who is entitled, under any applicable federal or state law, to enforce a warranty or service contract against the warrantor. Violation of or nonconformity with this section shall be considered an unfair trade practice.

Consumer product safety is another area for concern. It is found in Title 15, Section 2051 of the United States Code. Consumer credit protection legislation is found in Title 15, Section 1601. The goal here is disclosure pertaining to credit terms and costs of credit. Title 15, Section 1662 deals with advertisements of credit, including finance charges.

Credit Collections

Debt collection practices are regulated by the Federal Trade Commission, the FCC, and the individual states. Interstate transactions between creditors and collection agencies are considered commerce and are governed by federal statute.

The FCC has published a set of general guidelines for the collection of debts over the telephone. They should be analyzed before setting up a collection effort, for they concern harassment, hours you can call, and restrictions pertaining to repeat calls, callbacks, and follow-ups allowed by law.

You are prohibited from making debt collection phone calls at "off hours"; thus, it is a good policy to restrict such calls to the hours between 9 A.M. and 9 P.M. If you are calling between time zones, those hours are based on the area being called, not the area where the call originates.

Obey Rules of Courtesy and the Law in Making Collection Calls

No matter whether a delinquent account is a business firm or an individual, the collection procedure is substantially the same. The telephone, once used only rarely because of cost, has become the most common and effective collection tool.

The telephone enables you to make sure you are directing your collection effort to the right person. It enables you to vary your approach to fit the personality of your delinquent customer and to suit each situation. When using the telephone to call your past due accounts, you can find out if problems exist, negotiate a settlement, and demand action. By interjecting a pleasant note toward the end of the telephone conversation, you can usually retain your customer's good will.

The law prohibits you from making collection phone calls at unreasonable hours. It is a good policy to restrict such calls to the hours between 9 A.M. and 9 P.M., in the time zone in which your customer is located. Ask your attorney to determine how local ordinances may dictate your calling hours. To avoid any possibility of being accused of harassment, arrangements for you to make future telephone contact with your customer should be made during the initial call. You can always call, without prior arrangement, to follow up on the promise of a payment that was not made on time.

It is illegal to make threats over the telephone solely to frighten your customer into paying his or her bill. Telephone calls threatening bodily harm or property damage as a means of collection are strictly prohibited. If you find your customer persistent in not paying debts, you may tell him or her that you will be forced to assign the account to an attorney or collection agency. Once you threaten to turn an account over to a third person for collection, if the account does not pay, you must follow through. Otherwise, your customer will think anything you say in the future is just an idle threat, and will continue to ignore your requests and refuse to pay your bill.

Sequence of Successful Collections

A collection call has its own Sequence of Success. Step one is to verify the customer's name. A collection telephone call may legally be addressed only to the debtor or his or her spouse. In states where you are permitted by statute to gather information on a debtor by contacting nearby neighbors, relatives, or business associates, including his or her employer or supervisor, you are not allowed to indicate that the purpose of your call is to collect on an outstanding debt.

Step two is to introduce yourself and your company. In most states, it is illegal to use an alias when collecting money over the telephone. Other states require you to register any alias used when collecting money over the telephone.

The third step of the Sequence of Success for collection calls is to state the reason for your call; for example, "I'm calling to discuss your bill with us that is now past due."

Step four is to determine why the bill hasn't been paid; for example, "Mr. Customer, is there a reason why you haven't paid us yet?" With this question, you can appraise your customer's situation. If the reason for nonpayment was simply an oversight, go on to Step six and ask for payment. If there is a dispute or the customer is unable to pay all or part of the bill at this time, go to Step five. Disputes, real or imagined, are often used as a tool by a customer to prolong or even avoid payment of past due bills.

Step five is to carefully explain your terms to the customer and determine how and when he or she can make payment. If appropriate, suggest an alternative payment schedule you think the customer will find acceptable. Sometimes you will find your suggested payment plan immediately acceptable to your customer, but if it is not, discuss the matter with your customer until you come to an agreement.

If a disagreement occurs, you will still have a good chance for collection, if it can be resolved amicably. There is no advantage to winning an argument and losing the receivable. Occasionally, a customer will attempt to make vague or unrealistic arrangements that are unacceptable to you. When this happens, be firm. Establish the terms you will accept and stick to them. Remember, your primary objectives in making collection calls are to return your delinquent account to a regular paying basis, collect the money due you as quickly as possible, and retain your customer's good will.

Step seven in the Sequence of Success is to wrap up the details by restating the agreement just reached with your customer. Make sure you both fully understand how and when the account will be paid.

Step eight is to sell your name. Let the customer know that you are there to help and that he or she should call you with any future questions about the payment schedule.

Step nine is to smile and express thanks.

Step ten is to make yourself a note of the agreement you just reached.

Step eleven, depending on your company policy, is to confirm your understanding by letter to your customer.

Timing of Collection Calls

It is best to make your first collection call when an account is five calendar days late in making a payment. The first such call is always made by the sales account executive who usually sells the customer. The use of selling time is costly and it is best to limit the sales account executive's collection activities to the first call. With a first collection call being made five days after the obligation is due, more often than not, the late payment is an oversight, or "the check is in the mail."

The interaction of a mailgram and an automatic telephone system is currently being utilized widely to collect past due bills. Such equipment is programmed to send out mailgrams timed to arrive shortly before the telephone call. The call itself contains a taped message that asks the debtor when he plans to pay, then goes on to tell him that his answer will be recorded and placed in a file. The equipment records the debtor's answer, plays it back to him, and asks if there is anything he wants to add. This type of system is experiencing an approximate 54 percent success rate in collecting past due accounts, and does it cost effectively.

Successful collection professionals have found that the most effective method for collection of past due accounts involves an interplay between the telephone and written letters of correspondence. Always back up your calls with confirmation letters that verify both parties' intentions.

Always try to contact your customer at the earliest possible time of delinquency, and attempt to get some kind of mutual agreement on every call.

A recent statistical governmental study determined comparative effectiveness between collection letter writing and collection telemarketing.

Time	Effectiveness	
	Letter	*Telephone*
After two months	19%	40%
After three months	6%	25%

Obviously, the telephone is substantially more effective in collecting those delinquent accounts. Telemarketing can be a very fast, private, inexpensive, flexible, two-way collection process.

Precall Planning

Before you initiate your telemarketing collection effort, it is important to preplan your calling objectives, procedures, and even what words you will say. You must ask yourself the following questions:

1. Whose fault is it? You must determine and analyze how your company played a role in causing the delinquency. Are your accounting methods up to date? Were your billings correct? Were the shipments made and received? Have the late payments been noted?

2. What previous collection steps have been taken? Before making your collection call, you must know what letters, telephone calls, or personal visits have already been attempted, so you will understand where the situation is.

3. What is the pattern of payments so far? Is this customer consistently delinquent? How often is the customer delinquent? What collection steps were utilized previously?

4. With whom should I speak? You want to know who the decision maker is so you won't be wasting your time.

5. What repayment plan will I offer? You must know before you call what your options are as to what you can offer the customer as an agreeable repayment schedule. Can you accept just a partial payment? How long can you wait before bringing in your attorney?

6. What fact-finding questions will I ask? You must prepare the questions you will be asking so you will understand where you want the call to lead. What is the reason the customer is delinquent? Can the customer make a payment now? When will the account become current? How can you help the customer meet the schedule?

7. What is my opening statement? You must prepare your opening statements to identify yourself and your company and the reason for the call, and strategically take control of the conversation. Just as in a sales call, you must use attention-getting statements to grab your customer's interest and control the call.

Credit and collections is the name of the game to ensure your company is profitable. To a very large extent, modern business is conducted on a credit basis; thus, virtually every business at one time or another faces a collection problem. Slow collections inhibit further sales and future growth. A firm, courteous collection policy, executed over the telephone, is a necessary factor in maintaining any business in a healthy state. Use telemarketing, because it works.

Harassment Prohibited

Harassing a debtor with repeated phone calls is prohibited. Of course, callbacks to follow-up payment promises, instances where the debtor requested additional information, and when, during your initial contact, arrangements for future calls were made are excluded.

Telephone calls threatening bodily harm, damage to character, or property damage are strictly prohibited. It is illegal to make any threats solely to frighten your debtor into paying. The basic rules to follow in making threats are to be reasonable and realistic, and once you threaten to do something, then you must do it.

State laws pertaining to debt collection by telephone vary, but most resemble the Robbins-Rosenthal Fair Debt Collection Practices Act, California Civil Code, Sections 1788–1788.30. Under California law, "debt collectors" is broadly defined as persons who, in the ordinary course of business, on behalf of themselves or others, engage in debt collection. California law goes beyond Federal law in that it prohibits a debt collector from collecting, or attempting to collect, a consumer debt by means of the following conduct:

1. Using obscene or profane language
2. Causing a telephone to ring repeatedly or continuously so as to annoy the person being called
3. Placing telephone calls without disclosure of the caller's true identity and that of his or her company. The use of an alias is prohibited except by an employee of a licensed collection agency and then only if the alias used is registered with the state and the employee correctly identifies the agency he or she represents.
4. Causing expense to any person for long distance telephone calls, telegram fees, or charges for other similar communications by misrepresenting to such person the purpose of such telephone call, telegram, or similar communication

Sales Tax Problems

Sales taxes present a problem for telemarketers that is yet to be resolved. Firms receiving their orders in many states, California included, at "drop boxes" such as post office boxes, radio, and/or television stations, or any other address within that state, are required to obtain a registration certificate and make sales tax payments to that state.

If an 800 number response is actually received by an operator within one state, that state is currently claiming the right to collect sales tax on every such order, whether or not the offer was advertised within that state, where the order was received; this applies even if the order is forwarded out of state for fulfillment and shipment to another state.

This state sales tax issue is before the courts; surely, whichever way it goes, it will cause even more controversy. States with no sales taxes might end up being the haven for tomorrow's telemarketers.

Check Local Laws

It seems that everyone who could possibly claim jurisdiction over regulating telemarketing has! Regulatory dividing lines are blurred by many overlying circumstances, including the fact that the same telephone equipment can be used to sell products both inbound and outbound, in-state and out-of-state, in this country or out of the country, in-town or out-of-town, over toll-free lines and toll-lines, for legitimate companies and for con artists.

In 1977, the FCC initiated a formal inquiry to decide whether or not the telemarketing industry should be regulated to even more of an extent than it is currently. After 40 months of testimony, hearings, written reports, legal opinions, strong press, and much interaction with the American people, the FCC came to one conclusion—leave it alone, for now.

As America's fastest-growing industry and the future source of eight million new jobs, telemarketing will surely be confronted with new crises and controversies that will change the way things operate today. In the end, however, all it really will take is honesty, integrity, scruples, and ethical standards by the telemarketers of today, tomorrow, and tomorrow's tomorrow.

Because there are so many jurisdictions, it is the best policy always to consult your attorney before beginning any telemarketing program. Laws change almost daily from one municipality to another, so do your homework and do it well.

Chapter 17

The Ethics of Telemarketing

Throughout this book, reference has been made to the extraordinary need for a turnaround in the reputation of the telemarketing industry. A few bad apples and con artists have tarnished the telemarketing industry's good name with connotations of disrepute.

In December 1986, the third annual American Telemarketing Association Convention recognized the need for self-regulation. It drafted a 30-page report and outline for new guidelines of ethics to become standardized throughout the vast telemarketing interests in America.

Most professional corps of industry have standardized guidelines for conduct. Now it is time for the telemarketing industry to stand up and earn respect.

The following is a simple outline of the attributes of the professional and ethical telecommunicator:

The Professional Telecommunicator:

1. Recognizes selling over the telephone as a profession and, as a professional, understands that a customer expects, the business requires, and the law enforces a professional attitude and practice.
2. Always begins every telephone call with a *"Hello"* and ends it with a *"Thank You."*
3. Always uses the time-tested principles of honesty and full disclosure of all relations with customers. This means not engaging in illegal activities and continuing to work easily within the framework of all legal requirements, including a policy of making all customers fully aware and understanding of purchases.

4. Always adheres to a personal commitment of *never* using tactics of lying, cheating, or stealing, nor intentionally lying or embarrassing himself or herself or the entity being represented.
5. Is always conscious of the customer's needs—is so thorough in his or her work that there is never a need for others to follow up; always is dedicated to integrity, has a pleasant personality, and honestly enjoys the profession.
6. Always respects the rights of customers or prospects as to the acceptance or denial of calls.
7. Always, on every call, identifies himself or herself, the company represented, and the reason for calling.
8. Shall not call the designated prospect if the prospect has made this wish known.
9. Never oversells.
10. Knows that the secret of sales ability is speaking, therefore, always attempts to put his or her tools of voice tone, modulation, pace, pitch, and enthusiasm to best use.
11. Always takes legible notes of the responses and interaction in every telephone call.
12. Always *listens*.
13. Never uses vulgar, profane, or offensive language.
14. Never hangs up.
15. Always keeps informed about matters pertinent to the telemarketing industry, including laws, regulations, and self-discipline.
16. Never says bad things about competitors or their products.
17. Always avoids exaggeration, misrepresentations, or any concealment of any facts pertaining to the product being sold, terms, or any other facts.
18. Never interrupts a prospect.
19. Never calls unless it is appropriate.
20. Never harasses or uses any kind of high-pressure tactics.

Professionalism is a title that must be earned every day of the week, at every hour of each day, and on every telephone call made. Use these points as an ethical guideline and add more where you can, and you will become the professional and success you always have yearned to be.

Ethics is good for telemarketing; it is good for the customers and prospects, and it is just plain good for business.

Chapter 18

~~~~~~

Success Stories

Success . . . Winning . . . Profits . . .

These are all words that describe telemarketing's role in the business community today. America's fastest-growing industry has become the primary marketing phenomenon of the twenty-first century.

This chapter highlights just a handful of ringing success stories and testimonials from American and foreign-based businesses, some with payrolls of one person, others with employees in the thousands. Some market products selling for $.10, others market products selling for $10,000. They vary from inbound customer service centers, mail order houses, to outbound financial service operations.

Telemarketing has transformed itself from a tool for boiler room scam operations into the prime legitimate marketing system for companies like Burlington Northern Railroad, Time/Life Books, IBM, Xerox, Amway, and Century 21 Real Estate.

Telemarketing isn't solely a tool for commerce, as shown by the success stories achieved by government agencies and correctional industries programs. Telemarketing can work for almost any kind of enterprise.

New England Shrimp Company (NESCO)

Founded in 1955, NESCO is a fast-growing Massachusetts family business that specializes in shrimp and shrimp products. Using a combination of toll-free inbound telemarketing (called "Tele-Shrimp") and an aggressive outbound campaign, NESCO has successfully increased sales by over 18 percent since 1984.

Westinghouse Furniture Systems

As a major manufacturer of office furniture, Westinghouse Furniture Systems needed a way to generate qualified leads and reinforce its advertising without spending lots of time and money. Telemarketing has proved to be the answer, and it paid for itself in increased revenue in only nine months. Currently staffed with two telemarketers, Westinghouse Furniture Systems uses an 800 number to handle inquiries. Each telemarketer works staggered shifts to provide optimum coverage of the ten-hour workday. They work at CRTs and ask fact-finding questions of each inquiry to help qualify the leads for field reps. Combining this with minicomputer access, the telemarketers are able to instantly transmit the appropriate data to field reps by electronic mail. Recently, Westinghouse also tested outbound telemarketing and has initiated a 98 percent volume turnaround, to where outbound should be Westinghouse's marketing means of the future.

Century 21 Real Estate Brokers

With over 6,500 independent real estate brokers in the Century 21 International Directory, many firms have found remarkable success using toll-free 800 numbers to ease national inbound telemarketing. Most of the increased business has come from transfer referrals from other listed brokers. Utilizing many of the telemarketing techniques described in this book, several brokers have been able to turn these inquiries from just phone calls to sales and listings.

Continental Marketing

Based in Boise, Idaho, Continental Marketing has utilized telemarketing as a tool to sell life insurance. Continental has given the title of "telemarketing account specialists" to its teams of professional telemarketers. Telemarketing is an in-house operation for Continental, which established specific territories for the telemarketers who make cold-calls from prospect lists developed from Yellow Pages and insurance industry sources. Their goal is to contact independent insurance agents and attempt to convince them to sell the Continental product line. In 1986, the average Continental marketing representative earned over $40,000 on average sales of over $1 million each. In 1986, Continental had over 70 such employees, each making over 40 presentations per day.

Fingerhut

A company that specializes in mail order of general merchandise since 1947, Fingerhut is proud of its success with telemarketing. By using extensive lists of its customer base, Fingerhut has incorporated consistent follow-up telemarketing calls to help build up add-ons to existing orders. The lists that the telemarketers use are quite elaborate in that they often include specific customer profile information such as birthdates, names of children, and so forth. By integrating this information with a dedicated telemarketing operation that calls with suggested birthday gifts, Fingerhut achieved a 23 percent sales increase in just one year (1985).

The New York Times

The nation's most famous newspaper, *The New York Times*, has found tremendous success with telemarketing and currently sells over 75 percent of its subscriptions over the telephone. Using 67 telephones operated by Allegheny Communications, the *Times* has initiated campaigns that contact prequalified prospects twice annually. The prospect lists are put together from directories, carriers, and list brokers, and normally are targeted to college-degreed, medium to upper income, professional homes. These campaigns are made by two shifts of telemarketers working evenings and weekends, with follow-up confirmations made 24 hours later.

Overseas

In the past several years, telemarketing has made meteoric advances in the marketing technology of many overseas countries, including France and Britain. In France, many companies are using computers and telemarketing to help increase retail sales with outbound and inbound telemarketing campaigns. They are utilizing the special advantages of reinforcing print media with outbound and inbound professional sales reps. In Great Britain, several travel agencies have started using telemarketing to book travel accommodations, especially with the new 0800 toll-free systems that allow international toll-free calling.

Joanne's Fudge

This Minnesota firm was quite successful in selling "instant fudge" to beauty salons via a telemarketing program developed by the author. This program was so successful in its test campaign in the metro Minneapolis area that a national program is currently scheduled.

Spencer Enterprises

Telemarketing proved a tremendous help for this California real estate brokerage who wanted surveys and appointments with potential commercial leasing customers. The program was so successful in a short test that the field reps had real trouble keeping up with the appointments and listings.

Rug Doctor

Carpet cleaning supplies and franchises are just a few of the products and services successfully being marketed nationally by this California firm.

Windsor Vineyards

This California winery has found a golden niche in the wine market with its aggressive combination direct mail–telemarketing operation, which sells high quality, personalized wines as gifts to business and private parties.

Hadra

Telemarketing was quite effective as a surveying tool to find clients for custom preprinted circuit board products for this Massachusetts firm.

Thrifty Best Rubbish

The author was instrumental in designing a marketing plan that utilized extensive telemarketing to find new accounts for this California garbage collection firm. The telemarketing plan was so successful that the firm could not keep up with all of the new business.

Walt Disney Educational Media

Telemarketing proved extremely successful for this California company in placing filmstrips in grammar schools all across the country on a trial basis and then following up with conversion to sales.

Union Oil of California

The author developed and trained this California company's order takers and transformed them into telemarketers. Using the current customer base, telemarketing revolutionized the oil business in servicing gas stations all across the country.

Alza

This California firm found excellent results from a telemarketing program designed by the author to sell IUDs to nonbuying gynecologists.

DHL Air Courier

Telemarketing was the edge this California company needed to introduce its new air courier services as competition to Federal Express and Express Mail.

Holland Farms

Telemarketing can sell anything, as this company in California discovered after successfully selling jelly beans and cookies over the telephone as gift ideas.

Graphic Concepts

This California graphics company found great success using telemarketing to sell advertising for the Membership Directory of the San Jose Chamber of Commerce, which it created and published.

Duddy's

Probably one of the most exciting examples of how successful telemarketing has been in turning companies around can be found in the story of the Duddy organization. This tire wholesaler was one of the nation's first pioneers in telemarketing. Taking salespeople out of company vehicles and putting them behind desks and on the phone was really quite a gamble. Many people had a hard time adjusting to this provocative new marketing medium, and its beginnings were not easy, to say the least. Duddy made it work, though, for the tire industry, and the company skyrocketed from under $1 million in sales in 1962 to over $100 million in just 15 years. Today, even these numbers seem minuscule compared to the numbers telemarketing is achieving every day. It took guts, but it paid off. (The author learned his craft the hard way, by doing it—selling tires for the Duddy organization, and he owes everything to those days of hard knocks. Thanks Duddy.)

Correctional Telemarketing

Telemarketing has been a successful industry for over 25 years, but only in the last 5 years has it been used as a tool for correctional institutions.

In 1983, the State of Arizona implemented the nation's first correctional telemarketing program, when National Switchboard, a telemarketing company, employed some 20 female inmates to answer informational inbound telephone calls for 300 accounts, including Best Western Motels and Macy's.

This premiere program proved telemarketing's viability in the correctional environment. Productivity was high and it turned into an all-win situation for all concerned, including the inmates, the prison, and the private companies represented. Even society benefitted with employable, trained inmates on reentry to freedom.

A Personal Insight

In April 1985, the author of this book, as representative of TransContinental Telemarketing, approached the State of Minnesota Department of Corrections with the idea of establishing the nation's first outbound prison telemarketing program.

From a modest concept, this program developed into a super

successful, full-scale telemarketing operation consisting of up to 50 inmates conducting surveys and selling goods and services for private sector companies.

The following is a brief outline of some of the companies represented and some of the experiences and successes and failures we encountered.

Women's Correctional Facility, Shakopee, Minnesota: After the initial stages of selection, hiring, and training of staff and personnel, the prime motivation was to secure work for the new telemarketing crews. The first success stories resulted from representation for Burlington Northern Railroad and the 3M Company. For Burlington Northern, the new crews began a lead generation program. This operation turned out to be one of the most productive telemarketing operations in America. Burlington Northern had its own in-house operation, and this prison industries program was not designed to compete with private enterprises. But, as it turned out, it proved itself productive and cost effective. For the 3M Company, our women inmates presented prepared surveys with the goal of inviting specific business people to a free seminar created on behalf of 3M. The results were as desired: a full house.

Stillwater Men's Correctional Facility, Stillwater, Minnesota:

- *International Creative*—sold advertising on county maps.
- *Time/Life Books*—sold subscriptions to series of books.
- *WearAKnit*—sold schoolchildren safety patrol hats.
- *Grolier Encyclopedia*—sold Christmas children's books.
- *Everything for the Office*—sold local office supplies.
- *Guardian Financial*—surveyed to determine prospects for insurance.
- *Cooper Tire and Rubber*—sold tires to wholesale distributors.
- *Consolidated Readers*—sold subscriptions (night crews).
- *Sprint*—converted long distance carriers.

The keys to success in telemarketing are presented briefly in this book. Telemarketing can be your ticket to success, too, if you take the time to learn and practice the sales techniques and fundamentals of telephone selling. It can be a fun and profitable career, business, or challenge. So don't let this book sit on a shelf gathering dust. Read it. Learn it. Use it.

Appendix A

Telemarketing Organizations

The following is a brief list of some associations that are relevant to the telemarketing industry.

American Management Association
135 West 50th Street
New York, NY 10020
Telephone: (212) 586-8100

American Telemarketing Association
1800 Pickwick Avenue
Glenview, IL
Telephone: (800) 441-3335

Direct Marketing Association
Six East 43rd Street
New York, NY 10017
Telephone: (212) 689-4977

Direct Selling Association
1730 M Street, NW
Washington, DC 20036
Telephone: (202) 293-5760

North American Telecommunications Association
2000 M Street, NW
Washington, DC 20036
Telephone: (202) 296-9800

Telemarketing Managers Association
3100 West Lake Street
Minneapolis, MN 55416
Telephone: (612) 927-9220

Appendix B

Periodicals on Telemarketing

The following is a brief list of relevant periodicals for the professional telemarketing enthusiast.

Telephony   Telephony Publishing Corp.
                       55 East Jackson
                       Chicago, IL 60604
                       (312) 922-2435

Teleprofessional   TeleProfessional
                       1049J Camino del Mar
                       Box 123
                       Del Mar, CA 92014
                       (619) 755-6500

Telemarketing   Technology Marketing Publications
                       17 Park Street
                       Norwalk, CT 06851
                       (203) 846-2029

Marketing News   American Marketing Association
                       250 S. Wacker Drive, Suite 200
                       Chicago, IL 60606-5819
                       (312) 648-0536

DM News   Direct Marketing News Corp.
                       19 West 21st Street
                       New York, NY 10010
                       (212) 741-2095

Direct Marketing   Direct Marketing
                       224 Seventh Street
                       Garden City, NY 11530
                       (516) 746-6700

AIS 800 Report	Advertising Information Services, Inc. 353 Lexington Avenue New York, NY 10016 (212) 683-9070
1987 Telemarketing National Salary Guide	Telemarketing Recruiters, Inc. 114 East 32nd Street New York, NY 10016 (212) 213-1818
Eye on Telemarketing	Eye on Telemarketing, Inc. 13650 Gramercy Place Gardena, CA 90249 (213) 217-1770
Personal Selling Power	Personal Selling Power 1127 International Parkway Suite 102, Box 5467 Fredericksburg, VA 22405
The Telemarketer	Actel Marketing 200 Park Avenue, Suite 303E New York, NY 10166 (212) 674-2540
Telemarketing Insider's Report	LinBar Publishing, Inc. P.O. Box 572 Englishtown, NJ 07726 (201) 577-1118
Telephone Angles	United Communications Group 4550 Montgomery Avenue, Suite 700N Bethesda, MD 20814 (301) 656-6666
Telephone Selling	TeleMarketing Design, Inc. 5600 Birch Shawnee Mission, KS 66205 (913) 262-2626
The Van Vechten Report	ConMark International, Inc. 80 Scenic Drive, Suite 7 Freehold, NJ 07728 (201) 780-7020

Appendix C

Glossary of Telemarketing Terms

Asterisk Bills. A new form of legislation that requires publishers of telephone directories or prospect lists to place asterisks by the names of consumers or firms that do not wish to be solicited over the telephone.

Bird Dogging. Attempting to prospect for new customers by asking existing customers for referral names of friends, relatives, and acquaintances who could be potential customers.

Burnout. A situation where a telephone sales representative becomes exhausted, unmotivated, and tired of the job. This can be a normal psychological occurrence caused by long work shifts, monotony, stress, or low pay, and is usually a result of bad management, lack of supervision, or unprofessional training.

Buying Cycle. The time between when your customer buys once and when he or she is ready to buy again.

Buzz Words. Adverbs, adjectives, or other words that can spice up or flavor a vocabulary—the salesperson's tools of the trade.

Call Accounting. An equipment feature used to analyze calls by the following:

> Which extension used
> Time of call
> Date of call
> Length of call
> Number dialed

Call Diverter (also known as **Call Forwarding**). An equipment feature that diverts calls from one telephone number to another.

Call Guide. An outline used by telephone sales representatives to remind them of the necessary steps to a successful telephone call. For example:

Sequence of Success

1. Establish the objective for the call (precall planning).
2. Verify the prospect's name.
3. Make the prospect commit his or her time.
4. Introduce yourself.
5. Introduce the reason for the call.
6. Qualify the prospect.
7. Make your sales presentation.
8. Overcome objections.
9. Close the sale.
10. Get the required credit information.
11. Confirm the details.
12. Sell your name.
13. Bird dog (generate additional leads).
14. Smile and express thanks.

Call Parking. A call placed on "hold."

Canned Calls. Calls that utilize prepared word-for-word scripts.

CCR (Communicator Call Report). A report of an individual telephone sales representative's quantitative results from a shift of work. Some of the appropriate data that can be retrieved from such a report include:

Number of calls made
Number of completed calls
Number of no answers
Number of busy signals
Number of "yes" responses
Number of "no" responses
Number of "not in" responses

Close. The process whereby you ask for the order.

Closed-Ended Questions. A selling technique that utilizes questions that lead the prospect to only one predetermined goal—"yes" answers. For example:

"This is a good product, isn't it?"
"You aren't allergic to green, are you?"
"My price was the best, wasn't it?"

Cold-Calls. Any contacts with prospects unfamiliar to the salesperson, the company represented, or the product sold. Cold-calls are a salesperson's key to success. Approached professionally and confidently, cold-calls really should be "warm" calls.

Collections. Any attempt to collect past due accounts or receivables.

Communicator. A person employed to communicate messages or make presentations over the telephone.

Corporate Cowards. Managers who are content with the status quo.

Criss-Cross Directory (also known as "Reverse" Directories). A list or directory of prospects that is arranged by street address followed by name and telephone number.

CRT (Cathode Ray Tube). A widely used term to signify the computer monitors often used by telemarketers.

Data Base. Any collection of information.

Data Processing. Any manipulation of data for functions such as analysis, storage, sorting, classification, recording, dissemination, addition, or integration.

Demographics. A quantitative description of the vital statistics of a population. Some of the statistics determined include annual income, address, occupation, sex, age, etc.

Direct Mail. A marketing tool that uses the mail to send a sales message. Direct mail campaigns can be targeted to specific zip codes, neighborhoods, etc.

Ergonomics. The scientific study of how people adjust to their environment in the workplace. Some of the topics of concern include burnout, reinforcement, noise decibels, comfort zones, lighting, silent quotients, functionality, work surfaces, sound absorption, work flow procedures, work stations, adjustability of chairs, personalization, etc.

Follow-Up System. A feature in automated telemarketing that handles scheduling of callbacks, call cycling, and analysis.

Fulfillment. The shipping department of any business.

Hardware. Physical telephone equipment, including telephones, CRTs, modules, silent monitors, call directories, switchboards, junction boxes, etc.

Hold. The unhappy purgatory customers find themselves in when an inconsiderate person presses a button on a telephone and puts them in the long-lost holding pattern or parking space located somewhere between a live call and a dead call.

In-House Telemarketing. A telemarketing program that is operated within the existing company structure with existing personnel and management.

Inbound. Any calls that come into a telemarketing operation.

Inquiry. Any inbound call.

KISS ("Keep It Simple, Stupid"). A reminder to always keep presentations to the least complicated, most comprehensible format possible.

LCR (Low Cost Routing). An equipment feature that automatically routes outgoing calls to the least expensive telephone usage company available (i.e., AT&T versus Sprint versus MCI versus . . .).

Line. A communication wire that connects a telephone to a telephone system.

Line Capacity. The total number of telephones that a line can handle.

List. A register or directory of prospects.

Lotteries. A potential scam technique used by some unscrupulous telemarketing operations, normally involving some game of chance in which people buy chances for prizes.

Monitoring. The capability and practice of listening to phone conversations of telemarketing crews with or without their knowledge. Used quite effectively as a tool for training and verifying quality control of a telemarketing operation.

Noise Cancelling. An equipment feature that compensates for noise fluctuations and helps minimize background static on telephone calls.

Objection. Any expression or feeling of opposition or disapproval to a presentation, argument, or sales pitch. Objections stand between you and sales.

One Ring Dialer. A telephone that automatically dials a preselected telephone number when the receiver is taken off the hook.

Open-Ended Questions. Questions that the professional salesperson uses to control conversations and deter the customer from being able to say "yes" or "no." These questions use terms such as when, where, how, what, why, and who.

Optimum Reorder Time. The time when a customer's stock has been depleted by two-thirds of their full normal inventory. This is also the time most customers will be receptive to buying.

Outbound. Any calls made out of your telemarketing operation.

Phonathon. A fundraising campaign that utilizes either inbound or outbound telemarketing.

Prerecorded Messages. Any message that is recorded and played at a later time either by inbound or outbound telemarketing, normally used in conjunction with automatic dialers, computer-automated machines, or incoming answer machines.

Proactive Telemarketing. Any telemarketing that is initiated by a seller of a product or conducted by outbound calling.

Profit Disclosures. A new form of legislation in some states that requires telemarketers involved in fundraising to disclose the percentages of a donation that is spent on telemarketing expenses and how much actually goes to the charity.

Qualify. The attempt to identify a prospect's capabilities to buy the service or product being presented for sale. Some of the qualifications of concern can include credit ratings or financial abilities to buy, being the decision maker, and determination if the prospect uses this kind of product or service.

Special. A unique, distinctive, exceptional, or extraordinary reason for your customer to buy. It can be a price concession, an add-on feature, a unique assessment, a discontinued item, style, etc., but remember, it must be *special.*

Success Model. A training model used to show a trainee the right and desired methods for selling over the telephone. Normally, the success model utilizes examples of successful telephone presentations to give trainees insight to the sounds and styles of success.

Telecommunications. The communication of audio or video information by transmission of electromagnetic waves.

Telemarketing. The systematic use of the telephone to market goods or services, survey for information, or commercially service accounts.

Telemarketing Service Vendor. Anyone who sells telemarketing services.

TSR (Telephone Sales Representative). Anyone who sells, surveys, or makes presentations over the telephone. Also known as "communicators," "customer representatives," "sales account executives," etc.

Turnover. The percentage of total employees who leave a company and have to be replaced over a certain period of time.

VDT (Video Display Terminal). A computer terminal screen.

Video Teleconferencing. Any use of televisions and/or the telephone via microwave, closed circuit, etc., to present interactive and multiply integrated conferences of groups to more than one location on a "live" basis.

Voice Input. A feature of a telemarketing machine that functions because of audio instead of keyboard or physical inputs.

Voice Output. A feature of a telemarketing machine that enables the machine to "speak" using audio means.

WATS (Wide Area Telecommunication Service). A long distance discount service. Once the golden child of AT&T, WATS is now available through many long distance companies.

Index

Account executive, 109
  evaluation questionnaire, 116–119
Airline telemarketing, 72
Amortization of expenses, 35
Answering the telephone, 132
  techniques for, 137–138
Appointments, booking, guidelines
    for, 82–83
Area codes/time zones, 66
Assumptive close, 91, 168
Asterisk bills, 210
Automated Dialing-Recorded Message
    Players (ADRMPs), 9–10, 40
  legal issues, 210–211
Automatic call director (ACD), 39

Bands/service areas, WATS line, 47
Bird dogging, 85, 142–143
Burnout, 122
Buying, motivation to buy, 78–79
Buzz words, 125–127
  words with sales appeal, 127

Callback form, 177
Call forwarding, 45
Call-mail-call method, 100, 103, 150
Call monitoring regulations, 209–210

Call processors, computerized, 73–74
Call report card, 173–175
Call waiting, 45
"Canned"/prepared calls, 8–10
Closed-ended questions, and objec-
    tions, 161
Closing the sale, 166–168
  guidelines for, 167–168
  questions to client, 89–91
  types of closes, 167, 168
    assumptive close, 168
Cold-calls, 78, 83
  method for prospecting, 143–144
Collections, 216–221
  content of call, 217–218
  and harassment, 221
  hours/timing for, 216, 219
  precall planning, 220
  regulation of, 216
Commercial accounts, prospecting for,
    150
Compensation, 32–33
Complaints, 201–207
  handling of, 202–206
  pitfalls to avoid, 206–207
Computer-assisted telemarketing,
    72–73

Computerized call processors, 73–74
Conference calls, 44
Consultants, use of, 35
Correctional institutions, telemarketing
    program, 230–231
Cost sales ratios, 33–34
Credit card calls, 44
Criss-cross directories, use of, 144, 181
Cycling, telephone cycling, and exist-
    ing accounts, 171–172, 180

Demographics/psychographics, use of,
    prospecting, 142–143
DIAL-IT, 900 service, 52–53
Direct mail, and telemarketing,
    149–150
Director, corporate position, 107

Economic factors, 27–37
    amortization of expenses, 35
    "communicator hour," 34–35
    compensation, 32–33
    consultants, use of, 35
    cost sales ratios, 33–34
    in-house operations, use of, 30–32
    outside service bureaus, use of,
        29–30
    quotas, 33
    vendors, use of, 34
800 service, 48, 51–52
    800 Readyline, 51–52
    service options offered, 48, 51
Electronic mail, 38
Electronic yellow pages, 38
Equipment
    automatic call director (ACD), 39
    Automatic Dial Recorded Message
        Players (ADRMPs), 40
    "Baby Bells," listing of, 37–38
    computer-assisted telemarketing,
        72–73
    computerized call processors, 73–74
    headsets, 39
    interactive television, 70–72
    monitoring equipment, 39–40
    power dialer, with answer recogni-
        tion, 74
    resellers, 69
    telemarketing work station, 75–76

teleports, 69
Touch Tone instrument, 38–39
voice-data terminals, 74–75
voice mail, 38
Ethical issues, 223–224
Existing accounts, 169–180
    and customer payments, 180
    reasons for non-buying, 170
    record-keeping, 172–180
    and telephone cycling, 171–172, 180

Federal Communications Commission
    (FCC), 208, 222
Foreign Exchange service, 43

Goal setting, 16–17

Headsets, 39
Hiring salespersons, 105–106, 110–114
    characteristics needed, 110–111
    employment agencies, use of,
        111–112
    interviewing applicants, 112–113
    newspaper ads, use of, 111
    requirements of job and, 106
Home Shopping Network, 72
Home solicitation rules, 214–215

Inbound telemarketing, 189–200
    customer, information needed
        about, 196
    guidelines for sales campaign,
        192–195
    inquiries, handling of, checklist for,
        198–199
    "on-hold" technique, 200
    practical applications, list of, 195
    pre-call preparation, 190–191
    as sales opportunity, 190, 192,
        199–200
    sample script, 197
Incentives, 24–25
    pitfalls to avoid, 25
In-house operations, 30–32
    advantages/disadvantages of, 30–32
Interactive television, 70–72
International calls, 59, 61–64
    codes for foreign countries, 61–64

handling of, 80
to ships, 61
Interviews, telemarketing applicants,
    112–113

Job descriptions, 106–110
    corporate positions, 107–108
        director, 107
        manager, 107–108
        supervisor, 107, 108
    service agency positions, 108–110
        account executive, 109
        manager, 108
        sales director, 109
        sales representative, 109–110
        services manager, 109
        supervisor, 108–109
        telemarketing director, 109
        training manager, 109

Legal issues, 208–222
    asterisk bills, 210
    Auto-Dialed Message Players
        (ADRMP), 210–211
    call monitoring regulations, 209–210
    collections, 216–221
    home solicitation rules, 214–215
    900 number controversy, 213
    profit disclosures, 212
    registration, 212
    sales tax issue, 221–222
    scams, 211–212, 213
    solicitation hours, 213–214
Listening to customer, 126, 128,
    guidelines for, 162–163
Lists, 144–150
    leasing lists, 147
    list brokers, use of, 144–145
    list cards, 145–146
    publishers' lists, 148
    selection of, 147, 148
    Standard Rates and Data Service
        List (SRDS), 147–148
    testing of, 149
    without telephone numbers, 148–149
Local calls, 40, 43
Long distance calls, 40
    area codes/time zones, USA, 66
    international calls, 59, 61–64

person-to-person calls, 67
satellite transmissions, 67–69
station-to-station calls, 65
telephone log for, 42
telephone rates, 64–65
wrong number, 67
See also International calls; Services
    (telemarketing related)

Management, guidelines for, 123
Manager
    corporate position, 107–108
    service agency position, 108, 109
MCI, 57, 59
Megacom, 53
Metromail, 149
Monitoring equipment, 39–40
Monitoring system, 23

Negativity, avoiding, 130–132
New accounts, 97–107
    call-mail-call method, 100, 103
    checklist/guidelines for, 102–103
    product, presentation of
        features/advantages/benefits,
        97–99
    single item, first sale, 99–100
    specials, offering, 100
900 service, 52–53
    controversy related to, 213

Objections, 89, 91, 152–167
    and closed-ended questions, 161
    and closing sale, 166–168
    focusing on objections, 153
    ignoring objections, 162
    objections/responses, examples of,
        154–159
    and open-ended questions, 160–161
    psychology, use of, 161
    throw-back technique, 91
    training for, 159–160
"On-hold" technique, 200
Open-ended questions, and objections,
    160–161
Other common carrier (OCC), 56–57
    advantages/disadvantages of, 59
Outside service bureaus, use of, 29–30
Overseas telemarketing, 227

Payments from customers, and additional sales, 180
Performance report, sales, 101
Person-to-person calls, 67
Power dialer, 74
PRO America, 56
Professionalism, characteristics of, 223–224
Profit disclosures, 212
PRO plan, 54, 56
Prospecting, 140–151
  bird dogging method, 143–144
  cold-calling method, 143–144
  for commercial accounts, 150
  criss-cross directories, use of, 144
  for customer accounts, 150
  demographics/psychographics, use of, 142–143
  lists, 144–150
  reverse directories, use of, 144
  on telephone, guidelines for, 150–151
  Yellow Pages, 141
  See also Lists.
Prospects
  overlooked prospects, 182
  types of, 81–82
Public Announcement Service (PAS), 52

Quotas, 33

Reach-Out, 53, 54
Reach Out America, 53, 55
Readyline, 800, 51–52
Record-keeping, 172–180
  callback form, 177
  sales call performance checklist, 179–180
  sales call report card, 173–175
  sales call report form, 176
  statistical call report form, 178
Registration, of telemarketers, 212
Reorders, lack of, reasons for, 171
Reverse directories, use of, 144

Sales
  emotional appeal in, 99
  instinct to sell, 105
  new accounts, 97–104
  objections, 152–167
  performance report, 101
  perseverance, importance of, 104
  training customers, 104
Sales call performance checklist, 179–180
Sales director, 109
Salespeople, productivity of, 12–14
Sales presentation
  preparation for, 83–84, 85
  scripts, 87–96
Sales representative, 109–110
Sales tax issue, 221–222
Satellite transmissions, 67–69
  advantages of, 68–69
  placing a call, 68
  teleconferencing, 69–70
Scams, 211–212, 213
Screening calls, 132–133
Scripts, 87–96
  for close
    assumptive close, 91
    questions to client, 89–91
  guidelines for, 91–92
  inbound telemarketing, sample, 197
  number of words in, 89, 91
  for objections, 89, 91, 152–167
  outline script, 87
  overused words, listing of, 131–132
  positive/negative phrasing, examples of, 131
  sample scripts, 94–96
  Sequence of Success, in presentation, 88–89
  surveys, samples, 184–188
  testing/analysis of, 92–93
  value of, 87–88
  verbatim script, 87
Secretaries, handling of, 79–81
Sequence of calls, 78–85
  booking appointments, 82–83
  control of telemarketer, 81
  list of names, developing, 78, 84
  sales presentation, preparation for, 83–84, 85
  secretaries, handling of, 79–81
Services (telemarketing related)
  airline telemarketing, 72

call forwarding, 45
call waiting, 45
conference calls, 44
credit card calls, 44
800 service, 48, 51–52
   800 Readyline, 51–52
electronic mail, 38
electronic yellow pages, 38
Foreign Exchange service, 43
MCI, 57, 59
Megacom, 53
900 service, 52–53
other common carrier (OCC),
   56–57, 59
PRO America, 56
PRO plan, 54, 56
Reach-Out, 53, 54
Reach Out America, 53, 55
SPRINT, 58–59
teleconferencing, 69–70
tie-lines, 43–44
WATS line, 46–48
   two-way WATS, 52
Zenith/Enterprise, 45
Services manager, 109
Ships, calling of, 61
Simulated calls, 114–115
Smiling on telephone, 129–130
Solicitation hours, regulations of,
   213–214
Specials, offering, 100
SPRINT, 58–59
Standard Rates and Data Service List
   (SRDS), 147–148
Station-to-station calls, 65
Statistical call report form, 178
Supervisor
   corporate position, 107, 108
   service agency position, 108–109
Surveys, 181–188
   guidelines for, 181, 182–183
   sample scripts, 184–188

Taking messages, 133–134
Teleconferencing, 69–70
   costs related to, 70
   major projects in, 69–70
Telemarketing
   burnout in, 122

"canned"/prepared calls, 8–10
closing sale, 166–168
common mistakes in, 10
compared to eyeball-to-eyeball selling, 105, 124
complaints, 201–207
economic factors, 27–37
effectiveness of, 5–8
equipment/services/technology
   related to, 36–76
ethical issues, 223–224
existing accounts, 169–180
facility requirements, 18, 20–22
factors for success, 17
goal setting, 16–17
hiring salespersons, 105–106, 110–
   114
inbound telemarketing, 189–200
incentives, 24–25
job descriptions, 106–110
legal issues, 208–222
management, guidelines for, 123
management of, 22
monitoring system, 23
objections, 152–167
organizations for, 233
periodicals about, 234–235
prospecting, 140–151
prospects, types of, 81–82
salespeople, productivity of, 12–14
sequence of calls, 78–85
successful program
   characteristics of, 15
   guidelines for, 17, 19, 23–24
   success stories, 225–230
surveys, 181–188
telephone techniques, 124–139
terms related to, 236–240
training salespersons, 12, 114–121
trouble signs, 23
See also specific topics
Telemarketing Recruiters, Inc., 112
Telemarketing work station, 75–76
Telephone Look-Up Service, 149
Telephone techniques
   answering the telephone, 132,
   137–138
   best times to call, 138–139
   buzz words, listing of, 125–127

courtesies to callers, 135–137
enthusiasm, 128–129
good impression, creating, 125
listening to customer, 126, 128,
    162–163
negativity, avoiding, 130–132
screening calls, 132–133
smiling on telephone, 129–130
taking messages, 133–134
Teleports, 69
Television, interactive television, 70–72
Throw-back technique, objections, 91
Tie-lines, 43–44
Touch Tone instrument, 38–39
Training manager, 109
Training salespersons, 12, 114–121
about product, 159–160
overcoming objections, 159–160
simulated calls, 114–115
steps in process, 114
training guidelines, 115
voice training, 120–121

Vendors, use of, 34
Verifying desk, 91
Voice-data terminals, 74–75
Voice mail, 38
Voice training
    guidelines for, 120–121, 124–125
    relaxation exercises, 120–121
    taping calls, value of, 125

WATS line, 46–48
    bands/service areas, 47
    billing, 46
    disadvantages of, 46
    two-way WATS, 52
Work station (telemarketing), 75–76
Wrong number, long distance calls, 67

Yellow Pages, prospecting, 141

Zenith/Enterprise, 45